MW01252743

Overcoming Inequality in Latin America

Latin America is faced with the challenge of achieving the Millennium Developmental Goal to halve poverty in the region by 2015. Historically, this region has experienced persistently high levels of inequality and poverty, and the situation has deteriorated considerably over the past few years. This book analytically examines both the causes and consequences of inequality in Latin America.

Overcoming Inequality in Latin America adopts a multidimensional approach to understanding the fundamental causes of inequality in the region, focusing on the mechanisms that lead to higher inequality and emphasising the role of macroeconomics, trade rules, capital flows and the political electoral process. This book analyses how inequality has hindered development, how it interacts with a nation's economic, social and political processes, and how inequality constrains the above processes in ways that weaken the prospect of establishing and sustaining a dynamic, wealthy and creative society. Examining the key economic policies and reforms that have exacerbated the region's extremely high inequality levels, this book prescribes an alternative range of policy suggestions to help alleviate inequality and provide the foundations for more equitable development.

An international team of specialist contributors elucidate these crucial issues and the result is a book that will prove an invaluable resource across a number of fields including development economics and politics.

Ricardo Gottschalk is a Research Fellow at the Institute of Development Studies at the University of Sussex.

Patricia Justino is a British Academy Research Fellow at the Poverty Research Unit and the Department of Economics at the University of Sussex.

Routledge Studies in Development Economics

Overcoming Inequality in Latin America

Issues and challenges for the twenty-first century

Edited by Ricardo Gottschalk and Patricia Justino

160401

Routledge
Taylor & Francis Group

LONDON AND NEW YORK

First published 2006
by Routledge
2 Park Square, Milton Park, Abingdon, Oxon OX14 4RN

Simultaneously published in the USA and Canada
by Routledge
270 Madison Ave, New York, NY 10016

Routledge is an imprint of the Taylor & Francis Group

Typeset in Times New Roman by
HWA Text and Data Management, Tunbridge Wells
Printed and bound in Great Britain by
TJ International Ltd, Padstow, Cornwall

British Library Cataloguing in Publication Data
A catalogue record for this book is available from the British Library

Library of Congress Cataloging in Publication Data
A catalog record for this book has been requested

ISBN 0–415–36284–9

Contents

Illustrations

Figures

Tables

Contributors

Arnab Acharya was until recently a Research Fellow at the Institute of Development Studies at the University of Sussex. Dr Acharya has worked extensively on the issues concerning the delivery of basic goods to the poor in developing countries with a special interest in the delivery of health care, health systems and assessment of impact of health policy and projects. His past research includes theoretical research into cost-effectiveness analysis, game theoretical account of functioning of planned economies, impact of family planning programmes and theoretical issues in disease eradication programmes.

David Evans was until recently a Research Associate at the Institute of Development Studies at the University of Sussex. He has worked extensively on globalisation, regionalisation and poverty. Recently, he has worked extensively on the regional integration of Southern Africa and the identification of poor winners and losers from globalisation, especially the poverty impact of a potential WTO round of trade liberalisation. Has also worked on the impact of the reform of tariff and non-tariff trade barriers affecting EU trade with developed and developing country partners.

Ricardo Gottschalk is a Research Fellow at the Institute of Development Studies at the University of Sussex. He is experienced in macroeconomic research as well as having large familiarity with government work in Latin America. His work has covered a wide range of topics including capital flows to developing countries, the reform of the international financial architecture, financial crises and their impact on poverty; the sequencing of capital account liberalisation; the macroeconomics of the PRSPs; the links between macroeconomics and poverty and inequality; foreign debt and its connection with macroeconomic stability and sustainability of economic reforms in Latin America. He has co-edited, with Griffith-Jones and Cailloux, *International Capital Flows in Calm* *and Turbulent Times: The Need for New International Architecture*, University of Michigan Press, 2003. He has acted as international consultant to various development organisations and agencies, including UNCTAD, the European Commission, and the UK Department for International Development, and to developing country governments, including South Africa and Tanzania. He was the director of the MPhil Programme in Development Studies at IDS during 2001–4.

Stephany Griffith-Jones is a Professor at the Institute of Development Studies at the University of Sussex. Her expertise includes work on global capital flows, with special reference to flows to emerging markets, the macro-economic management of capital flows in Latin America, eastern Europe and sub-Saharan Africa, proposals for international measures to diminish volatility of capital flows and reduce the likelihood of currency crises and the analyses of national and international capital markets.

Patricia Justino is a British Academy Research Fellow at the Poverty Research Unit and the Department of Economics at the University of Sussex. Her areas of specialisation are applied microeconomics and quantitative development economics. She has worked extensively on the measurement of monetary and non-monetary dimensions of inequality and their effects on social development and economic growth in Brazil and India. Previous research has included the measurement and modelling of poverty (static and dynamic) (India, Brazil and Vietnam), the role of social security and redistribution on economic growth (India and Vietnam) and welfare and the impact of trade liberalisation and trade reforms on household income mobility (Vietnam). She is co-founder and co-director of the Leverhulme-funded *Households in Conflict Network*, a collaborative effort between European researchers to analyse the impact of socio-political conflict on inter- and intra-household welfare. She has also been involved in several policy-oriented projects for the World Bank, UNDP, the UK Department for International Development and the Minority Rights Group International.

Jenny Kimmis was, at the time of writing, a Research Officer in the International Finance Team at the Institute of Development Studies at the University of Sussex. Her research interests include the impact of financial globalisation on the poor, the policies of the international financial institutions in middle-income countries, global governance and socially responsible investment. Previously she worked as a Policy Advisor for Oxfam UK and as Credit Analyst for the National Bank of Mexico.

Julie Litchfield is the Director of the Poverty Research Unit at Sussex (PRUS) and Senior Lecturer in Economics at the University of Sussex.

She has extensive expertise in the measurement and analysis of poverty, income inequality and income distribution in Latin America using large complex household survey data-sets. She has published studies of poverty and inequality in Chile, Brazil, Vietnam, China and Zambia. Julie Litchfield is also a Research Associate of the Distributional Analysis Research Programme at STICERD, London School of Economics.

Aaron Schneider is a Research Fellow at the Institute of Development Studies at the University of Sussex. His research interests include questions of political economy and the causes of and links between power and wealth in Latin America. Present interests include questions of federalism, decentralisation, party systems, public finance, fiscal adjustment and budgeting in Latin America.

Cecilia Ugaz is currently at the UN, Geneva. She was until recently a Research Fellow at the Institute of Development Studies at the University of Sussex. She has large research expertise in Latin America and has done substantial work on institutional development, poverty alleviation and fiscal/redistributive issues. The main focus of her research is private/public partnerships in social and infrastructure service provision. She has recently conducted research combining micro and macro/institutional analysis to assess the effect of infrastructure privatisation on poverty in Latin America.

Laurence Whitehead is the Director of the new Centre for Mexican Studies at the University of Oxford. He is also an Official Fellow in Politics at Nuffield College, Oxford University, and Senior Fellow of the College. His most recent work has focused on international aspects of democratisation, and on the relationship between democratisation and economic liberalisation in Latin America.

Preface

This book was born out of a deep unease among a group of academics at the Institute of Development Studies (IDS) and the Poverty Research Unit (PRUS), both at the University of Sussex, with the persistently high levels of inequality in Latin America. The theme has naturally attracted enormous attention from academics, the international policy community and all those who are concerned with, and committed to, poverty reduction, justice and equal rights, and sustainable development in the region and across the world. However, two issues in particular have caught the attention of the Sussex-based group of academics, and turned them to the task of addressing them through a collection of papers that culminated in this book.

The first was the recognition that the types of inequality entrenched in Latin America through its history and institutions have clearly hindered the region's prospects of development and poverty eradication. The task was therefore to take stock of this issue and thereby improve our understanding of how inequality may hinder development, how it interacts with a nation's economic, social and political processes, and how it constrains these processes in ways that weaken the prospect of establishing and sustaining a dynamic, wealthy and creative society. The second was the shared view that inequality, already extremely high in the region, may have worsened even further due to a combination of inappropriate macroeconomic policies and wrong timing, sequencing and speed of economic reforms. The task was therefore to examine the channels through which certain policies and reforms may have deteriorated inequality in the region even further, and to propose alternative policies that can truly support broad based growth and development.

To address these multidimensional processes, the book has contributions from academics of different areas of expertise. Patricia Justino and Julie Litchfield, from PRUS, are poverty and inequality experts who mapped the different types of inequality in Latin America, suggested through careful analysis reasons for their existence, and discussed their negative economic, social and political implications. As a political scientist with long-term experience in Latin America, Laurence Whitehead brought an added, insightful contribution to the political analysis of inequality. Arnab Acharya, Aaron Schneider and Cecilia Ugaz, the first two political economists and the third an economist based at IDS at the time of the project, dealt in turn with the specific issue of the political economy of the electoral process. Their aim was to understand the role of inequality in specific distributive outcomes in Latin America. Finally, and turning to economic issues, Ricardo Gottschalk, Stephany Griffith-Jones, Jenny Kimmis and David Evans, all from IDS, examined how specific economic policies and reforms that have been extensively adopted in Latin America since the mid-1980s at least, have to a large extent failed to address inequality, and may have even contributed to further inequality in the region. While Gottschalk, a macroeconomist with long-term work experience in Latin America, has addressed the interaction between macroeconomics and inequality, Griffith-Jones and Kimmis, both international finance experts with close links with Latin America, looked at the financial crises that the region has experienced in the past decade, and the role played by the international financial institutions during the crises. Finally Evans, drawing on his life-long work on international trade issues, examined trade policy reforms and the possible channels through which these reforms may affect growth, poverty and distribution in the Latin American context.

The book is mostly analytical, although with a strong policy dimension attached, as one would expect given the topic's enormous policy significance, as well as the strong policy focus underlying the work of most of the book contributors and of the institutions to which they are affiliated. Of course, we expect the book can contribute in important ways to the debate on inequality in Latin America, and serve through its analysis and policy recommendations as a guide to those country and international policy actors committed to social justice in their efforts to help overcome inequality in the region.

Acknowledgements

A number of people have contributed to this book. The editors would like to thank in particular the book publishers for their encouragement and support, the book contributors for their time and dedication in preparing and revising the chapters, Sue Holloway for detailed comments on earlier versions of various chapters, and three anonymous reviewers for helpful comments and suggestions for improvement.

Ricardo Gottschalk and Patricia Justino
Brighton, December 2004

Abbreviations

CCL	Contingent Credit Line
CDF	Comprehensive Development Framework
CGE	Computable General Equilibrium
CIID	Centro Internacional de Investigaciones para el Desarrollo
CPI	Consumer Price Index
CU	Customs Unions
DFID	UK Department for International Development
ECA	Export Credit Agencies
ECLAC	Economic Commission for Latin America and the Caribbean
ESAF	Enhanced Structural Adjustment Facility
EU	European Union
FDI	Foreign Direct Investment
FTA	Free Trade Area
GATT	General Agreement on Tariffs and Trade
GDP	Gross Domestic Product
GTAP	Global Trade Analysis Project (Purdue University)
HIPC	Heavily Indebted Poor Countries
H–O	Heckscher–Ohlin
IADB	Inter-American Development Bank
IBGE	Instituto Brasileiro de Geografia e Estatistica
IDS	Institute of Development Studies
IFAD	International Fund for Agricultural Development
IFI	International Financial Institutions
IIF	The Institute of International Finance, Inc.
IMF	International Monetary Fund
LA	Latin America
LAC	Latin America and the Caribbean
MDB	Multilateral Development Bank

MERCOSUR	in English translation, 'common market of the southern cone'
NAFA	North American Framework Agreement
NAFTA	North American Free Trade Area
NEC	National Executive Committee
NGO	Non-governmental Organisations
OECD	Organisation for Economic Co-operation and Development
OR	Open Regionalism
PFL	Partido da Frente Liberal *(Liberal Front Party)*
PRGF	Poverty Reduction and Growth Facility
PRSP	Poverty Reduction Strategy Paper
PRUS	Poverty Research Unit at Sussex
PSIA	Poverty and Social Impact Analysis
PT	Partido dos Trabalhadores *(Workers' Party)*
PUNE	Party Unanimity Equilibrium
RTA	Regional Trade Agreement
SAP	Structural Adjustment Programme
SDRM	Sovereign Debt Restructuring Mechanism
SME	Small and Medium-sized Enterprise
SOE	State-Owned Enterprise
SRF	Supplemental Reserve Facility
SRI	Socially Responsible Investment
STICERD	Suntory and Toyota International Centres for Economics and Related Disciplines
UN	United Nations
UNCTAD	United Nations Conference on Trade and Development
URR	Unremunerated Reserve Requirement
WIDER	World Institute for Development Economics Research
WTO	World Trade Organisation

1 Introduction

Ricardo Gottschalk and
Patricia Justino

Why inequality matters in Latin America

Latin America has some of the highest levels of socio-economic inequality in the world. These high levels of inequality pose a serious threat to recent development undertakings, not only because inequalities may seriously undermine efforts to eliminate poverty and destitution, but also because persistent inequalities waste financial and human resources, erode social cohesion and, consequently, pose serious constraints to the process of social and economic development.

Economic growth is typically accompanied by a certain level of inequality. Different people have different abilities and different initial endowments of physical and human capital. It is therefore extremely difficult to ensure that all population groups benefit equally from potential economic gains. Not all types of inequality are adverse. In fact, inequalities that result from rewards to risk-taking, enterprise, skill acquisition and saving may create important incentives for technological advance and increased productivity. However, other types of inequality that may arise from lack of opportunities, social and political exclusion and other forms of discrimination, from a colonial legacy or from political connections and inherited wealth, are likely to be associated with the exclusion of some population groups from the process of development and may pose constraints to the establishment of fully functioning market economies.[1] This is particularly problematic in developing countries, where the number of poor vulnerable households is relatively high.

Large evidence has shown that countries with high levels of inequality achieve significantly lower economic growth (Datt and Ravallion, 1992; Kanbur and Lustig, 1999). Moreover, it makes growth less effective in reducing poverty (Birdsall and Londoño, 1997; Ravallion, 1997; Hanmer and Naschold, 2000). Recent empirical and theoretical results show that inequality can harm economic growth and socio-economic development via several social, economic and political mechanisms. Conversely, more equitable distributions of income and assets can result in improved opportunities for the poor and, consequently, to better living standards. They can also result in improved economic growth. Indeed, recent studies have shown that the investment of public funds on the reduction of inequality can generate important welfare benefits. They may take the form of programmes of public employment, investment in education, land reforms and the reinforcement of legal and political rights. Moreover, these forms of redistribution can benefit the poor without distorting investment decisions (Bénabou, 1996).

There are therefore a number of reasons why inequality is a central issue and why researchers and policy makers should be concerned about it. Focusing on Latin America, an extensive literature has shown that a large number of individuals and households remain poor due to the persistence of high levels of economic, social and political inequalities. They are poor, not because they live in poor countries, but because high levels of inequality create exclusion and pockets of persistent poverty amongst certain population groups (World Bank, 2003b). Given the extremely high levels of inequality in Latin America, not only is the region's level of income insufficient for poverty eradication, but also its pace of growth. Hanmer *et al.* (1999) have shown that, unless extremely high, growth alone will not be sufficient to halve poverty by 2015.

Inequality: concepts and dimensions

Although it is commonly accepted that poverty and inequality are related phenomena, the two concepts are not equivalent. The crucial difference between the concepts of poverty and inequality lies in their main focus: when examining poverty, whether we are concerned with material deprivation or less tangible, psychological dimensions of poverty, we focus on people, families and/or households that lie below some poverty line. When talking about inequality, we no longer focus solely on poor people but on the whole distribution.[2] When this difference between poverty and inequality is taken into account it becomes clear that changes in inequality do not necessarily have to be associated with changes in poverty. Furthermore, it is possible to conceive of situations where poverty (measured by the percentage of individuals and/or households below a poverty line) can fall yet inequality increase. For instance, in circumstances where the whole population is equally poor, if one person moves above the poverty line, poverty estimates will decrease whilst inequality would have increased. Furthermore, as empirical evidence discussed throughout this book will demonstrate, although a high level of inequality is usually associated with high levels of poverty (e.g. Nicaragua, Honduras), relatively low levels of inequality[3] can easily coexist with both low (e.g. Uruguay, Argentina) and high degrees of poverty (e.g. Peru).[4]

Inequality is a multidimensional phenomenon. Despite the fact that most studies of inequality tend to concentrate on the analysis of income inequality, inequalities arise due to other economic, social and political factors. This is the perspective taken in this book. In this sense, the concept of inequality can be associated with the concept of social exclusion. The concept of social exclusion was originally developed as a form of categorising conceptually population groups that were left at the margin of social insurance systems in Europe: the mentally and physically handicapped, single parents, etc. (Behrman *et al.*, 2002). Throughout the 1980s, the concept started to be adopted by most social sciences and its original meaning extended to form a framework for thinking about deprivation and poverty in terms of material and non-material disadvantages – such as poor educational opportunities, low wages, employment insecurity and so forth – and the nature of social justice (as emphasised by the question 'equality amongst whom?'), social participation, lack of social integration and lack of power (Behrman *et al.*, 2002). This interpretation of the concept of social exclusion is closely related to the notion of inequality, when considering inequality in its many dimensions (economic, social, political and cultural). However, similarly to inequality and poverty, inequality and exclusion are not equivalent notions. Whilst inequality refers to differences in income, assets and access to social and political institutions between various population groups, it does not necessarily imply that those groups will be excluded from accessing those economic, social and political institutions. Being excluded will, however, imply the existence of inequalities, when exclusion is not voluntary. As argued by Sen (1985), there is a need to consider and distinguish between (i) the realisation of one's objectives irrespective of one's own role, and (ii) their realisation as a result of one's efforts. Social exclusion can, in the context of (i), be understood as a manifestation of extreme forms of inequality. Involuntary forms of exclusion – which result from the absence of opportunities for large segments of society (Behrman *et al.*, 2002) – can, thus, be understood as a consequence of extreme forms of economic, social and political inequality.

Impacts of inequality

Social impact of inequality

Persistently high levels of inequality have important social effects. High inequality may result in reductions in the stock of human capital available in each economy when it leads to the persistence of illiteracy and poor health amongst disadvantaged groups. Dilapidated stocks of human capital will, in turn, decrease individuals' capacity to access better jobs and higher incomes. For instance, Ribero and Nuñez (1999) show that disability and stature (an indication of nutrition status) influence significantly the earnings capacity of men and women. This will, in turn, reflect in the countries' inability to pursue higher rates of economic growth (Saint-Paul and Verdier, 1992; Galor and Zeira, 1993; Perotti, 1993). Zoninsein (2001a, 2001b) show that in Latin American countries the poor could have sizeable earning gains through access to education (and from removal of education inequalities between population groups).

The persistence of social, economic and political inequalities amongst certain socio-economic groups may, furthermore, increase social discontent and, consequently, the propensity of individuals and population groups for engaging in criminal activities, violence and even civil wars. In fact, inequality has been associated with increased risk of crime (Becker, 1967; Sala-i-Martin, 1996). In Latin America, Fajnzylber *et al.* (1998) have found that increases in income inequality raise crime rates (homicide and robbery). This evidence is supported by the findings reported in Cruz *et al.* (1998), Rubio (1998), Briceño-León *et al.* (1997), and Stewart (1998, 2002) for Colombia, El Salvador, Nicaragua, Guatemala, Venezuela and Mexico during the 1990s. An extensive literature has also provided empirical evidence for a positive relationship between inequality and various forms of social and political conflict (Lichbach, 1989; Gupta, 1990). Although in many countries some level of inequality may coexist with social peace, not all societies will have high levels of tolerance for persistent inequalities (Hirschman, 1981). When tolerance breaks, inequality can lead to the accumulation of discontent amongst some population groups to a sufficiently high level to damage social cohesion (Alesina and Perotti, 1993; Bénabou, 1996; Stewart, 1998; Elbadawi, 1999; Dollar *et al.*, 2000).

Economic impact of inequality

High inequalities restrain the demand capacity of poor and middle-income countries. Murphy *et al.* (1989) have shown that internal demand can change as a response to more equal distributions of income. Decreases in income inequality imply a wealthier middle class (enlarged by those coming out of the poorer classes), which are the most significant consumers of manufactured goods. Consequently, the reduction of inequalities is likely to induce an increase in private consumption and, consequently, an enlargement of internal markets and higher prospects for economic growth.

High inequality affects demand capacity in normal times, but equally important, it makes aggregate demand more volatile when the economy is hit by a shock. For instance, a shock typically causes an increase in unemployment, affecting the poor disproportionately. Because the poor lack physical and financial assets, they will respond to a fall in income through reducing demand. Given that they constitute the majority of the population in a country where inequality is high, aggregate demand is strongly affected (Furman and Stiglitz, 1998 and discussion in Chapter 3).

High levels of inequality may also impede the establishment of pro-poor trade policies and magnify possible negative distributional impacts caused by international economic shocks. Most Latin American countries have been through large programmes of economic liberalization in recent years, of which trade liberalization has been one of the largest components (Wood, 1994; Taylor, 2000; McCulloch *et al.*, 2001; Winters, 2002). As discussed by David Evans in Chapter 5, these programmes are likely to have affected, and have been affected by, the level and persistence of inequality in each country. On the one hand, existing inequalities will affect the establishment of pro-poor trade policies. The larger the number of poor people in relation to richer people, the more challenging will be the implementation of socially protective policies in political, financial and targeting terms. On the other hand, trade liberalization policies may induce short-term social and economic shocks of various degrees. Those shocks may result from the emergence of new markets, changes in relative prices, the remuneration of different factors of production and the disappearance of traditional economic relations. These, in general, will affect disproportionately the poorest segments of the population. Consequently, the larger the initial level of inequality in a given country, the larger the negative impact of economic shocks on its development and economic growth potential.

Political impact of inequality

High inequalities may also hinder the political participation of vulnerable households and poor local communities. Arnab Acharya, Aaron Schneider and Cecilia Ugaz in Chapter 6 provide an in-depth analysis of these mechanisms. Most political analyses of inequality are based on standard median-voter models. These models predict that, when inequality in a certain society is high, the median voter is located closer to the vast majority of poor voters. In those circumstances, policies targeted at the median voter should be pro-poor. However, the reality observed in most high-inequality countries is that the provision of public goods will tend to systematically exclude the poor (World Bank, 2003a). The link between inequality and political participation takes place in a perverse way when the poor cannot afford to vote or are bought out by richer votes, which prevents the poor from voicing their demands in equal weight to the rich.

Political and social policy decisions in developing countries are frequently determined by the interests of elites and the protection of their own social, political and economic welfare. Powerful families and larger enterprises have a considerable influence on government policies in many developing countries.

It is thus possible to imagine a situation where high inequality may lead to lower rather than higher tax rates, when the richer population groups are capable of influencing the design of the tax system through the political system (Chapter 3). Lower taxes, in turn, may affect economic growth negatively, if the country is below its optimal tax level (Furman and Stiglitz, 1998). Thus, as shown in Chapter 3, many countries in Latin America have low tax rates as a proportion of the GDP. In some cases this may reflect structural deficiencies in the tax systems associated with their stages of development. However, political lobbying on the part of the elite may also partly explain these governments' low tax capacity (see Sachs, 1990). In richer countries, like Argentina, that seems to be the case.

Previous work on inequality in Latin America and book structure

Inequality in Latin America has been a topic increasingly revisited by scholars since the early 1990s, initially with the aim of assessing the impact on poverty and distribution of adjustment policies and economic reforms Latin American countries adopted in response to the debt crisis of the 1980s (see, for example, Morley, 1995; Lustig, 1995; Stallings and Peres, 2000). Their work was to an important extent motivated by the persistently high levels of inequality in the continent. Given this, their question was how the region could possibly bear further inequality increases arising from the adjustment efforts. Following the adjustment experiences of the 1980s, the social protection model in Latin America became increasingly seen as clearly inadequate to meet the region's critical social demands and needs. This inadequacy, as well as alternative social protection mechanisms, has been explored by scholars, worth mentioning in this regard is the work by Tokman and O'Donnel (1998).

The 1990s saw important initiatives in the region such as affirmative action to address issues of race and ethnicity (see Chapter 2), which are at the basis of social exclusion and therefore closely related to inequality, as well as the creation of social welfare programmes targeted at the poor. These initiatives have been the subject of careful analysis by studies undertaken by the international organisations such as the Inter-American Development Bank (IADB) and the World Bank, and seen as examples of areas where progress has been made and, from the policy perspective, as elements of a possible new strategy for the future (see for example, Buvinic and Mazza, 2003; World Bank, 2003b). Nowadays, there is a widely held view that the continent's high and persistent inequality constitutes a major obstacle for the achievement of the Millennium Development Goals, thereby becoming a central policy challenge. In response to this, the World Bank study has proposed a number of policy initiatives that, it believes, can contribute to a more balanced, equitable development in Latin America.

Our book fits in with this literature by identifying inequality as a central issue and challenge facing Latin America. It is motivated by our strong belief that persistent inequalities as those observed in the Latin American region will undermine efforts to reduce poverty and destitution due to the emergence of poverty traps caused by the impossibility of economic and social mobility of certain population groups. Moreover, persistently high inequalities will also impact negatively on crucial economic, social and political variables and will thus seriously undermine the success of any development strategies. This will in particular have important consequences for the challenge of achieving the Millennium Development Goal of halving poverty worldwide by 2015.

There are therefore a number of concerns and policy challenges this book aims to address, which makes it overlap with other work on inequality. However, unlike previous work which is predominately empirical, the book's contribution will be mainly analytical. It approaches the problematic of inequality from different thematic areas, namely macroeconomics, trade policy, the political economy of the electoral process, and international finance, whose links with inequality have not been sufficiently explored in the past. The book therefore fills an important research gap, aiming to contribute to our understanding of how inequality operates in Latin America, how it interacts with and constrains macro, trade and international finance policies and the political process, and how it affects growth and development.

Following this introduction, Chapter 2 discusses different types of inequality – economic (income, employment and land), social (health, education and social security) and political (access to political power and legal institutions) – and their different dimensions – regional, urban/rural and group – and provides an analysis of their true extent in Latin America. It also examines why inequalities arise in the first place, how they interact and why some inequalities persist across time.

Chapter 3 examines the interaction between the macro-economy and inequality. It focuses on the analysis of macroeconomic policies adopted by Latin American countries in the post-reform context of fairly liberalized economies. It shows that high levels of inequality in the region have contributed to the level of economic, social and political vulnerability of Latin American countries to external shocks. Whilst the larger economies (e.g. Argentina and Brazil) have been vulnerable to financial shocks associated with volatile private capital flows, the smaller economies (e.g. Bolivia, El Salvador, Guatemala, Honduras) have been vulnerable to exogenous shocks, such as terms of trade shocks and natural disasters. The inability to respond appropriately to these shocks has resulted in major setbacks in the region's fight against poverty and inequality. At the same time, high levels of inequality across the continent have worked as a constraint to the adequate management of macroeconomic policies and have increased the volatility effects of shocks, which have aggravated inequality even further.

Chapter 4 follows on the discussion of financial shocks facing the larger economies but changes the focus by taking an international perspective. Specifically, it reviews the recent financial crises that took place in Mexico, Argentina and Brazil and argues that in order for policy reforms currently being implemented in Latin America to help increase economic growth and reduce poverty, important changes need to take place in international policies. In particular, the international community (the International Monetary Fund, the World Bank and the Inter-American Development Bank) needs to coordinate efforts to reduce the extent and impact of financial crises and help to manage them if and when they occur. Furthermore, the international financial institutions need also to encourage the adoption of social policies such as greater investment in human capital, tax reforms and asset redistribution if better distribution is to become a key policy objective in Latin America.

Chapter 5 examines the links between inequality and trade liberalization. It focuses on the analysis of the distributional impact of trade policies and trade policy reforms in a group of Latin American countries. The chapter uses a powerful simplification of the basic Hecksher–Ohlin model to discuss the links from trade policy and factor accumulation to the pattern of trade and the returns to skill and natural resources, which, in turn, will affect inequality. In order to develop this analysis, the chapter assembles a large data set that includes macro variables illustrating trade policy reforms, trade patterns and income distribution in Latin America. This data set is used as a basis for the discussion of some connections that can and cannot be made between those variables. The chapter shows that, in the short run, trade policy reform affects income distribution through changes in prices and changes in the allocation of factors of production. In the medium and long run, trade affects income distribution through specialization and change in the relative demand for factors of production, changes in productivity, changes in tariff revenue and expenditure and through long-term growth and growth volatility. The chapter also argues that macroeconomic policies, especially exchange rate policies and capital account liberalization, affect the impact of trade on income inequality. The chapter in addition examines unilateral, regional and global changes in trade policies in selected Latin American countries and concludes that (i) historically, unilateral trade policy reform has had greater impact on economic welfare and economic growth than policies designed to achieve regional integration, whereas (ii) future trade policy reforms that bring greater access of Latin American economies to northern markets will have large static and dynamic effects on economic efficiency.

Chapter 6 analyses the reasons why redistributive policies have failed in Latin America, by examining the case of the privatization of utilities. Under state ownership, utilities were inefficient and often failed to reach the poor. However, after privatization, universal service provision remained elusive and tariffs rose. In the first part of the chapter, the authors try to provide an explanation for the regressive policy bias in public sector utilities and discuss what can be done about it. Political economy theories of elections and policy making suggest that rational politicians seeking re-election should enact policies that appeal to the median voter. Given the skewed distribution of wealth in Latin America policies targeted at the median voter should be pro-poor, as noted earlier. However, Latin American countries experience some of the most regressive policies in the world. The authors thus ask: why Latin American policy makers, supposedly interested in winning elections, would choose policies that alienate poor voters and why nonetheless voters seem to support them. Using an array of tools from the emerging field of political economics, the authors show that the answer to that question can be directed to a multidimensional issue space, in which redistribution is not the only issue, and internal partisan politics is the best way to understand the policy maker and voter choices.

The final chapter provides a discussion of what can be done to reduce the extent of inequality in Latin America by governments and the civil society and the international community, including what role they can play in influencing both national and international policies aimed at reducing and/ or avoiding inequalities. It also draws lessons applicable to other developing countries.

Challenges for addressing inequality

As will be seen throughout this book, the crucial question is how much are society and the state in Latin America willing to intervene in order to reduce dysfunctional inequalities. Most Latin American governments have in place some form of distributional systems governed by an array of fiscal policies. However, even if fiscal policies are progressive, inequalities do not arise exclusively from disparities in wages and other earnings. As discussed in Chapter 2, inequalities are determined also by the opportunities and choices each individual faces and by forms of discrimination inherent in society.

Furthermore, income transfers may not be the most adequate policy for inequality reduction, as they may result in increased forms of social exclusion when stigma is attached to means-tested transfers (Atkinson, 1987). Reducing inequalities will thus require more pro-active state interventions in establishing equality of initial opportunities, as well as acting against forms of discrimination that exist in most societies. In other words, redistribution should refer not only to the redistribution of incomes, wealth and assets but also to the guarantee of equal choices and the redistribution of social and political rights.

This is not, strictly speaking, a conventional form of redistribution, as targeted poor households will not necessarily benefit from an increase of disposable income as they would with income transfers. It constitutes, however, a form of redistribution of assets (human capital and political assets) that will hopefully allow their recipients to be more productive and less excluded socially (Bourguignon, 2002). This will not be a pure form of redistribution of assets from one population group to another – since that would involve large social costs and would hence hardly be a feasible option – but will rather redistribute income from the rich, or the whole population, into the accumulation of assets among the poor (Bourguignon, 2002). Other relevant policies include the guarantee of equal access to job opportunities by all groups in the population, independently of gender, religion or ethnicity. Governments can also promote the protection of cultural differences, the right to use different languages, different ways of living and different artistic expressions, as well as establishing equal rights of access to economic, social, political and legal institutions by all population groups.

The guarantee of equal choices and opportunities and the redistribution of social and political rights are likely to face similar difficulties to the redistribution of incomes, wealth and assets, both at the economic and political level. The lack of capital and insurance markets and the extent of budget restrictions that characterize most Latin American countries may constrain the implementation of efficient redistributive systems and education and health programmes. In addition, the persistence of traditional labour structures may impede a change in social attitudes crucial to the reduction – and elimination – of discrimination and forms of segregation, not only in the labour market but in all areas of society. Finally, policies that guarantee more equal opportunities and a more equal distribution of social and political rights are also likely to face opposition from established elites as such policies may be perceived as a direct challenge to their economic and political influence.

The redistribution of financial resources and social and political rights require thus political determination on the part of the government, as well as the support of elites and a change of social attitudes. It requires also increased demand from the general population for redistribution and a more active participation of the civil society in holding the various governments to account on all issues related to redistribution and lobbying for the three types of intervention suggested above.

Several groups may have an important role to play in the process of inequality reduction in Latin America. Local small and medium enterprises are important sources of employment in most developing countries. Without a change in attitudes in local labour markets towards discrimination, segregation and other bad job practices, little will be achieved in terms of reducing social inequalities. Labour unions can also play an active role in the reduction of inequalities, as they will be able to influence both local job practices undertaken by public and private enterprises and lobby for the interests of otherwise disadvantaged groups in the design of national policies (Freeman and Medoff, 1984). In order to perform those tasks, labour unions need, however, to be well-organized, benefit from efficient communication channels, have well-managed and transparent accounts and be able to voice actively the demands of the workers they represent.

It is also particularly important that local communities are made aware of the devastating effects of inequality and the need to increase their demand for better and more extensive redistribution of incomes and social and political rights. The political participation of local communities, citizens' associations and local governments, and the strengthening of their demands for more redistributive policies, is thus crucial for the reduction and avoidance of persistent inequalities in Latin America.

International agencies can also have an important role to play in the process of inequality reduction. These institutions are generally in a good position to help increase awareness amongst national policy makers for the problem of inequality and the need to resolve it. They can also participate in building governments' technical capacity to deal with the various issues, by providing technical advice and support to individual governments in the design of adequate policies, such as the implementation of progressive tax systems in countries that experience serious budget constraints; policies that counteract the power of elites and their antagonism towards the redistribution of income, assets and wealth and social and political rights; policies that promote larger efficiency in administrative tasks (more qualified staff, wider use of computers, etc.); polices that increase the availability of more equal opportunities for all social groups (for instance, the establishment of universal secondary education, the increase of efficiency in the administration of public health systems and better targeting systems in the distribution of social benefits and other socially protective policies); policies aimed at directly reducing discrimination and segregation in the labour markets and in the access to social and judicial services, such as more transparent procedures in job applications and the use of indigenous languages in the design of legal documents; and the creation and provision of financial arrangements that provide credit, and thus higher financial auto-sufficiency, to poor people.

Notes

1 Killick (2002) makes an important distinction between functional and dysfunctional inequalities.
2 In the poverty measurement literature this is reflected in the focus axiom that requires poverty measures to be invariant to changes in the poverty indicator (e.g. income) above the poverty line (Sen, 1973).
3 Inequality levels in Latin America lie very much at the top end of the scale of observed inequality levels across all developing countries, hence it is not possible to observe low levels of inequality except in comparison to the Latin American average.
4 See Kanbur (1987) and Fields (1980). Fields shows evidence on other countries where trends in poverty and inequality have moved in opposite directions. See also World Bank (1990).

Bibliography

Alesina, A. and Perotti, R. (1993) *Income Distribution, Political Instability and Investment*, Working Paper no. 4486. Cambridge, MA: National Bureau of Economic Research.

Atkinson, A.B. (1987) 'Income Maintenance and Social Insurance', in A. Auerback and M. Feldstein (eds) *Handbook of Public Economics*, Amsterdam: Elsevier Science Publishers.

Becker, G.S. (1967) 'Crime and Punishment: An Economic Approach', *Journal of Political Economy*, 76(2), 169–217.

Behrman, J.R., Gaviria, A. and Székely, M. (2002) *Social Exclusion in Latin America: Introduction and Overview*, IADB Working Paper no. R-445. Washington, DC: Inter-American Development Bank.

Bénabou, R. (1996) *Inequality and Growth*, Working Paper no. 2123. Cambridge, MA: National Bureau of Economic Research.

Birdsall, N. and Londoño, J.L. (1997) 'Asset Inequality Matters: An Assessment of the World Bank's Approach to Poverty Reduction', *American Economic Review*, 87, 32–7.

Bourguignon, F. (2002) 'From Income to Endowments: The Difficult Task of Expanding the Income Poverty Paradigm'. Paper prepared for the conference on 'Conceptual Challenges in Poverty and Inequality Analysis', Cornell University, 16–17 April. Paris: DELTA, Ecole des Hautes Etudes en Siences Sociales.

Briceño-León, R., Perdomo, R.P., Navarro, J.C., Màrquez, P., Castillo, A. and Zubillaga, V. (1997) *La Violencia en Venezuela: Dimensionamiento y Políticas de Control*, Working Paper R-373. Washington, DC: Inter-American Development Bank.

Buvinic, M. and Mazza, J. (2003) *Social Inclusion and Economic Development in Latin America*, Washington, DC: Inter-American Development Bank.

Cruz, J.M., González, L.A., Romano, L.E. and Sisti, E. (1998) *La Violencia en El Salvador en los Años Noventa. Magnitud, Costos y Factors Posibilitadores*, Working Paper R-338. Washington, DC: Inter-American Development Bank.

Datt, G. and Ravallion, M. (1992) 'Growth and Redistribution Components of Changes in Poverty Measures: A Decomposition with Applications to Brazil and India in the 1980s', *Journal of Development Economics*, 38(2), 275–95.

Dollar, D., Easterly, W. and Gatti, R. (2000) *What Causes Political Violence? A Research Outline*, Washington, DC: World Bank: Development Research Group.

Elbadawi, I. A. (1999) *Civil Wars and Poverty: The Role of External Interventions, Political Rights and Economic Growth*, Washington DC: World Bank.

Fajnzylber, P., Lederman, D. and Loayza, N. (1998) *Determinants of Crime Rates in Latin America and the World: An Empirical Assessment*, World Bank Latin American and Caribbean Studies. Washington, DC: World Bank.

Freeman, R.B. and Medoff, J.L. (1984) *What Do Unions Do?*, New York: Basic Books.

Furman, J. and Stiglitz, J. (1998) *Economic Consequences of Income Inequality*, Federal Researve Bank of Kansas City Papers and Proceedings, 221–63.

Galor, O. and Zeira, J. (1993) 'Income Distribution and Macroeconomics', *Review of Economic Studies*, 60(1), 35–52.

Gupta, K.D. (1990) *The Economics of Political Violence: The Effect of Political Instability on Economic Growth*, New York: Praeger.

Hamilton, C.V., Huntley, L., Alexander, N., Guimaraes, A.S.A. and James, W. (2001) *Beyond Racism: Race and Inequality in Brazil, South Africa and the United States*, London: Lynne Rienner.

Hanmer, L. and Naschold, F. (2000) 'Attaining the International Development Targets: Will Growth Be Enough?', *Development Policy Review*, 18, 11–36.

Hanmer, L., Jong, N.D., Kurian, R. and Mooij, J. (1999) 'Are the DAC Targets Achievable? Poverty and Human Development in the Year 2015', *Journal of International Development*, 11(4), 547–63.

Hirschman, A.O. (1981) *Essays in Trespassing: Economics to Politics and Beyond*. Cambridge, MA: Cambridge University Press.

Kanbur, R. and Lustig, N. (1999) *Why is Inequality Back in the Agenda?*, Washington, DC: World Bank.

Killick, T. (2002) *Responding to Inequality*, Inequality Briefing Paper no. 3. London: DFID and ODI.

Lichbach, M.I. (1989) 'An Evaluation of "Does Economic Inequality Breed Political Conflict?" Studies', *World Politics*, 41, 431–70.

Lustig, N. (1995) *Coping with Austerity: Poverty and Inequality in Latin America*, Washington, DC: Brookings Institution Press.

McCulloch, N., Winters, A. and Cirera, X. (2001) *Trade Liberalisation and Poverty: A Handbook*, London: CEPR.

Morley, S. (1995) *Poverty and Inequality in Latin America: The Impact of Adjustment and Recovery in the 1980s*, Baltimore, MD and London: Johns Hopkins University Press.

Murphy, K.M., Shleifer, A. and Vishny, R. (1989) 'Income Distribution, Market Size, and Industrialization', *Quarterly Journal of Economics*, CIV(3), 537–64.

Perotti, R. (1993) 'Political Equilibrium, Income Distribution and Growth', *Review of Economic Studies*, 60(4), 755–76.

Ravallion, M. (1997) *Can High-Inequality Developing Countries Escape Absolute Poverty?* Washington, DC: World Bank.

Ribero, R. and Nuñez, J. (1999) *Productivity and the Household Investment in Health – The Case of Colombia*. Working Paper R-354. Washington, DC: Inter-American Development Bank.

Rubio, M. (1998) *La Violencia en Colombia. Dimensionamiento y Políticas de Control*. Working Paper R-345. Washington, DC: Inter-American Development Bank.

Sachs, J.D. (1990) 'Social Conflict and Populist Policies in Latin America', in R. Brunetta and C. Dell'Aringa (eds) *Labour Relations and Economic Performance*, Basingstoke: Macmillan and International Economic Association.

Saint-Paul, G. and Verdier, T. (1992) *Education, Democracy and Growth*, Discussion Paper no. 613. London: Centre for Economic Performance Research.

Sala-i-Martin, X. (1996) *Transfers, Social Safety Nets and Economic Growth*, IMF Working Paper WP/96/40, Washington, DC: International Monetary Fund.

Sen, A.K. (1985) *Commodities and Capabilities*, Oxford: North-Holland.

Stallings, B. and Peres, W. (2000) *Growth, Employment and Equity: The Impact of the Economic Reforms in Latin America and the Caribbean*, Washington, DC: ECLAC and Brookings Institution Press.

Stewart, F. (1998) *The Root Causes of Conflict: Some Conclusions*, Queen Elisabeth House, Working Paper Series no. 16, Oxford: University of Oxford.

—— (2002) *Horizontal Inequalities: A Neglected Dimension of Development*, Queen Elisabeth House, Working Paper Series no. 81, Oxford: University of Oxford.

Taylor, L. (2000) *External Liberalization, Economic Performance, and Distribution in Latin America and Elsewhere*. Working Paper no. 215. Helsinki: UNU/WIDER.

Tokman, V. and O'Donnel, G. (1998) *Poverty and Inequality in Latin America: Issues and Challenges*, Notre Dame, IN: University of Notre Dame Press.

Winters, L.A. (2002) 'Trade, Trade Policy and Poverty: What Are the Links?', *World Economy*, 25, 1339–67.

Wood, A. (1994) *North–South Trade, Employment and Inequality: Changing Fortunes in a Skill-Driven World*, Oxford: Clarendon Press.

World Bank (2003a) *World Development Report 2003*, Washington, DC: World Bank.

—— (2003b) *Inequality in Latin America and the Caribbean: Breaking With History?* Washington, DC: World Bank.

Zoninsein, J. (2001a) 'The Economic Case for Combating Racial and Ethnic Exclusion in Latin American and Caribbean Countries', IDB mimeo.

—— (2001b) 'GDP increases from Ending Long-Term Discrimination Against Blacks', in C.V. Hamilton, L. Huntley, N. Alexander, A.S.A. Guimaraes, and W. James (eds) *Beyond Racism: Race and Inequality in Brazil, South Africa and the United States*, London: Lynne Rienner.

2 Inequality in Latin America

Dimensions and processes

Patricia Justino, Julie Litchfield and Laurence Whitehead

Introduction

Latin American countries have some of the highest levels of income inequality in the world with an average Gini coefficient[1] above 0.50 since the 1960s (Table 2.1).[2] Although there were significant reductions in income poverty in Latin America during the 1990s (Table 2.2 and Appendix B), income inequality hardly changed during the same period.[3] High levels of inequality pose a serious threat to recent development undertakings, not only because inequalities may undermine efforts to eliminate poverty and destitution, but also because persistent inequalities waste financial and human resources, erode social cohesion and, consequently, pose serious constraints to the process of social and economic development.

High levels of inequality have indeed crippled efforts to reduce poverty in the Latin American region. While poverty decreased in the 1970s in Latin America, it nearly doubled during the 'lost decade' of the 1980s. In the

Table 2.1 Income inequalities in Latin America and the rest of the world

	1960	*1965*	*1970*	*1975*	*1980*	*1985*	*1990*	*1995*
OECD countries	0.40	0.37	0.38	0.37	0.36	0.36	0.36	0.37
Latin America and the Caribbean	0.52	0.50	0.54	0.54	0.52	0.55	0.55	0.56
North Africa and the Middle East	0.50	0.47	0.50	0.49	0.41	0.47	0.39	0.35
Sub-Saharan Africa	0.52	0.51	0.56	0.44	0.42	0.46	0.53	0.45
South Asia	0.39	0.37	0.37	0.38	0.38	0.39	0.36	0.30
East Asia and the Pacific	0.40	0.38	0.36	0.40	0.39	0.40	0.40	0.38

Source: Deininger and Squire (1996) and World Income Inequality Dataset, UNU/ WIDER (http://www.wider.unu.edu/wiid/wiid.htm).

Table 2.2 Income poverty in Latin America and the rest of the world[1]

	1981	1984	1987	1990	1993	1996	1999	2001
Europe and Central Asia	0.7	0.5	0.4	0.5	3.7	4.2	6.3	3.7
Latin America and the Caribbean	9.7	11.8	10.9	11.3	11.3	10.7	10.5	9.5
North Africa and the Middle East	5.1	3.8	3.2	2.3	1.6	2.0	2.6	2.4
Sub-Saharan Africa	41.6	46.3	46.8	44.6	44.0	45.6	45.7	46.9
South Asia	51.5	46.8	45.0	41.3	40.1	36.6	32.2	31.3
East Asia and the Pacific	57.7	38.9	28.0	29.6	24.9	16.6	15.7	14.9

Source: World Bank, World Development Indicators (http://www.worldbank.org/research/povmonitor).

Note
1 Refers to the percentage of the population living below US$1 per day.

1990s, the poor still constituted, on average, a large percentage of the total Latin American population, despite higher rates of economic growth (Birdsall and Londoño, 1997; IADB, 1998). This is due in part to the persistence of income inequality. Persistent forms of income inequality are also likely to be correlated with other forms of social and political inequalities such as disparities in employment conditions (between, for instance, skilled and non-skilled workers), differences in the access to land and other physical assets, discrepancies in the use of and access to health, education and other social services, and variations in the rights of access to political power (reflected, for instance, in the membership of labour unions and the exercise of voting rights) and access to legal institutions. The successful achievement of the Millennium Development Goals of halving poverty by 2015 in a context of equitable and sustainable development may thus be put at risk if inequalities continue to rise in Latin America.

In this chapter, we examine the extent of inequality in Latin America and discuss some structural processes that may explain the persistence of inequalities in the region across time and amongst certain socio-economic groups. By inequality we refer not only to differences in income or consumption expenditure between population groups that hinder the welfare of these groups, but also to discrepancies in social and political indicators. The persistence of inequalities due to social exclusion and difficulties in accessing social services and socio-political institutions has undermined efforts to decrease income inequality, has increased group and individual vulnerability and has created poverty traps caused by the impossibility of social and physical mobility. In Latin America, the most affected groups are typically African descendants and/or indigenous populations, who are often found more likely to be poor, have lower education, lower nutrition levels and worse access to health care and other social institutions than any other population groups (Justino and Litchfield, 2003). Just as income is only one aspect of poverty, income inequality is only one aspect of inequality and other aspects (in particular, social, cultural and political) may have had an important role in the processes and inputs that have led to the well-documented persistence of large inequalities amongst groups and individuals in Latin America.

In the section below, we analyse the extent of economic, social and political inequalities in Latin America across several vertical and horizontal dimensions, namely rural and urban areas,[4] different racial groups and different ethnicities. In the third section, 'Determinants of persistent inequality in Latin America' we present a simplified framework for thinking about the persistence of inequalities in Latin America. We argue that inequalities arise and persist because individuals start from unequal initial circumstances, which are maintained by social and market forces. The final section summarises the evidence and concludes the chapter.

Inequalities in Latin America

Failures to reduce poverty in Latin America have been associated not only with increased inequalities in income, as described above, but also with inequalities in the access to social and political institutions, in particular with inadequate access of some population groups to resources, markets and socio-political institutions and their exclusion from political power, media access, access to health care, education and employment and access to markets for land, credit and technology. This enlarged concept of inequality is, however, associated with important analytical difficulties due to the subjectivity it entails. One of the most significant difficulties is the lack of adequate disaggregated data. Household surveys are one of the richest sources of information on the different forms of inequality. Unfortunately, representative household surveys are not available for all Latin American countries. And when they are available they tend to cover recent years and thus do not allow the construction of an historical picture of monetary or non-monetary inequalities in Latin America. They also tend not to cover remote rural areas, a particularly serious problem as these are areas inhabited by groups likely to be found at the bottom of any economic, social or political distribution of assets and rights.[5] Household surveys and cross-country datasets are also rather poor in terms of non-monetary variables, which has imperilled the analysis of socio-political inequalities. Despite these difficulties, information available in various studies of Latin America has allowed us to build a strong picture of the extent of the various dimensions of inequality in Latin America and fill in an important gap in the literature on inequality in Latin America, which, more often than not, focus solely on income inequality.

Economic inequalities

Although income inequality is by far the largest component of economic inequalities in Latin America, some evidence has shown that large disparities have also been found in the earnings and employment opportunities of skilled and unskilled workers and in the distribution of an important asset – land.

Poor people are often found to be employed in low-earning activities. It is, however, difficult to measure accurately the extent of employment inequalities in developing economies due to the presence of large informal sectors and the persistence of underemployment amongst the poorest households. In addition, it is also difficult to discern the direction of any cause-effect in the relationship between employment and inequality. However, empirical evidence collected for Latin America (though not extensive) has shown that employment inequalities have been closely associated to overall inequality levels. Attanasio and Székely (1999) find that 11.3 per cent of total poverty in Latin America is explained by differences in wages between sectors of activity using skilled and unskilled labour. They also show that 21.5 per cent of all poverty in Latin America is associated with differences across occupational groups. This value hides some regional discrepancies: while in Nicaragua the extent of poverty explained by inequalities across occupational groups is a mere 1.2 per cent, in Mexico and Chile that estimate raises to over 40 per cent.

Land is often one of the most important assets held by the poor and, although other physical assets (livestock, equipment, etc.) may affect their welfare, access to land is usually the asset most closely associated with the probability of an individual or household being poor in developing countries (Rodriguez and Smith, 1994; IFAD, 2001; Deininger and Olinto, 2000). As such, it is not surprising that differences in access to land explain to a large extent the persistence of inequalities in developing countries. This is because people at the bottom of economic, social and political distributions of assets and rights in developing countries tend to concentrate in rural areas. Land is important for their economic survival and for their prospects of social mobility. In most developing countries, land is also synonymous of social and political power. Table 2.3 shows the extent of land inequality in Latin America.[6]

Land inequality in Latin America has been very high over the last six decades and has shown little signs of reduction. This may well explain, to a

Table 2.3 Land Gini concentration index in Latin America

	1941–50	1951–60	1961–70	1971–80	1981–90
Argentina	–	0.8625	0.8730	–	0.8598
Bolivia	–	–	–	–	0.7677
Brazil	0.8329	0.8347	0.8370	0.8521	–
Chile	–	0.9330	–	–	–
Colombia	–	0.8598	–	0.8592	0.7742
Costa Rica	0.8072	0.7820	0.7913	0.8133	–
Cuba	–	–	–	0.6061	0.6339
Dominican R.	0.7962	0.7999	0.7900	0.8197	–
Ecuador	–	0.8642	–	0.8155	–
El Salvador	0.8309	–	0.8386	0.8075	–
Guatemala	0.8588	0.8280	–	0.8484	–
Honduras	–	0.7512	–	0.7788	–
Mexico	0.5915	0.6216	0.7470	–	–
Nicaragua	–	0.8009	–	0.3177	–
Panama	0.7129	0.7326	–	0.7778	0.8712
Paraguay	–	0.8583	–	0.9281	0.9390
Peru	–	0.9350	0.9355	0.9105	–
Uruguay	–	0.8200	0.8147	0.8034	0.8400
Venezuela	–	0.9270	0.9244	0.9096	–
USA	0.7035	0.7152	0.7165	0.7455	0.7536
UK	0.7206	0.7166	0.6939	0.6754	0.6214
France			0.5165	0.5772	0.5821

Source: IFAD (2001).

large extent, the level of inequality between rural and urban areas in Latin America, as well as regional disparities. Land inequalities are also often closely related with inequalities in other assets. One of the impacts of land inequality economists have studied extensively relates to the importance of land for access to credit and, consequently, how land inequality determines inequalities in other asset endowments. Attanasio and Székely (1999) report the results of a simulation showing that in Colombia, if the poor had the same access to credit as the non-poor, poverty might be reduced considerably. Similar results were found for Costa Rica. The Costa Rica study shows further that having access to some kinds of capital through credit markets is as important as owning the asset itself.

The income extracted from land is also important (Escobal *et al.*, 1999). In a study of poverty in Costa Rica, Trejos and Montiel (1999) show that over 90 per cent of all poor farmers could move out of poverty if they increased land productivity levels. This suggests that what is important is not only inequality in the access to land but also disparities in access to better land quality, new technologies and new markets. The importance of land inequality in explaining overall asset and other inequalities has been further emphasised by Birdsall and Londoño (1997), who find that 0.5 percentage points of the difference in overall annual growth and 1.4 percentage points of the difference in annual income growth of the poor between Latin America and East Asia is explained by Latin America's greater initial land and education inequality.

There is thus a large scope for land reform policies to contribute towards the reduction of inequality in Latin America. Land reforms have, however, rarely been successful in reducing inequality in developing countries. This failure is often attributed to the absence of effective mobilisation of the lower classes in rural areas, the lack of linkages to political parties and to serious redistributive programmes, and the political and social power of the landowners (Herring, 1983, 1991). However, a new style of reform has been tried in South Africa, Colombia and Brazil. These land reform programmes rely on voluntary land transfers based on negotiation between buyers and sellers, mediated through local government. The role of the local government is to establish a legal framework and provide part of the purchase price to eligible beneficiaries (Deininger, 1999; Killick, 2002). If successful, these land reforms may increase the accumulation potential of small businesses and of households with small home enterprises and, therefore, contribute towards the decrease of asset inequality in Latin America.

Social inequalities

Social inequalities are particularly acute in Latin America and take place in three important sectors: health care, education and the distribution of social security benefits. These inequalities are determined not only by the access of some population groups to health, education and other social services, but also by the quality of these services. Most Latin America countries have in place universal primary education and primary health care, as well as basic social insurance and social assistance programmes. In fact, social expenditure on health, education and social security in Latin America during the 1990s was quite progressive, in the sense that it reached most of the poor (Stallings and Peres, 2000). However, it is often found that these sectors are organised along a two-tier system, whereby some population groups have to rely on badly organised and poorly designed public services, whereas better-off groups have access to private insurance, private hospitals and private schools.

Health inequalities

Latin America has some of the highest levels of health inequality in the world (Wagstaff, 2000; Wagstaff and Watanabe, 2000). Table 2.4 illustrates the access to health and sanitation in several Latin American countries, disaggregated by rural and urban areas. In some countries, like Costa Rica, health inequalities are quite small. However, for instance, in Paraguay, while 65 per cent of the urban population has access to adequate sanitation and 70 per cent to safe drinking water, only 14 per cent of the rural population has adequate sanitation and a mere 6 per cent has access to safe drinking water.

The design of health systems in Latin America is likely to be an important cause of these inequalities. In most Latin American countries, health systems are characterised by little continuity in policy implementation, large waiting lists, low health financing and low social spending. In addition, the allocation of services within public health systems in Latin America is seldom done according to need and hardly any links exist between primary care and hospital care. This results in the existence of a large non-accountable hospital

Table 2.4 Access to health and sanitation in Latin America

	Adequate sanitation (1990–7)		Safe drinking water (1995)		Health services (1985–95)	
	Urban	Rural	Urban	Rural	Urban	Rural
Bolivia	74	37	88	43	77	52
Brazil	80	30	80	28	–	–
Chile	90	–	99	47	–	–
Colombia	97	56	90	32	–	–
Costa Rica	95	70	100	99	100	63
Dominican R.	76	83	88	55	84	67
Ecuador	95	49	81	10	70	20
Guatemala	95	74	97	48	47	25
Honduras	–	57	91	66	80	56
Nicaragua	34	35	93	28	100	60
Panama	–	–	99	73	95	64
Paraguay	65	14	70	6	90	38
Peru	89	37	91	31	–	–
Trinidad & Tobago	99	98	100	88	100	99
Venezuela	64	30	79	79	–	–
Average	81	52	90	49	84	54

Source: IFAD (2001).

sector, characterised by high costs and little professional regulation (in terms of working hours, private practice, quality of care, etc.) (DFID, 2001). Birdsall and Hecht (2000) report that in Brazil, in the mid-1980s, almost 80 per cent of all public health spending was aimed at curative high-cost hospital care, concentrated in urban areas and in the south (the most affluent area). In Peru, in 1984, Lima benefited from almost 47 per cent of the government's budget for patient-related care, even though Lima has only 32 per cent of the country's population. This situation changed very little in the past years.

In many Latin American countries, health expenditure is fairly progressive because only the poor use subsidised government health centres and hospitals. However, the large subsidies provided by the government to social security-based health care for the middle-classes counteracts initial progressivity. In Brazil, for instance, households in the top income quintile received around 38 per cent of all public subsidies for health (Birdsall and Hecht, 2000). One of the few exceptions is Costa Rica, where the richer fractions of the population must contribute towards the social security-based health fund, even if they resort to private doctors and hospitals. Another exception is Chile, where a single national health fund has been established, in an effort to promote equity in health. This fund has allowed Chile to cover another 15 per cent of the population that, until recently, was not covered by the social insurance system (Birdsall and Hecht, 2000). These examples may, therefore, provide viable alternatives for the unequal, inefficient and costly health systems currently in place in most other Latin American countries.

There is a large scope for changes in health policies in Latin America to contribute towards the decrease of social inequalities in the region. This should certainly be a central element in government policies in Latin America, as better health access improves nutrition, decreases mortality rates and increases the human capital availability in the country. It also increases the chances of individuals accessing better jobs and, consequently, higher wages. In an analysis of how public and private investments in health in Colombia relate to future earnings of individuals, Ribero and Nuñez (1999) find that (i) one more day of disability decreases male rural earnings by 33 per cent and female by 13 per cent, (ii) having a disability in a given month decreases earnings of urban males by 28 per cent and urban females by 14 per cent, and (iii) having one more centimetre of stature (which is related to the quality of child nutrition) increases urban female earnings by 6.9 per cent and urban male by 8 per cent. This strongly suggests that policies oriented toward eliminating health differences would result in reduced inequalities across all other dimensions.

Education inequalities

Deinenger and Squire (1996) report, based on a cross-country analysis, that public schooling benefits the bottom 40 per cent of the population the most. This result suggests that access to education is vital to achieving equality. Tables 2.5 and 2.6 illustrate the extent of inequalities in the access to education in Latin America. Education inequalities in Latin America, measured by the Gini coefficient for a distribution of school attainment (defined by years of school completed), decreased in the four decades represented in Table 2.5. However, despite this decrease and, although education inequality is lower in Latin America than in other developing regions (North Africa and the Middle East, sub-Saharan Africa and Asia), it is almost twice the level of education inequality in OECD countries and in formally centrally planned economies.

The Gini coefficients for education in Latin America hide discrepancies across the region (Attanasio and Székely, 1999). Table 2.6 shows the level of illiteracy in four Latin America countries. As with health inequalities, the table reveals that illiteracy is much higher in rural areas in Latin America than in urban areas. Illiteracy is also higher for females than for males, which highlights the fact that gender inequalities in Latin America may indeed be higher than what is commonly suggested.

Inequality in education reflects itself in inequalities in labour participation and earnings, as groups with higher education levels tend to have higher rates of participation in the labour market and higher earnings, particularly for females. Although there are a few exceptions (Brazil, Honduras and

Table 2.5 Education and income inequalities in Latin America and the rest of the world

	1960	1965	1970	1975	1980	1985	1990	1995
OECD countries	0.21	0.21	0.21	0.23	0.21	0.21	0.21	0.24
North Africa and Middle East	0.86	0.86	0.83	0.83	0.78	0.71	0.65	0.53
Sub-Saharan Africa	0.83	0.74	0.75	0.73	0.67	0.64	0.63	0.75
South Asia	0.86	0.80	0.78	0.76	0.77	0.73	0.69	0.62
East Asia and the Pacific	0.51	0.49	0.41	0.39	0.35	0.32	0.31	0.39
Latin America and the Caribbean	0.50	0.51	0.48	0.45	0.44	0.44	0.39	0.43
Formally centrally planned economies	0.33	0.36	0.32	0.56	0.53	0.45	0.35	0.23

Source: Checchi (2000): 13.

Table 2.6 Illiteracy rates in selected Latin American countries

	Year	Total		Male		Female	
		Urban	Rural	Urban	Rural	Urban	Rural
Bolivia	1976	16.0	55.3	6.6	37.7	24.3	67.8
	1992	8.9	36.1	3.7	23.0	13.5	49.4
Brazil	1976	14.4	40.6	12.0	39.4	16.6	41.9
	1991	10.7	31.1	–	–	–	–
Costa Rica	1950	8.1	27.9	6.1	26.7	9.7	29.3
	1973	4.9	17.0	4.0	16.6	5.7	17.5
Guatemala	1973	28.2	68.6	20.0	59.9	35.5	77.6
	1994	16.8	47.8	11.2	38.5	21.6	56.9

Source: IFAD (2001).

Guatemala), universal primary education is in place in most of Latin America. The central problem currently faced by Latin American countries is the improvement of the quality of education and the implementation of universal secondary education (Londoño, 1996; IADB, 1999). Education inequalities in Latin America are reflected in the fact that, while the rich continue in education until they finish university, the poor typically leave school at the end of primary education. When higher levels of education are associated with higher returns to education, as in Latin America (Attanasio and Székely, 1999), inequalities will rise in all areas affected by education returns (earnings, job achievements) between those with higher levels of education and those with only primary school education.

It is thus important that governments in Latin America not only increase the access to education overall, but ensure also that more of the poor progress to and complete secondary school. This implies also improving the quality of primary schools attended by the poor (Londoño, 1996). Inequalities in both the quantity and quality of social services is bound to reflect themselves on wage inequalities and labour market segmentation (IADB, 1999), as better schooling is also associated with greater social mobility (Lam and Schoeni, 1993; Behrman *et al.*, 1998; Dahan and Gaviria, 1999; Binder and Woodruff, 1999).

Inequality in access to social security

The extent of social inequality in Latin America is demonstrated not only in the health and education sectors but also in the access to the social security benefits. Most countries in Latin America have implemented systems of social security; however, coverage by those systems varies substantially across different countries and population groups. Most systems have, in fact, resulted in the 'stratification of social security' (Mesa-Lago, 1983), whereby the most powerful groups (the military, civil servants and the labour aristocracy) benefit from the best systems. This has resulted in very regressive systems with the higher strata benefiting from better systems than the lower income groups (mostly uninsured). For instance, in 1973 in Brazil, people with less than one unit of minimum legal salary contributed with 17.2 per cent of their income towards the social security system, whereas the contribution of those with more than nine units of minimum legal salary was of 11.5 per cent. The more powerful the pressure group, the earlier it receives social protection, the greater the degree of coverage, the less costs it has to cover and the more generous the benefits it receives (Mesa-Lago, 1983).

Governments have slowly tried to change this situation. The pioneer was Chile which, in 1981, implemented a privately managed and funded defined-contribution system, controlled by the government. The Chilean model was recently adopted by Peru, Argentina, Colombia, Uruguay and Mexico. Evidence has shown, however, that in practice the systems have not met their redistributive objectives of transferring income from the rich to the poor and disparities in the coverage of rural and urban workers remain (CIID, 1999). There is also evidence for a negative impact of the new systems on new gender inequalities: at the time of retirement, women receive lower pensions than men (due to their longer life expectancy), as well as receiving lower salaries and spending less time in the labour market (due to their reproductive role) (CIID, 1999). These systems nevertheless represent a positive departure from the regressive pay-as-you-go systems that were previously in place.

Political inequalities

Political inequalities are notoriously difficult to quantify as they are determined by many subjective factors.[7] In addition, survey respondents tend to avoid revealing their political attitudes and activities. As a consequence, very few household surveys contain information that can be quantified or even used to infer on the extent of political inequalities. We have nonetheless attempted to discuss two important areas of inequality in political outcomes: access to political power and to legal institutions.

Inequalities in access to political power

High levels of inequality may create barriers that prevent the poor from equal political participation as the rich and, consequently, from voicing their demands in equal weight to the rich. Gacitúa and Sojo (2000) argue that, in Latin America, democracy failures (in particular, clientism and corruption) have resulted in the exclusion of large sectors of the poor population from involvement in political life. They have also resulted in the 'over'-representation of the non-poor and in the favouring of alliances between the non-poor and the poor on terms that are disempowering to the latter. Thus, the non-poor accumulate political advantages both through their domination of the state apparatus, the legal system, and the parties and through their informal social power, as landowners, bankers, employers, media voices, academics, and the controllers of pervasive patron–client relations. Of course the situation varies from country to country, and from one historical setting to the next, but the politically powerful remain heavily concentrated among a narrow and unrepresentative stratum of society – white, male, university educated (often abroad), urban, propertied, with privileged access to the legal system and embedded within highly personalised support networks.

In addition to these objective characteristics, the traditionally powerful non-poor are subjectively unified by a variety of (partly unspoken and unanalysed) beliefs about the status quo, their place within it, and the debts they owe to each other. All this makes for a durable and flexible system of elite domination and perpetuation, and it structures and limits the political spaces available to the majority of poorer and less privileged citizens.

Although this stereotypical image of a closed dominant oligarchy self-consciously dedicated to the protection of its own privileges may not be present in all Latin American countries, the general view is that, despite an appearance of pluralism and even ideological discord, the dominant political groupings operate within a tacit and socially understood framework of assumptions about their privileges, entitlements and impunities. When these assumptions come under threat (e.g. from democratisation or from political movements demanding redistribution) ranks are closed and underlying realities become more visible.

The influence of elites simultaneously accentuates and is accentuated by the low organisational capacity of poorer groups. Empirical evidence in support of this argument is, unfortunately, scarce. Escobal *et al.* (1999) estimate that membership of social organisations is closely associated with poverty in Peru. In Colombia, there was an effort after 1982 to restore democracy in local governments and reallocate sectoral functions to municipalities (Moore and Putzel, 1999). Some evidence has suggested that democratic decentralisation has increased the representation of non-elites, although other problems have limited the reduction of inequalities in the country.

We need to ask how the poor majority can make their voices heard, and perhaps redress these structural political inequalities given the formal and informal advantages concentrated in the hands of elite groupings.[8] One possibility is to seek a powerful oligarchic patron who is willing to build a multi-class clientele system. The PFL in Brazil is a good demonstration of how this may be successfully accomplished. In this case those poor citizens who are willing to throw their weight behind a traditional oligarchic establishment may obtain both material and possibly even political advantages derived from its electoral success. But within this framework there will be strong disincentives to autonomous organisation or consciousness raised by the poor (against the rich). The model is at best one of conditional empowerment through vertical channels.

An alternative possibility is to organise strategic segments of the poor majority in autonomous structures directed against the prevailing patterns of privilege and inequality. The PT in Brazil has followed that route (notably in greater São Paulo under Lula) with success comparable to that of the PFL in a different region of the country. Here the model is one of radical mobilisation on a horizontal axis. Note this too has its limitations. The strategic segments of the poor majority that can be organised (trade unionists in the industrial belt) may not be the neediest of the poor, and their interests may not coincide fully with those of the unorganised. More seriously, they may be unable to achieve lasting and socially legitimate redistribution unless they can find allies within dissident elite sectors. Over time the horizontal model may therefore depart from its ideological origins, and come to look more like the multi-class vertical structure championed by its competitor. This is not to say that the PT and the PFL become indistinguishable, either in social composition or in ideology. But as they become more successful and entrenched they may come increasingly to reflect the inequalities and hierarchies of the surrounding society.

This does not mean that it is impossible to rectify the entrenched political inequalities (both formal and informal) discussed above. Democratisation, decentralisation, division and diffusion of powers, subsidiarity, and accountability can all be advanced in ways that gradually increase the responsiveness of the political system to the interests and aspirations of the poor majority. But if so this will come about through protracted (and erratic) processes of social contestation and political learning. It cannot be simply decreed from above or read off from some predictable set of institutional prescriptions.

Inequality in access to legal institutions

Inequalities in the access to political power will determine closely the performance of legal institutions. Typically public legal systems, systems of protection of property, prisons and so forth benefit citizens largely in proportion to their levels of wealth or investment (Bénabou, 2000; Genn, 1999). Although it is not easy to detect who chooses to litigate, developed countries have recognised that the poor do not bring up legal grievances when the law would permit them to do so (Genn, 1999).

In the context of Latin America, the Inter-America Development Bank has begun, since 1994, to fund an 'access to justice' project (Domingo and Sieder, 2001), in order to guarantee equality in legal protection for deprived population groups, particularly the poor, ethnic minorities and women. These groups have traditionally been denied equal access to Latin America's judicial system (Hammergren *et al.*, 2002). Courts are typically located in urban areas and other zones where deprived groups do not live and may have difficulties in accessing. The groups often cannot afford the normal costs of judicial processes. Even those supposed to be free may include hidden costs – counsel, documents, bribes, transportation, etc. – that are above the limited financial capacity of the poor. In addition, the type of language and concepts used are often difficult to grasp by those with limited literary abilities and those that speak minority languages. The view that the judicial system in Latin America is characterised by discrimination and prejudice contributes towards distrust and altogether avoidance by most citizens (Hammergren *et al.*, 2002). In view of this situation, it is important that the new 'access to justice' policies address the degree of discrimination and encourage the spread of information in order to reduce the extent of inequalities within the Latin American judicial systems.

Determinants of persistent inequality in Latin America

Inequalities in Latin America are very large and have shown little sign of improvement in recent decades, despite large social, economic and political changes that have taken place across the region. One question that has worried development practitioners and policy makers in Latin America is why these inequalities have been so difficult to reduce.

The understanding of persistent inequalities and the processes of inequality formation have concerned social scientists for a long time and we do not intend to review this vast literature that can traced back to Greek philosophy. Our intention in this section is to present a simplified framework for thinking about persistent inequalities that can be practically translated into policy recommendations for Latin American countries. We argue that inequalities arise and persist because individuals start from unequal initial circumstances, which are maintained by social and market forces. In other words, inequalities arise because different individuals face different opportunities and choices. These may be determined by individual circumstances, social and family networks and initial endowments of physical and human capital or by forms of discrimination inherent to the various societies (defined by historical processes or otherwise). In addition, inequalities arise and persist due to the existence of unequal distribution systems in the economy. The absence of systematic actions against those three factors – initial opportunities, forms of discrimination and unequal distribution systems – explains, in turn, why inequalities persist across time.

Initial opportunities

Inequalities will arise when people face different opportunities. These are often determined by family relations and surrounding social environments (social capital). The relationship between the social and economic position of individuals and family circumstances and the issue of how different generations move along the income and social strata (i.e. intergenerational mobility) have been extensively analysed by social scientists.

Inequality can be transmitted through family relations via several means. One is through wealth inheritances. When credit markets are imperfect, which is the case in most Latin American countries, dynasties with little initial wealth will face limited investment opportunities and remain poor. Other means include the transmission of productive abilities and efficient human capital investments across generations, as well as family transmission of ambition and other tastes that are conducive to high productive ability (Piketty, 1998). Dahan and Gaviria (1998) examined the experience of Latin American countries and found that families tend to accentuate overall inequality of income and earnings. In a later paper, Dahan and Gaviria (1999) use sibling correlations in schooling to measure differences in intergenerational mobility. They argue that if there is perfect social mobility, family background would not matter and siblings would behave as two random people chosen from the total population. If, on the other hand, family background matters, then siblings would behave in a similar fashion. They find that intergenerational mobility is quite low in Latin America, which registers a coefficient of 0.49 (indicating that siblings behave quite similarly), against a coefficient of 0.20 for the US.

In addition, Attanasio and Székely (1999) found that a child's attainment in school (average number of years spent in school) and family education in Latin America are strongly positively correlated. This is likely to be explained by the fact that more educated parents put more input into their children's education. Alternatively, less educated parents may face financial difficulties that prevent them from borrowing the funds necessary to see their children through a certain number of years of school. In order to investigate these two hypotheses, they look at household surveys for Bolivia, Costa Rica, Chile, El Salvador, Paraguay and Venezuela. These household surveys ask children and young adults not enrolled in school why they are not attending school. Attanasio and Székely estimate that around 25 per cent of all 21-year-olds from the first quintile (bottom 20 per cent of the income distribution) answer that they are not enrolled in school because they lack the necessary resources, while 17.8 per cent do not attend because they are working. Amongst those in the top decile of the income distribution, only 9 per cent give lack of financial resources as the reason why they are not in school. In addition, poorer children tend, in general, to attend lower scoring schools than children from better-off families. These facts, allied with better family connections and larger initial wealth of children from richer families, further contribute towards the deepening of inequalities across generations.

Other social relations may equally explain the emergence of inequalities in society due to the access to different initial opportunities and choices. One key example is local segregation into unequal communities. Bénabou (1993) examines the likelihood that public goods and educational opportunity are greater in richer neighbourhoods than in the poorer neighbourhoods.[9] The lower cost of acquisition of human capital in a given area is an incentive factor that, combined with higher wages for skilled labour, induces increases in land prices which, in turn, exclude lower income groups from moving into those neighbourhoods. As segregation is practised by upper-income groups, the cost of acquisition of human capital rises in poorer neighbourhoods due both to deterioration of public goods and the lack of spill-over effects that usually originated from larger pool of skilled labour. Cutler and Glaeser (1997) (quoted in Piketty, 1998) find that a one standard deviation decrease in segregation would eliminate one-third of the black–white differential in schooling and employment outcomes in the USA. Other econometric studies have, furthermore, suggested that neighbourhood characteristics, such as average educational level of the adults, contribute to poverty-inducing factors, such as teenage pregnancy and low-level schooling achievement among the young (Durlauf, 2000). In addition, Wilson (1987) (quoted in Piketty, 1998) argues that residential segregation may contribute towards labour market discriminations and, consequently, to differences in initial opportunities between those individuals who live in better areas and those who live in less desirable residential districts. Furthermore, because credit constraints tend to accentuate forms of residential segregation, credit imperfections, local segregation and discrimination can operate together and lead to a cumulative process of socially inefficient persistent inequality (Piketty, 1998). Molina *et al.* (2002) find that individual and neighbourhood-level interactions between ethnicity and segregation in Bolivia are significantly and negatively correlated with income and schooling attainment.

Forms of discrimination

Discrimination and unequal initial opportunities often go hand in hand, although the existence of discrimination against specific population groups is usually difficult to prove empirically. It is also difficult to prove that inequalities between population groups and the exclusion of some groups from the access to social, economic and political institutions are a result of discrimination (Justino and Litchfield, 2003). We can nevertheless deduce causality from the fact that exclusion and poverty are generally higher among some population groups (such as indigenous people, households of African descendance or women), and that inequalities between these groups and the rest of the population tend to persist and/or become worse over time (Justino and Litchfield, 2003).

Race and ethnicity are complex issues. In Latin America, they are usually defined as having a maternal language other than Spanish (or Portuguese in Brazil). They are one of the most important correlates of inequality in Latin America, as African descendants and indigenous peoples often constitute the majority of the poor in many Latin American countries. In fact, in Latin America, countries with large ethnic groups are the most unequal ones (Gacitúa and Sojo, 2000). This also coincides with people's perceptions of inequality in the region. When asked to mention the most discriminated groups in their countries, the vast majority of the answers concentrated on three groups: African descendants, indigenous people and the poor (Behrman *et al.*, 2002).

These perceptions are reflected in most social indicators (literacy, school attendance, malnutrition, infant mortality, access to services, etc.), which are much worse for indigenous populations than for society as a whole (World Bank, 1993). Health inequalities are particularly high. In Peru, 27 per cent of all children under age five suffer chronic malnutrition. The situation in Ecuador is similar. In the Amazon region of Peru, this figure reaches 70 per cent, and, in places such as Atalaya, with an Ashaninka population, the value is 91 per cent (World Bank, 1993). Disparities in education between indigenous groups and the rest of the population are also strong in Latin America. In Mexico, 63 per cent of the indigenous population (most of them living in the state of Chiapas) are illiterate compared to 42 per cent of the non-indigenous population. In Colombia, the primary school enrolment rate for indigenous children is around 11 per cent and 44 per cent of adults in the indigenous population are illiterate. In terms of access to services, in Mexico, for instance, indigenous people have a poor record in terms of housing quality and access to services such as piped water, electricity and communications (World Bank, 1999).

One way in which discrimination can result in persistent inequalities is through what the literature refers to as 'self-fulfilling beliefs'. Persistent inequality through self-fulfilling beliefs derives from the fact that lower classes internalise that they will not be able to climb the social ladder and therefore assume behaviours that will keep them at the bottom of the distribution (Bourdieu, 1986; Akerlof and Kranton, 2000). Inequality between two social groups with homogeneous characteristics generated from self-fulfilling beliefs can make inequality between population groups more persistent than it would otherwise be (Piketty, 1998).

This situation is reinforced by the fact that individuals tend to identify themselves with certain groups. Once groups assume a strong identity, mobility between groups is generally low and the way in which certain groups are perceived by society changes very slowly. Inequalities between groups – i.e. horizontal inequalities (Stewart, 2002) – constitute an important dimension of development. Family connections, segregation of neighbourhoods and discrimination are strong mechanisms through which those group inequalities not only arise but also persist across time. Persistent inequalities between different population groups may create unfair situations, where some groups benefit from access to good schools and better health care and have a high political influence, whereas others suffer from serious deprivation.

Non-progressive distributional systems

Inequalities can arise and persist, not only due to different initial opportunities and discrimination, but also as a result of unequal distribution systems. One of the most significant examples is the existence of inefficient and non-progressive, or even regressive, fiscal systems. Most tax systems in developing countries are not progressive (Killick, 2002). In a survey of tax incidence in a sample of 20 developing and in transition countries, Chu *et al.* (2000) found that tax systems were progressive in just over a third of cases. About a fifth of all cases were regressive and the remainder neutral. This results from the fact that implementing progressive tax systems in developing countries is very difficult, given the existence of weak governments, influenced by elites and affected by corruption, political interests, the persistence of high tax evasion and the existence of very small taxable income bases (Radian, 1980; Newbery and Stern, 1987).

Most Latin American countries face a combination of insufficient tax resources and uneven tax systems (Shome, 1999; Tanzi, 2000). While bottom tax rates (both personal and corporate) have increased in the late 1990s, top tax rates have decreased steadily in Latin America, particularly in the case of corporate taxes. This trend is likely to be closely related to the process of globalisation Latin American economies have experienced since the early 1990s and reflects difficulties in taxing factors of production that are internationally mobile (Shome, 1999). Both personal income tax rates and corporate income tax rates are, furthermore, on average, lower in Latin American countries, than in OECD countries, which suggests that Latin American countries benefit, on average, from lower tax revenues than OECD economies (Shome, 1999). Macroeconomic crises, high inflation and political opposition explain, to a very large extent, why governments in Latin America have a limited capacity to collect taxes.

The extent of poverty and the need for social protection policies in developing countries imply, however, that governments need not only to increase tax revenues (in order to maintain and/or increase social protection policies) but also to design progressive tax systems whereby the poor benefit from a transfer of resources from the rich. Solutions to address some of the problems will, of course, be country-specific and depend on the particular needs of each economy. A large literature has issued viable recommendations for various developing countries (see Jenkins, 1995; Shome, 1999). One feasible solution would be to combine traditional fiscal systems with policies directed at increasing the physical and capital endowments of those at the bottom of economic, social and political distributions. Policies such as the promotion of rural development, incentives to encourage labour-intensive investment, investment in infrastructure that reduces the remoteness of many poor population groups, social policies that promote educational, health and social capital and so forth, would guarantee that disadvantaged groups do not slip further down the distribution scale (Killick, 2002). The implementation of those policies need not create a further burden on already stressed fiscal systems and may, in fact, contribute towards social stability and lay the foundations for a more efficient and legitimate market economy.

In terms of fiscal policy alone, some Latin American governments have implemented novel tax initiatives. Some of the most important were the setting up of gross asset taxes (essentially a minimum tax on enterprises' assets that force companies to use their assets productively and do not avoid evasion on profit taxes), taxes on bank debits (introduced in Colombia to make up for lost revenues when value-added tax (VAT) rates were reduced and in Ecuador to replace income taxes) and the simplification of taxes for small tax payers (Tanzi, 2000). Other tax initiatives being pursued include VAT and excise taxes which replace the old tariffs and export taxes on traded goods. Although changes in excises have not been very pronounced, most Latin American countries have experienced significant increases in VAT, sales taxes and turnover taxes. These have been accompanied in most cases by a decrease in income taxes, which, on the whole, are more difficult to collect. The continuing implementation of progressive redistributive systems, whether tax systems of other redistributive policies, will be an important factor in the reduction of economic, social and political inequalities in Latin American countries.

Conclusions

This chapter analysed the extent of economic, social and political inequalities in Latin America, across different geographic and socio-economic population groups. The empirical evidence discussed suggested that Latin American countries not only have some of the highest levels of income inequality in the world, but are also characterised by serious social and political inequalities, in the access to educational and health institutions, social security services, political power and legal institutions. The levels of economic, social and political inequality in Latin America are likely to affect significantly social and economic development in the region. Although some level of inequality may derive from the fact that market economies reward successful risk-taking strategies and skill acquisition, a large fraction of inequality that has taken place during the development process of most Latin American countries has been largely dysfunctional. Some of the processes that explain the persistence of dysfunctional inequalities in Latin America include unfairness in the distribution of initial opportunities (transmitted and maintained through family and community relations), the presence of discrimination in the labour markets and in the access to social, economic and political institutions, and the incidence of non-progressive distributional systems.

Successful development strategies can only be implemented in Latin America when dysfunctional forms of economic, social and political inequalities are reduced or avoided altogether, as high levels of persistent inequalities may result in significant negative economic, social and political outcomes. The reduction and avoidance of high inequalities requires, in turn, a combination of policies that simultaneously establish just distributional systems (of financial resources and social and political rights), guarantee equal access to social and economic opportunities across all segments of the population and eliminate all forms of discrimination and segregation. The implementation of such a policy framework will depend on the coordination of efforts, not only from national governments, but also from the civil society and the international community.

Appendix A: the measurement of inequality

The axiomatic approach

Just as the poverty measurement literature is rife with debates over issues such as definitions, poverty lines, equivalence scales and the measures used to aggregate the information on those identified as poor into a summary statistic, the inequality measurement literature has a long and equally impressive pedigree. Although important studies of poverty and inequality were published much earlier (see, for instance, Rowntree, 1901), the subject really took off during the 1970s, after the publication of A. B. Atkinson's article 'On Economic Inequality' in 1970 and the first edition of A. K. Sen's 'On the Measurement of Inequality' in 1973.[10] Since then inequality measurement has been studied using an axiomatic approach of a prescribed set of desirable properties of inequality measures. Most measures of inequality are now assessed with a reference to those first axioms and others that have been suggested as the literature on the subject developed.[11]

The most important axioms currently used in the measurement of inequality include the Pigou–Dalton transfer principle, the income scale independence, the principle of population, the principle of anonymity and decomposability.

We begin with some notation.[12] Define a vector **y** of incomes, $y_1, y_2 \dots y_i \dots y_n$, with $y_i \in \Re$ and where n represents the number of units in the population (such as households, families, individuals or earners for example). Let I(y) be an estimate of inequality using a hypothetical inequality measure.

The Pigou–Dalton Transfer Principle (Dalton, 1920; Pigou, 1912). This axiom requires the inequality measure to rise (or at least not fall) in response to a mean-preserving spread: an income transfer from a poorer person to a richer person should register as a rise (or at least not as a fall) in inequality and an income transfer from a richer to a poorer person should register as a fall (or at least not as an increase) in inequality (see Atkinson, 1970, 1983; Cowell, 1985; Sen, 1973). Consider the vector **y**′ which is a transformation of the vector **y** obtained by a transfer δ from y_j to y_i, where $yi > yj$, and $yi + \delta > yj - \delta$, then the transfer principle is satisfied if $I(y') \geq I(y)$. Most measures in the literature, including the Generalised Entropy class, the Atkinson class and the Gini coefficient, satisfy this principle, with the main exception of the logarithmic variance and the variance of logarithms (see Cowell, 1995).

Income Scale Independence. This requires the inequality measure to be invariant to uniform proportional changes: if each individual's income changes by the same proportion (as happens say when changing currency unit) then inequality should not change. Hence for any scalar $\lambda > 0$, $I(\mathbf{y}) = I(\lambda \mathbf{y})$. Again, most standard measures pass this test except the variance since $var(\lambda y) = \lambda^2 var(y)$. A stronger version of this axiom may also be applied to uniform absolute changes in income and combinations of the form $\lambda_1 y + \lambda_2 1$ (see Cowell, 1999).

Principle of Population (Dalton, 1920). The population principle requires inequality measures to be invariant to replications of the population: merging two identical distributions should not alter inequality. For any scalar $1 > 0$, $I(y) = I(y[\lambda])$, where $y[\lambda]$ is a concatenation of the vector **y**, λ times.

Anonymity. This axiom – sometimes also referred to as symmetry – requires that the inequality measure be independent of any characteristic of individuals other than their income (or the welfare indicator whose distribution is being measured). Hence for any permutation $\mathbf{y'}$ of **y**, $I(\mathbf{y}) = I(\mathbf{y'})$.

Decomposability. This requires overall inequality to be related consistently to constituent parts of the distribution, such as population sub-groups. For example, if inequality is seen to rise amongst each sub-group of the population then we would expect inequality overall to also increase. Some measures, such as the Generalised Entropy class of measures, are easily decomposed and into intuitively appealingly components of within-group inequality and between-group inequality: $I_{total} = I_{within} + I_{between}$. Other measures, such as the Atkinson set of inequality measures, can be decomposed but the two components of within- and between-group inequality do not sum to total inequality. The Gini coefficient is only decomposable if the partitions are non-overlapping, that is the sub-groups of the population do not overlap in the vector of incomes.

Cowell (1995) shows that any measure $I(y)$ that satisfies all of these axioms is a member of the Generalised Entropy (GE) class of inequality measures.

Measures of inequality

The most commonly used measures of income inequality fall into two categories (Sen, 1997): (1) positive measures, which make no explicit use of any concept of social welfare and capture the extent of inequality by using statistical measures of relative income variation (the range, the relative mean deviation, the variance, the coefficient of variation, the standard deviation of logarithms, Theil's entropy measure and the Gini coefficient); and (2) normative measures based on the explicit formulation of a social welfare function (Dalton's measure and Atkinson index).

The measurement of inequality implies the choice of a welfare variable, of a receiving unit and a period of analysis. Each of these decisions involves both technical issues, relying on what is practical or available, and conceptual issues, relating to how inequality is conceived. The welfare variables most often used in economic studies are income and consumption expenditure. Consumption expenditure data is usually of better quality than income data in developing countries, particularly given the extent of self-employment in family farms and firms, where incomes are difficult to disentangle from profits (Deaton, 1997). Consumption expenditure may also provide a more accurate picture of inequality in current living standards in poor economies, and it is argued is a better indicator of 'permanent' or long-run living standards. Recent studies have also considered non-monetary welfare variables such as education outcomes and health status (Checchi, 2000; Wagstaff, 2000; Justino *et al.*, 2004). The most common unit of analysis is the household, with total household consumption or income equivalised by the size and/or composition of the household. Survey data does not allow the analysis of intra-household distributions (between men and women and between children and adults). Some household surveys allow also the calculation of inequality based on individual level data, such as earnings. The measurement of inequality implies a decision over which period inequality should be measured, such as a reference week, month or year preceding the survey. New household surveys and the use of panel data have, however, allowed the study of inequality over longer periods of time. This has allowed researchers to analyse the persistence of inequalities, their causes and their consequences (McCulloch and Calandrino, 2001; Glewwe *et al.*, 2000; Litchfield and Justino, 2004).

The choice of an inequality measure is, however, more than just a technical choice as different indices represent implicitly different value judgements. The most important refers to the relative weight to be given to the different parts of the distribution (McKay, 2002). While, for instance, GE(0) and GE(1) (see below) give greater weight to incomes in the lower part of the distribution, the Gini coefficient attaches more weight to those households or individuals in the middle of the distribution and the coefficient of variation and GE(2) emphasise the top of the distribution. It is thus possible to observe only very small changes in inequality as measured by the Gini coefficient, but very large changes in GE(2) because of increases in gaps between income or consumption values in the upper tail.

Which measure should be believed, or relied upon for policy recommendations? There is no straight answer to this: much depends on the policy objective and whether policy makers are concerned about gaps between the very rich and the rest of society or gaps between the middle and lower parts of the distribution. Table A1 summarises the most common measures of inequality currently used in the literature.

Table A1 Measures of inequality

Measures	Formulas	Definition and comments
		Positive measures
Range	$E = y_{max} - y_{min}$	• Compares the extreme values of an income distribution. • $0 \leq E \leq n$. $E = 0$ means that income is equally divided; $E = n$ if one person receives all the income. • E ignores the distribution of income between the extremes.
Coefficient of variation	$C = V^{1/2} / \bar{y}$	• Independent of mean income; concentrates on the relative variation of incomes (unlike V). • A transfer from a richer person to a poorer person will always reduce the value of C (i.e. C passes the Pigou–Dalton test). • However, a transfer from a person with \$500 to a person with \$400 or from a person with \$100,100 to a person with \$100,000 causes C to fall by exactly the same amount because C is much more sensitive to transfers in the upper tail.
Gini coefficient	$G = \dfrac{1}{2n\bar{y}(n-1)} \sum_{i=1}^{n} \sum_{j=1}^{n} \lvert y_i - y_j \rvert$	• Measures average difference between all possible pairs of incomes in the population expressed as a proportion of total income. • $0 \leq G \leq 1$; $G = 0$ indicates perfect equality and $G = 1$ means that one individual holds the whole income. • G is sensitive to transfers from rich to poor at every level. • G is closely related to the Lorenz curve of the distribution: it is the ratio of the difference between the line of absolute equality (the diagonal) and the Lorenz curve.[1]

- G provides only a partial ordering of income distribution (two identical Gini coefficients can represent different shaped Lorenz curves that intersect each other). Same could be true of other inequality measures – simply because they are summary measures.
- G attaches higher weight to people in the middle of the distribution; thus it does not fulfil the transfer sensitivity axiom.
- G is a mean independent measure: if the incomes of everyone were to double, the Gini coefficient would not be altered.

Generalised entropy measure

$$GE(\alpha) = \frac{1}{\alpha^2 - \alpha} \sum_{i=1}^{n} (\bar{y} - y_i)^2$$

- α is a measure of the sensitivity to inequality at different parts of the distribution. Lower values of a place greater weight on inequality in the lower tail (e.g. among the poor) while higher values, particularly $\alpha \geq 2$, are more sensitive to inequality in the upper tail (e.g. among the rich).
- All members of the $GE(\alpha)$ class satisfy all of the axioms listed above.
- $GE(\alpha)$ class of measures are ordinally equivalent to the Atkinson class (i.e distributions are ranked in the same way) where $\alpha = 1 - \varepsilon$, for all values of $\varepsilon > 1$.

Normative measures

Dalton's measure

$$D = 1 - \frac{\sum_{i=1}^{n} U(y_i)}{nU(\bar{y})}$$

- Measures the ratio of actual social welfare to the maximal social welfare (i.e. level of total utility that would be obtained if incomes were equally divided).
- D is not invariant with respect to positive linear trans formations of the utility function.

continued…

Table A1 continued

Measures	Formulas	Definition and comments
Atkinson's measure	$A = 1 - \left[\dfrac{1}{n} \displaystyle\sum_{i=1}^{n} \left(\dfrac{y_i}{\overline{y}} \right)^{1-\varepsilon} \right]^{1/(1-\varepsilon)}$	• Measures the percentage of current income needed to achieve our current level of welfare if all incomes were equally distributed. • ε is a measure of inequality: as ε rises more weight is attached to transfers at the lower end of the distribution and less weight is attach to transfers at the top. • A is a decomposable and subgroup consistent index but less intuitive than the $GE(\alpha)$ decomposition.

Source: Cowell (1995).

Notes

1 A Lorenz curve is essentially a line that joins in a graph the percentages of the population arranged from the poorest to the richest (represented on the horizontal axis) and the percentage of income enjoyed by the bottom x% of the population (shown on the vertical axis).
y_i = income of person i; $\overline{y}$ = arithmetic mean income; n = total population; $U(.)$ = utility function.

Appendix B

Table B1 Poverty and inequality in Latin America in the 1990s (selected countries)

Country	Year	Population (millions)[6]	GDP per capita $US 1985[7]	Headcount	Poverty gap	Squared poverty gap	Gini coefficient
Argentina	1991[3]	33.0	5136	25.5	–	–	–
	1993[3]	33.8	5796	17.6	–	–	–
	1996[1]	35.2	6052	18.4	4.6	2.3	0.48
	1998[1]	36.1	6716	17.9	4.5	2.3	0.49
Bolivia	1990[1]	6.6	1658	65.6	32.8	20.2	0.55
	1993[1]	7.1	1752	63.4	30.7	18.3	0.53
	1995[1]	7.4	1831	63.6	29.7	17.4	0.53
	1996[1]	7.6	1862	62.1	35.2	24.8	0.59
	1997[1]	7.8	1896	62.3	34.5	24.2	0.59
	1999[1]	8.1	1987	61.4	36.9	27.4	0.60
Brazil	1992[1]	152.7	3882	48.3	23.8	15.0	0.57
	1993[1]	155.0	4013	49.7	24.5	15.5	0.60
	1995[1]	159.4	4307	44.7	21.3	12.9	0.59
	1996[1]	161.5	4369	41.6	19.7	12.0	0.59
	1997[1]	163.7	4449	41.3	19.5	11.9	0.59
	1998[1]	165.9	4413	41.9	19.1	11.5	0.59
	1999[1]	168.1	4412	41.3	18.7	11.1	0.59
Chile	1990[1]	13.1	4338	32.4	12.0	6.1	0.55
	1992[1]	13.5	4890	19.8	6.0	2.8	0.52
	1994[1]	14.0	5354	22.7	7.6	3.7	0.56
	1996[1]	14.4	6174	18.3	6.0	2.9	0.56
	1998[1]	14.8	6701	16.1	5.3	2.6	0.56

continued…

Table B1 continued

Country	Year	Population (millions)[6]	GDP per capita $US 1985[7]	Headcount	Poverty gap	Squared poverty gap	Gini coefficient
Colombia	1991[1]	35.7	3297	42.4	18.3	10.7	0.57
	1993[1]	37.1	3495	44.7	20.0	11.9	0.60
	1995[1]	38.6	3766	38.8	16.1	8.8	0.57
	1997[1]	40.0	3813	38.4	17.3	10.8	0.58
	1998[1]	40.8	3836	37.8	16.5	9.9	0.57
	1999[1]	41.5	3666	39.4	17.2	10.1	0.56
El Salvador	1995[1]	5.7	2130	58.6	26.4	14.5	0.51
	1997[1]	5.9	2158	61.3	28.4	15.4	0.52
	1998[1]	6.1	2192	64.0	33.5	21.3	0.56
	1999[1]	6.2	2235	64.0	33.4	21.3	0.55
Guatemala	1990[2]	8.7	2127	–	–	–	0.60[4]
	1998[5]	10.8	2457	33.8	11.8	–	0.56
Honduras	1990[2]	4.9	1377	–	–	–	0.54
	1991[2]	5.0	1364	–	–	–	0.50
	1992[1]	5.2	1385	75.9	45.0	31.5	0.55
	1993[2]	5.3	1429	–	–	–	0.54
	1996[1]	5.8	1396	76.3	44.2	30.2	0.53
	1997[1]	6.0	1424	74.7	47.3	35.4	0.59
	1998[1]	6.2	–	74.9	46.7	34.9	0.59
	1999[1]	6.3	–	75.3	47.4	35.4	0.58
Mexico	1992[1]	86.4	6253	16.2	5.0	2.3	0.53
	1994[1]	89.6	6419	15.3	4.6	2.1	0.54
	1996[1]	92.7	6119	21.2	7.3	3.6	0.53
	1998[1]	95.8	6620	21.2	8.0	4.2	0.54

Nicaragua						
1993[1]	4.2	1186	70.7	41.2	28.9	0.57
1998[1]	4.8	1485	72.7	40.9	28.1	0.60
Peru						
1991[1]	22.0	2170	41.9	18.1	10.3	0.46
1994[1]	23.2	2434	44.0	18.7	10.8	0.48
1997[1]	24.4	2732	43.2	19.3	11.4	0.51

Sources: 1. Székely, Miguel (2001) 'The 1990s in Latin America: Another Decade of Persistent Inequality, but with Somewhat Lower Poverty', *IADB Working Paper no. 454*, Washington DC: Inter-American Development Bank. 2. Deininger, Klaus and Squire, Lyn (1996) *A New Data Set Measuring Income Inequality*, World Bank (http://www.worldbank.org/research/growth/dddeisqu.htm). High quality sample only. 3. World Bank, Global Poverty Monitoring (http://www.worldbank.org/research/povmonitor/regional). 4. World Income Inequality Indicators (WIID) (http://www.wider.unu.edu/wiid/wiid.htm). 5. World Development Indicators 2001. 6. Global Development Finance and World Development Indicators. 7. Penn World Tables 5.6.

Notes
Székely (2001) results are based on a study of 76 household surveys that cover 17 Latin American countries between the years 1989 and 2000 and represent about 95 per cent of the population in the region. To accomplish comparability the author made sure that the definition of income sources was the same within each country over time. Whenever there were changes in the survey questionnaire, due, for instance, to a more detailed breakdown of income sources covered, the minimum common denominator in the series for each individual country was identified and used as welfare indicator for all years. Poverty measures are based on the use of household per capita income as welfare indicator. To compute those estimators the author (i) uses a PPP $2-a-day poverty line (1985 prices) as criteria for separating the poor from the non-poor, and (ii) adjusts household per capita incomes to make them equal to PPP-adjusted private consumption per capita (1985 prices) from the National Accounts.

Notes

1   The Gini coefficient is a measure of inequality that varies between zero and one. A coefficient close to one indicates that very few people own most of the income (i.e. high income inequality). A coefficient equal to zero indicates perfect income inequality. Appendix A provides a technical summary on inequality measurement.
2   This has been the case since at least the Second World War (Deininger and Squire, 1996; WIDER, 2000; Milanovic, 2002; Bourguignon and Morrison, 2002; Sala-i-Martin, 2002).
3   See also Appendix B, which provides inequality and poverty estimates for several Latin American countries during the 1990s.
4   Attanasio and Székely (1999) find that rural/urban differences in Latin America account for around 12.2 per cent of poverty in the region. For instance, in Colombia in 1995, poverty in rural areas was 57.9 per cent, in contrast with 23.3 per cent in urban areas (World Bank, 1998).
5   For example, the Brazilian household surveys exclude the rural population of the North of the country (the states of Rondônia, Acre, Amazonas, Roraima, Pará and Amapá) which is where one would expect to find some of the Amazonian indigenous peoples (Litchfield, 2001).
6   See also Deininger and Olinto (2000).
7   For some recent attempts using legislative malapportionment as a measure of inequality in political representation see Samuels and Snyder (2001).
8   This issue is addressed in further detail in Chapter 6.
9   See also Borjas (1999).
10   See also, for instance, Anand (1983), Cowell (1995) and Sen (1997).
11   See Cowell (1985) on the axiomatic approach. Alternative axioms to those listed in this technical appendix are possible and the appropriateness of these axioms has been questioned. See Amiel (1998), Amiel and Cowell (1998), Harrison and Seidl (1994) amongst others for questionnaire experimental tests of the desirability of these axioms, and Cowell (1999), for an introduction to alternative approaches to inequality.
12   What follows draws on Litchfield (1999).

Bibliography

Akerlof, G.A. and Kranton, R.E. (2000) 'Economics and Identity', *Quarterly Journal of Economics*, CXV(3), 715–53.

Amiel, Y. (1998) 'The Subjective Approach to the Measurement of Income Inequality', in J. Silber (ed.) *Income Inequality Measurement: From Theory to Practice*, London: Kluwer.

Amiel, Y. and Cowell, F.A. (1998) 'Distributional Orderings and the Transfer Principle: A Re-examination', *Research on Economic Inequality*, 8, 195–215.

Anand, S. (1983) *Inequality and Poverty in Malaysia: Measurement and Decomposition*, World Bank Research Publication. Oxford: Oxford University Press.

Atkinson, A.B. (1970) 'On the Measurement of Inequality', *Journal of Economic Theory*, 2, 244–63.

—— (1983) *The Economics of Inequality*, 2nd edn, Oxford: Clarendon Press.

Attanasio, O. and Székely, M. (1999) *An Assets Based Approach to the Analysis of Poverty in Latin America*, Washington, DC: Inter-American Development Bank.

Bénebou, R. (1993) 'Workings of a City: Location, Education and Production', *Quarterly Journal of Economics*, 108(3), 619–52.

—— (2000), 'Unequal Societies: Income Distribution and the Social Contract', *American Economic Review*, 90(1), 96–129.

Behrman, J.R., Birdsall, N. and Székely, M. (1998) *Intergenerational Schooling Mobility and Macro Conditions and Schooling Policies in Latin America*, IABD Working Paper no. 386. Washington, DC: Inter-American Development Bank, Office of the Chief Economist.

Behrman, J.R., Gaviria, A. and Székely, M. (2002) *Social Exclusion in Latin America: Introduction and Overview*, IADB Working Paper no. R-445. Washington DC: Inter-American Development Bank.

Binder, M. and Woodruff, C. (1999) *Intergenerational Mobility and Educational Attainment in Mexico*, Department of Economics, University of New Mexico and Graduate School of International Relations and Pacific Studies, UCSD.

Birdsall, N. and Hecht, R. (2000) *Swimming Against the Tide: Strategies for Improving Equity in Health*, Washington, DC: Inter-American Development Bank, Office of the Chief Economist.

Birdsall, N. and Londoño, J. (1997) 'Asset Inequality Matters: An Assessment of the World Bank's Approach to Poverty Reduction', *American Economic Review*, 87, 32–7.

Borjas, G.J. (1995) 'Ethnicity and Human–Capital Externalities', *American Economic Review*, 85(3), 365–90.

Bourdieu, P. (1986) *Distinction: A Social Critique of the Judgment of Taste*, London: Taylor & Francis.

Bourguignon, F. and Morrison, C. (2002) 'Inequality Among World Citizens: 1820–1992', *American Economic Review*, 92(4), 727–44.

Checchi, D. (2000) *Does Educational Achievement Help to Explain Income Inequality?*, UNU/WIDER Working Paper no. 208. Helsinki: UNU/WIDER.

Chu, K., Davoodi, H. and Gupta, S. (2000) *Income Distribution and Tax, and Government Spending in Developing Countries*, WIDER Working Paper no. 214. Helsinki: UNU/WIDER.

CIID (1999) *Social Security Reform in Latin America*, Canada: Centro Internacional de Investigaciones para el Desarrollo.

Cowell, F.A. (1985) 'Measures of Distributional Change: An Axiomatic Approach', *Review of Economic Studies*, 52, 135–51.

—— (1995) *Measuring Inequality*, London: Prentice-Hall/Harvester Wheatsheaf.

—— (1999) 'Measurement of Inequality', in A.B. Atkinson and F. Bourguignon (eds) *Handbook of Income Distribution*, Amsterdam: North-Holland.

Cutler, D.M. and Glaeser, E.L. (1997) 'Are Ghettos Good or Bad?', *Quarterly Journal of Economics*, 112, 827–72.

Dahan, M. and Gaviria, A. (1998) *Parental Actions and Siblings' Inequality*, IADB Working Paper no. 389. Washington, DC: Inter-American Development Bank, Office of the Chief Economist.

—— (1999) *Sibling Correlations and Social Mobility in Latin America*, IADB Working Paper no. 395. Washington, DC: Inter-American Development Bank.

Dalton, H. (1920) 'The Measurement of the Inequality of Incomes', *Economic Journal*, 30, 348–61.

Deaton, A. (1997) *The Analysis of Household Surveys: A Microeconometric Approach to Development Policy*, Baltimore, MD: Johns Hopkins University Press.

Deininger, K. (1999) 'Making Negotiated Land Reform Work: Initial Experience from Colombia, Brazil and South Africa', *World Development*, 27(4), 651–72.

Deininger, K. and Olinto, P. (2000) *Asset Distribution, Inequality and Growth*, World Bank Policy Research Paper 2375. Washington, DC: World Bank.

Deininger, K. and Squire, L. (1996) *A New Data Set Measuring Income Inequality*, Washington, DC: World Bank. Online. Available HTTP: <http://www.worldbank. org/research/growth/dddeisqu.htm> (accessed October 2003).

DFID (2001) *Reforming Latin America Health Sectors: Can Inequalities be Reduced?* Presentation at CPD Seminar, London: Department for International Development.

Domingo, P. and Sieder, R. (2001) *Promoting the Rule of Law: Perspectives on Latin America*, Washington, DC: Brookings Press.

Durlauf, S.N. (2000) 'The Membership Theory of Poverty: The Role of Group Affiliations in Determining Socio-economic Outcomes', Dept. of Economics, University of Wisconsin, mimeo.

Erikson, R. and Goldthorpe, J. H. (1992) *The Constant Flux: A Study of Class Mobility in Industrial Societies*, Oxford: Clarendon Press.

Escobal, J., Saavedra, J. and Torero, M. (1999) *Los Activos de los Pobres en el Perú*, IADB Working Paper R-361. Washington, DC: Inter-American Development Bank.

Gacitúa, E. and Sojo, C. (2000) *Social Exclusion and Poverty Reduction in Latin America and the Caribbean*, Washington, DC: World Bank.

Genn, H. (1999), *Paths to Justice,* Oxford: Hart Publishing.

Glewwe, P., Gragnolati, M. and Zaman, H. (2000) *Who Gained from Vietnam's Boom in the 1990s?: An Analysis of Poverty and Inequality Trends*, Policy Research Working Paper no. 2275, Washington, DC: World Bank.

Hammergren, L., Magalmi, A.L., Negrete, L., Ramirez, A. and Tellez, R. (2002) *The Juicio Ejecutivo Mercantil in Mexico's Federal District Courts*, Washington, DC: World Bank.

Harrison, E. and Seidl, C. (1994) 'Perceptional Inequality and Preferential Judgements: An Empirical Examination of Distributional Axioms', *Public Choice*, 79, 61–81.

Herring, R.J. (1983) *Land to the Tiller: The Political Economy of Agrarian Reform in South Asia*, London: Yale University Press.

—— (1991) 'From Structural Conflict to Agrarian Stalemate: Agrarian Reforms in South India', *Journal of Asian and African Studies*, XXVI(3–4), 169–88.

IADB (1998) *Magnitude, Custos Econômicos e Políticas de Controle da Violência no Rio de Janeiro*, IADB Working Paper R-347. Washington, DC: Inter-American Development Bank.

—— (1999) *Facing Up to Inequality in Latin America: Economic and Social Progress in Latin America 1998–9 Report*, Baltimore, MD: Johns Hopkins University Press.

IFAD (2001) *Rural Poverty Report 2001*, Oxford and Rome: Oxford University Press for IFAD.

Jenkins, G.P. (1995) *Perspectives for Tax Policy Reform in Latin America in the 1990s*, Taxation Research Series 22. Harvard, MA: Harvard Institute of International Development.

Justino, P. and Litchfield, J. (2003) *Economic Exclusion and Discrimination*. London: Minority Rights Group International.

Justino, P., Litchfield, J. and Niimi, Y. (2004) *Multidimensional Inequality: The Case of Brazil*, PRUS Working Paper no. 24. Poverty Research Unit at Sussex, University of Sussex.

Killick, T. (2002) *Responding to Inequality*, Inequality Briefing Paper no. 3. London: DFID and ODI.

Lam, D. and Schoeni, R.F. (1993) 'Effects of Family Background on Earnings and Returns to Schooling: Evidence from Brazil', *Journal of Political Economy*, 101(4), 710–40.

Litchfield, J. (1999) 'Inequality: Methods and Tools', Text for World Bank's Web Site on Inequality, Poverty, and Socio-economic Performance: Online. Available HTTP: <http://www.worldbank.org/poverty/inequal/index.htm> (accessed October 2003).

—— (2001) 'Poverty, Inequality and Social Welfare in Brazil 1981–1995', PhD thesis, London School of Economics, University of London.

Litchfield, J. and Justino, P. (2004) 'Poverty Reduction in Vietnam: What Do the Numbers Tell Us?', *Journal of the Asian Pacific Economy*, 9(2): 145–69.

Londoño, J.L. (1996) *Poverty, Inequality and Human Capital Development in Latin America 1950–2025*, World Bank Latin American and Caribbean Studies. Washington, DC: World Bank.

McCulloch, N. and Calandrino, M. (2001) 'Vulnerability and Chronic Poverty in Rural Sichuan', mimeo, Institute of Development Studies, University of Sussex.

McKay, A. (2002) *Defining and Measuring Inequality*, Inequality Briefing Paper no. 1. London: DFID and ODI.

Mesa-Lago, C. (1983) 'Social Security and Extreme Poverty in Latin America', *Journal of Development Economics*, 12, 83–110.

Milanovic, B. (2002), 'True World Income Distribution, 1988 and 1993: First Calculation Based on Household Surveys Alone', *Economic Journal*, 112(476), 51–92.

Molina, G.G., de Rada, E.P. and Jiménez, W. (2002) *Social Exclusion: Residential Segregation in Bolivian Cities*, IADB Working Paper no. R-440. Washington, DC: Inter-American Development Bank.

Moore, M. and Putzel, J. (1999) *Thinking Strategically About Politics and Poverty*, IDS Working Paper no.101. Brighton: Institute of Development Studies.

Newbery, D. and Stern, N. (eds) (1987) *The Theory of Taxation for Developing Countries*, Oxford: Oxford University Press.

Pigou, A.F. (1912) *Wealth and Welfare*, London: Macmillan.

Piketty, T. (1998) 'Theories of Persistent Inequality and Intergenerational Mobility', in A. Atkinson and F. Bourguignon (eds) *Handbook of Income Distribution*, Amsterdam: North-Holland.

Radian, A. (1980) *Resource Mobilization in Poor Countries*, London: Transaction Books.

Ribero, R. and Nuñez, J. (1999) *Productivity and the Household Investment in Health – The Case of Colombia*, Working Paper R-354. Washington, DC: Inter-American Development Bank.

Rodriguez, A. and Smith, S. (1994) 'A Comparison of Determinants of Urban, Rural and Farm Poverty in Costa Rica', *World Development*, 22(3), 381–97.

Rowntree, B.S. (1901) *Poverty: A Study of Town Life*, London: Macmillan.

Sala-i-Martin, X. (2002) *The World Distribution of Income (estimated from individual country distributions)*. NBER Working Paper #8933. Cambridge, MA: National Bureau for Economic Research.

Samuels, D. and Snyder, R. (2001) 'Devaluing the Vote in Latin America', *Journal of Democracy*, 12(1), 146–59.

Sen, A.K. (1973) *On Economic Inequality*, Oxford: Clarendon Press.

—— (1985) *Commodities and Capabilities*, Oxford: North-Holland.

—— (1997) 'From Income Inequality to Economic Inequality', *Southern Economic Journal*, 64(2), 384–401.

Shome, P. (1999) *Taxation in Latin America: Structural Trends and Impact of Administration*, Working Paper WP/99/19. Washington, DC: International Monetary Fund.

Stallings, B. and Peres, W. (2000) *Growth, Employment and Equity: The Impact of Reforms in Latin America and the Caribbean*, Washington, DC: ECLAC and Brookings Institution Press.

Stewart, F. (2002) *Horizontal Inequalities: A Neglected Dimension of Development*, Queen Elisabeth House, Working Paper Series no. 81. Oxford: University of Oxford.

Tanzi, V. (2000) *Taxation in Latin America in the Last Decade*, Working Paper 76. Stanford, CA: Center for Research on Economic Development and Policy Reform, Stanford University.

Trejos, J.D. and Montiel, N. (1999) *El Capital de los Pobres en Costa Rica: Accesse, Utilización y Rendimiento*, IADB Working Paper R-360. Washington, DC: Inter-American Development Bank.

Wagstaff, A. (2000) 'Socioeconomic Inequality in Child Mortality: Comparisons Across Nine Developing Countries', *Bulletin of the World Health Organization*, 78(1), 19–29.

Wagstaff, A. and Watanabe, N. (2000) *Socioeconomic Inequalities in Child Malnutrition in the Developing World*, Working Paper 2434, Washington, DC: World Bank.

Wilson, W. (1987) *The Truly Disadvantaged: The Inner City, the Underclass, and Public Policy*, Chicago, IL: University of Chicago Press.

World Bank (1993) *Poverty Assessment of Peru*, Washington, DC: World Bank.

—— (1998) *Poverty Assessment of Colombia*, Washington, DC: World Bank.

—— (1999) *Poverty Assessment of Ecuador*, Washington, DC: World Bank.

—— (2001) *World Development Report 2000–2001*, Washington, DC: World Bank.

World Institute for Development Economics Research (2000) *UNU/WIDER-UNDP World Income Database Version 1.0.*

3 The interactions between inequality and the macroeconomy in Latin America in the post-reform context

Ricardo Gottschalk

Introduction

This chapter examines the macroeconomy and inequality in Latin America. The main aim is to understand how these two dimensions interact with each other in a region characterised by high levels of inequality. The concern with inequality reflects, and is a response to, a widespread recognition that the international targets of halving extreme poverty by 2015 will not be met in Latin America through growth alone; for this to effectively happen, inequality should be substantially reduced as well.[1]

The chapter focuses mainly on those policies Latin American countries have been adopting in a post-reform context of fairly liberalised economies. Of particular importance for the analysis is the liberalisation of foreign trade and in particular the capital account of the balance of payments. Countries with fairly liberalised capital accounts face similar issues concerning macroeconomic management. A major issue refers to the limited room national governments have for conducting macroeconomic policies. Given the constraints domestic policy makers face, not unusually they are led to take macroeconomic policy decisions that have important welfare implications, more often negative than positive.

The chapter focuses on nine Latin American countries: Argentina, Bolivia, Brazil, Colombia, El Salvador, Guatemala, Honduras, Nicaragua and Peru. All of them have to some extent liberalised their capital account. As a result, countries like Argentina and Brazil managed to attract substantial amounts of external private capital flows during the 1990s, although a marked decline in these flows was observed in the later years of the decade. Other countries have been less successful in attracting such flows, and therefore have relied more heavily on official flows to finance their balance of payments. Thus, these two categories of countries – those that have attracted different types of private flows and those that have not – have faced somewhat different macroeconomic problems and challenges. The chapter attempts to identify which policy issues are relevant to each category of countries. At the same time, the chapter shows that some issues are common to these two categories of countries, therefore requiring similar policy responses.

For example, a common issue facing Latin American countries have been their high vulnerability to shocks (financial or otherwise) which resulted in high degree of volatility in key macroeconomic variables, such as output, employment, wages and real exchange rate. As will be argued, Latin American countries failed to respond adequately to these shocks, due to lack of instruments to prevent them, and/or to mitigate their effects. The inability to respond appropriately to these shocks resulted in major setbacks in the region's fight against poverty and inequality. At the same time, the high levels of inequality across Latin America may have worked as a constraint to macroeconomic policies, and contributed to increased volatility and further inequality in the region.

The chapter is organised in six sections. The following section 'Monetary policy, inflation and inequality' starts with an analysis of how monetary policy and inflation may affect poverty and inequality. It then discusses how in the specific Latin American context inflation may have harmed the poor and worsened income distribution in the region. Looking at monetary policy and inflation is important, given the region's past history of high inflation. The third section 'Macroeconomic management in the context of private capital flows' proceeds by discussing macroeconomic policies adopted, and issues faced, by those Latin American economies that had access to private capital flows in the 1990s. The main issues highlighted are the constraints these countries have faced to pursue autonomous macroeconomic policies, the macroeconomic instability they have been subject to in the recent past, and the lack of counter-cyclical mechanisms at their disposal that can be used to reduce instability and/or attenuate its negative effects. The fourth section 'Macroeconomic issues concerning countries that did not attract different forms of private capital flows' analyses macroeconomic issues faced by those economies that remained dependent on official flows. The chapter identifies as the main issues their lack of instruments to enhance economic growth and to deal with major external shocks, which tend to affect most strongly the poorest. The fifth section 'Inequality, and macroeconomic policies and performance' briefly reviews the literature on the effects of inequality on macroeconomic policies and macroeconomic performance, with reference to Latin America. The final section concludes.

Monetary policy, inflation and inequality

It is broadly accepted that monetary policy is a powerful macroeconomic management tool, with important poverty and inequality effects.[2] The inequality effects can be examined both in the short and long run.

In the short run, an expansionary monetary policy may lead to higher aggregate demand and increased output growth; as a consequence, jobs are created (probably leading to lower unemployment levels) and, due to a tighter labour market, wages tend to increase. Both these factors contribute to lower poverty levels, through increased average income. To the extent the newly created jobs are mainly for unskilled labour, it can also have positive distribution effects.

The poverty and distribution effects tend to be temporary, however, especially when initial spare capacity is not large, with inflation kicking in quite rapidly as a result. This is because, in response to higher inflation, a tight monetary policy may be adopted, which leads to reduced economic activity and therefore neutralises the positive poverty and distribution effects associated with the expansionary phase. It is further argued that the effects during the phases of expansion and contraction are not symmetric, with the latter being larger than the former, with a net result of increased poverty and worsened inequality over the whole economic cycle.[3]

Thus, in the short run, although an expansionary monetary policy can indeed reduce poverty and inequality, these effects tend to be temporary and, due to asymmetries, net negative over the whole economic cycle.

In the long run, monetary policy may affect poverty mainly through long-run growth. On the one hand, a prudent monetary policy may affect growth positively by signalling a stable economic environment, which is more conducive to investment. On the other hand, if the monetary policy is conducted erratically and marked with periods of excessive monetary expansion, it can influence the average level of inflation and cause macroeconomic volatility. These factors, in turn, can affect long-run growth negatively, increase poverty and worsen income distribution as well. Uncertainty is the main channel through which inflation can influence growth,[4] essentially because it can affect the efficiency of the role of price signals, leading to misallocation of resources, which in turn lowers factor productivity (Fischer, 1993; Smyth, 1994; Kormendi and Meguire, 1985). In addition, inflation can lower growth by discouraging investors, due to expectations it creates regarding higher macroeconomic volatility.

The effects of inflation and higher macroeconomic volatility on equality, in turn, may take place through different channels. The channels leading to negative effects include: depressed wages, especially of the unskilled workers due to their lower levels of organisation, and lower human capital investment, which is an important mechanism to reduce inequality in the long run. In addition, higher inflation and macroeconomic instability can harm the poor to the extent these factors affect labour-intensive industries disproportionately. The channels leading to positive effects could include transfers from creditors to debtors when inflation is unanticipated (assuming that creditors are mainly rich and debtors, poor), and a possible taxation shift from labour to capital.

Numerous empirical studies have supported the claims that inflation levels can harm the poor through less growth. These include work by Barro (1996), according to which average inflation correlates negatively with growth.[5] It has also been tested whether the relationship between inflation and growth is linear. Empirical work has shown that inflation may affect growth negatively only after a certain level.[6] It is believed that the threshold for inflation levels to start affecting growth is at 20 per cent (see, for example, Griffin, 2001).[7]

Looking specifically at the relationship between inflation and inequality (rather than inflation and poverty, via growth), Bulir (2001) finds that stabilisation efforts that succeed in defeating hyperinflation contribute significantly to the reduction of income inequality levels. However, he finds that bringing inflation further down to very low levels has no additional inequality reduction effects, thus showing the existence of non-linearity between inflation levels and inequality as well.

In view of the evidence supporting the non-linearity hypothesis, particularly regarding the relationship between inflation and growth, some academics have argued that developing countries could pursue moderate fiscal and/or monetary expansionary policies in order to stimulate aggregate demand and output, even if such policies led to some inflation. Provided the latter did not go beyond a certain level, it would not hurt long-term growth.

How does all what has been discussed thus far relate to Latin America's macroeconomic policies and experiences in the past?

First, many Latin American countries suffered in the 1970s and 1980s from high inflation, a phenomenon believed to have contributed to poor growth performance and, through various mechanisms, higher inequality as well. It is also well known that some countries faced the problem of high and chronic inflation, and a few of these even had periods of hyperinflation – Argentina, Bolivia, Brazil, Nicaragua and Peru are the main cases in point.

In response to high inflation and its harmful effects on growth, poverty and distribution, Latin American governments have since the early 1990s set price stability as a major policy objective. Tolerance, even to moderate inflation levels, has since then become very low. Partly as a result of more prudent monetary and fiscal policies, generally adopted under IMF and World Bank stabilisation and economic reform programmes, and partly as a result of higher exposure to foreign competition through foreign trade liberalisation, these countries succeeded in bringing inflation to low levels (see Table 3.1).[8] As discussed further below, lower inflation has had an important positive

Table 3.1 Annual inflation in Latin America (selected countries)

Country	Consumer price index (%)						
	1980–90	*1995*	*1999*	*2000*	*2001*	*2002*	*2003*[1]
Argentina	437.6	1.6	−1.8	−0.7	−1.5	41.0	3.6
Bolivia	222.7	10.6	3.1	3.4	0.9	2.4	3.3
Brazil	330.2	22.4	8.9	6.0	7.7	12.5	11.0
Colombia	23.7	19.5	9.1	8.8	7.6	7.0	6.1
El Salvador	19.0	11.4	−1.0	4.3	1.4	2.8	2.6
Guatemala	13.9	8.6	4.9	5.1	8.9	6.3	5.8[2]
Honduras	7.8	26.8	10.9	10.1	8.8	8.1	7.2
Nicaragua	618.8	10.9	7.2	9.9	4.8	3.9	5.3[2]
Peru	332.1	10.2	3.7	3.7	−0.1	1.5	1.9

Source: ECLAC 2001 and 2002.

Notes
1 Preliminary.
2 One year inflation until October 2003.

distributive effect. This has been a very impressive achievement given these countries' past history of high inflation. The successful stories included countries like Argentina and Brazil, which had suffered from high and chronic inflation for many years. The higher inflation observed in 2002 in Argentina was due to the financial crisis in the same year (see discussion below).

In the Latin American continent, the strong aversion to high inflation has to do with the perception that not only does it limit growth, but, as mentioned above, it can also have negative inequality effects. The inequality effects can take place through different channels. An important channel refers to the functioning of the labour markets. In Latin America, the very poor, which tend to be self-employed or under-employed, normally are poorly organised, thus lacking the means to protect their earnings against inflation. This is true for both rural and urban workers. The latter tend to be concentrated in the services sector. Strong labour unions exist, but their members tend to be better off semi- or skilled workers from the most dynamic segments of the manufacturing sector, such as the car industry in Brazil, and public sector employees.

Another important factor that has made the poor suffer disproportionately from inflation in the past in certain countries of Latin America relates to the banking system. The poor in their majority do not have access to bank current accounts; they instead hold cash and therefore are subject to inflation tax. The rich and affluent, on the other hand, have access to remunerated bank accounts in which their current income can be protected against inflation.

In addition, they can protect their personal savings through access to inflation-corrected financial instruments.

A further possible negative effect from inflation on the poor that may have been relevant in Latin America relates to the fact that the consumption basket of the poor is less diversified than that of the rich. In a context in which high inflation is also associated with high price dispersion, the poor as compared to the rich have less room to change their consumption pattern in response to a change in relative prices, and this might also have implied important distributive effects.

Even the possible positive distributive effects associated with inflation may not be observed in the poorer Latin American countries. For instance, the fact that unanticipated inflation results in transfer from creditors to debtors may not benefit the poor, as in some countries the poor are not debtors. In most cases, the main debtors are businesses of all sizes, and tax payers. As regards the latter, the fact that they may benefit from unanticipated inflation means that the government – their main creditor – may lose. Even when inflation is anticipated, the government may lose due to the Olivera–Tanzi effect, which is the loss of tax revenue due to the time lag between tax generation and tax collection. When this happens, the poor lose, as the response to such revenue erosion normally takes the form of cuts in social expenditure, which hurts particularly the poor and aggravates inequality.

The Latin American experience with inflation suggests that the higher the initial inequality, the higher the inequality effects of inflation through various mechanisms, as described above.

Due to the differentiating effects of inflation on different segments of the population, in most cases with a strong bias against the poor, stabilisation programmes that have successfully defeated hyperinflation brought about immediate major positive distributive effects in Latin America.[9]

To illustrate this point, following the Real stabilisation plan adopted in Brazil in 1994, Brazil's workers, especially the poor ones, benefited from a significant increase in their real incomes. According to data provided by the Brazilian *Instituto Brasileiro de Geografia e Estatistica* (IBGE), the average real wage of those in the top 10 per cent of the total income group increased 24 per cent, the real wage of those in the bottom 50 per cent increased 35 per cent, and those in the 10 per cent bottom, 83 per cent. This meant not only higher income to all workers, but also a better income distribution among them, as the wage ratio of the top 10 per cent to the bottom 10 per cent declined from 72 to 49. The massive increase in real wages of the poorest reflected a higher minimum wage and the end of wage erosion over the indexation cycle, which used to occur when inflation was high (Dornbusch, 1997, based on various sources).

As mentioned earlier, commitment to stability and prudent macro policies seem to have played an important role in bringing about price stability in the region (see ECLAC, 2002). However, even in the context of achieved price stability, Latin American countries continued to face serious macro-economic problems. The next section analyses the problems faced by those countries that attracted large amounts of private capital flows during the 1990s, while the subsequent section discusses problems and challenges faced by those countries that continued to depend on official flows as their main source of external finance.

Macroeconomic management in the context of private capital flows

Among the countries that are the focus in this chapter, Argentina and Brazil have been the two cases that have experienced large surges of private capital flows, thus attracting proportionately more flows than the other countries (see Table 3.2).

The surge of capital flows in these countries during the 1990s caused a number of problems, the main of which were: (1) strong pressures towards currency appreciation and/or excessive monetary expansion; and (2) costly

Table 3.2 Net private capital flows, 1990–9 (in US$ millions and as a % of the total flows to Latin America)

Countries' GDP share in total LA GDP[1]	Portfolio equity		Bonds		Bank lending		FDI	
	Value	%	Value	%	Value	%	Value	%
Argentina: 16%	1132	12.3	4871	35.7	578	5.4	5442	16.5
Brazil: 30%	2785	30.2	2594	19.0	4808	45.0	9909	30.1
Middle-income countries[2]: 10%	902	9.8	914	6.7	1100	10.3	3844	11.7
Low-income countries[3]: 5%	8	0.1	10	0.1	97	0.9	1845	5.6

Source: ECLAC (2001).

Notes
1 Based on 1999 current prices.
2 The middle-income category comprises those Latin American countries with per capita GDP between US$2.000 and US$4.000 in 1997. These are: Colombia, Costa Rica, Jamaica, Panama and Peru.
3 This low-income category comprises those Latin American countries with per capita GDP of less than US$2.000 (at market exchange rate) in 1998. These are: Bolivia, Dominican Republic, Ecuador, El Salvador, Guatemala, Guyana, Haiti, Honduras, Nicaragua and Paraguay.

attempts to combat excessive liquidity. Moreover, given that such flows were volatile, they caused the additional problem of (3) high volatility in key macroeconomic variables, such as real output, employment, wages and exchange rate. Since the Russian crisis, when these flows started to dry up, thus becoming scarce rather than abundant, those countries with overvalued exchange rates and accumulated foreign liabilities faced the further problem of (4) full-blown crises (i.e. Brazil in early 1999 and Argentina in late 2001). All these problems, which we discuss in turn, have had negative poverty and inequality effects.

Currency appreciation and/or excessive monetary expansion

In the 1990s, countries that were adopting fixed exchange rate regimes in the context of surges of capital inflows witnessed accumulation of foreign reserves and monetary expansion. Moreover, real exchange rate appreciation took place due to continued increase in domestic prices of non-tradable goods[10] associated with economic expansion.[11] Countries adopting more flexible exchange rate regimes also witnessed monetary expansion due to excessive capital inflows, as these countries tended to intervene in the foreign exchange markets (thus accumulating reserves) in order to avoid excessive nominal (and real) exchange rate appreciation.

The main reason for avoiding exchange rate appreciation was that this could deteriorate the country's international competitiveness, with negative effects on the country's foreign trade balance. Despite efforts made by many countries, currency appreciation was observed during the 1990s (see Table 3.3).

Where appreciation was significant, exports lost dynamism and imports increased. As a consequence, some countries experienced a turn around in their foreign trade balance that was very fast and quite dramatic. These trends in trade flows brought about negative growth and poverty effects, as, first, with lower export growth, the export and export-related sectors witnessed a lower rate of job creation. In countries where export sectors are labour intensive (and in particular based on unskilled labour), distributive effects also took place. Second, higher imports impacted on the ability of import-competing industries to generate employment, with distributive effects where, again, such industries are labour intensive (e.g. clothes, shoes industries).

Data from ECLAC (2002) shows that in Latin America, employment in the tradables sector grew very little – only 1.7 per cent per annum on average – against total employment growth of 3.3 per cent (p. 25). Moreover, these data show that in South America employment in manufacturing grew only 1.1 per cent per annum on average, compared to total employment growth of 2.9 per cent. According to ECLAC, lower manufacturing employment

Table 3.3 Real exchange rate for selected Latin American countries[1] (index 1988 = 100)

Year	Argentina	Brazil	Colombia	Mexico	Peru
1988	100	100	100	100	100
1990	80	72	114	90	51
1991	58	87	115	82	43
1992	50	103	114	76	42
1993	46	98	107	73	47
1994	46	98	87	75	44
1995	48	88	85	110	44
1996	49	82	79	98	44
1997	48	82	74	85	44
1998	47	85	80	86	45
1999	43	129	91	78	49

Source: ECLAC.

Note
1 Real effective exchange rates. Downward movement indicates appreciation.

growth reflected production and trade specialisation patterns based on natural resources, which certainly was influenced by real exchange rate appreciation, a trend observed over most of the 1990s in the larger economies, like Argentina and Brazil. Econometric work presented by Weller (cited by Stallings and Peres, 2000) shows that employment creation in selected Latin American countries (Argentina, Brazil, Chile, Colombia, Costa Rica and Mexico) between 1985 and 1998 were primarily determined by real exchange rates, in addition to output expansion.

Costs associated with combating excess liquidity

As seen above, the accumulation of international reserves that resulted from capital inflows led to monetary expansion. To reduce excessive liquidity in the system, countries used sterilisation instruments.[12] This policy, however, had a fiscal impact associated with increased government financial liabilities. To reduce major fiscal imbalances caused by growing quasi-fiscal costs,[13] Latin American countries pursued primary fiscal surplus (which excludes interest payments). This was achieved through cuts mainly in social expenditures.

Brazil is a case in point. In a context of capital inflows, the Brazilian Central Bank had to mop up the excess supply of foreign exchange in order to avoid a further appreciation of the domestic currency, and to conduct sterilisation operations to avoid excessive monetisation. The situation was further aggravated when the country suffered from contagion from financial crises elsewhere – Mexico, Asia and Russia. Contagion led to the opposite problem of having to attract private capital flows. The answer to that was to push up domestic interest rates, which made debt service of an expanding debt stock of mostly short-term maturity very large.

This policy proved to be very costly in fiscal terms, as it contributed to the build-up of a very vulnerable fiscal position. The country's overall primary public deficit increased from –0.4 per cent of GDP in 1995 to a balanced position in 1998. However, the nominal deficit (i.e. after including interest payments) became very large, ranging from 7.2 per cent of GDP in 1995 to 8.0 per cent in 1998.[14] Interest payments of a growing public debt therefore became largely responsible for the country's deficit in the 1990s. Between 1995 and 1998, total net public debt increased markedly, from 30.5 per cent to 42.7 per cent of GDP. This rapid debt increase was in part a result of high interest rates; this benefited government debt holders, which are the wealthy, whereas the poor were harmed by cuts in public expenditure on social programmes, required to raise resources to service the debt.[15]

High volatility in key macroeconomic variables

The macro-management problems discussed above started with the need to avoid excessive exchange rate appreciation, caused by capital inflows. The volatility of flows that characterised the second half of the 1990s in Latin America further aggravated the macro-management problems, as the Brazil case illustrates.

The main problem with volatility of capital flows was that it was translated into high macroeconomic volatility in the real economy (ECLAC, 2002). This volatility, characterised by phases of economic expansion and contraction, was observed throughout the 1990s, when private flows came in, and went out, in large amounts.

The expansionary phases, initiated with surges of capital flows, were fuelled mainly by domestic credit and liquidity expansion, which tended to be excessive despite efforts to contain these. Although less relevant in the Latin American case, further demand pressures also came from wealth effects, caused by asset price increases. The expansion was mainly consumption-led; most new jobs were created in the non-tradable sectors (e.g. services in urban areas), at least partially offsetting the low rate of job creation in the tradable sector due to exchange rate appreciation (see above). According to ECLAC (2002), in Latin America, employment in the non-tradables sector increased by 4.1 per cent per annum on average during the 1990s, a growth rate considerably higher than the 3.3 per cent growth rate for total employment (see above).

Capital reversals led, in turn, to economic contraction due to adjustment efforts in the form of higher interest rates and fiscal tightening, undertaken with the intention of attracting capital back to the country. Due to high interest rates, fiscal tightening, widespread unemployment and falling real wages, contraction tended to be deep and have major negative poverty and inequality effects.

In addition to such negative short-term effects, the volatility of such key macroeconomic variables – output, employment, real wages – created uncertainty among agents thereby undermining investment and long-term growth. Moreover, specifically in the area of the exchange rate, the volatility of capital flows caused excessive exchange rate variability, which could also hurt long-term growth – and the poor as a result with likely distributive effects – through creating higher uncertainty among exporters, affecting in particular those that are risk averse. In the poorer countries, risk-averse exporters tend to be the majority, given their lack of access to hedging instruments (which could be used against exchange rate risk).

Thus, although as seen earlier, Latin American countries succeeded in reducing inflation, which was an important source of economic instability in the 1970s and 1980s, economic instability continued to be a main feature in Latin America in the 1990s, due to the volatile behaviour of capital flows (ECLAC, 2002). The adoption of prudent monetary and fiscal policies reinforced this boom-bust cycle. This is because these policies were mainly pro-cyclical.

According to Lustig (2000), macroeconomic volatility in Latin American leads to higher poverty, and slows down long-term trends in improvements of social indicators, such as schooling attainment and health, thus reducing the poor's ability to overcome poverty (p. 5). The consequences to the poor of sharp macroeconomic downturns are therefore far reaching, rather than limited to income decline caused by higher unemployment.

Crisis caused by capital flows reversals

Following the Asian and especially the Russian crisis, private capital flows to developing countries declined markedly (except for FDI), reaching zero levels in 2001, being just slightly positive in 2002 (see Griffith-Jones, 2003 and various recent IMF and IIF reports), and recovering significantly only in 2003 (IIF, 2004). The period of decline caught Argentina and Brazil in a particular vulnerable position as both countries had overvalued exchange rates, large current account deficits and large foreign liabilities in the late 1990s.

In Brazil, the adjustment to the sharp decline in capital flows took the form of large currency devaluation in January 1999. According to Goldfajn (2003) capital reversals were a process led by residents and then followed by foreigners. The Brazilian legislation for capital outflows by residents is fairly open, thus permitting residents to take their financial resources out of the country mainly through legal channels.

Brazil's currency crisis was relatively less costly, with a quicker recovery than other crises in the late 1990s, however. This milder outcome was partly explained by macroeconomic and microeconomic features specific to Brazil, such as the existence of relatively high reserves when the currency was floated and a private sector with low levels of indebtedness and hedged against exchange-rate risk.

Unlike in Brazil, in Argentina the adjustment to the drying-up of capital flows in the second half of 1998 happened not through exchange rate devaluation, which was maintained fixed and therefore overvalued, but in the real economy, through a sharp decline in output, employment and real wages.[16] As this type of adjustment resulted in a prolonged and deep recession, it gradually undermined international lenders and investors' confidence in the country's ability to meet its growing external debt obligations and to sustain its fixed exchange rate regime, which did not allow for substantial exchange rate realignment. Lenders' and investors' perception was that economic growth was needed for the country to be able to reduce its foreign liabilities as a proportion of the GDP, and that for the GDP to recover, exports had to increase, which required exchange rate devaluation.

The Argentinean debt default in December 2001 followed by currency and banking crises in early 2002 led to further GDP contraction, job losses and street protests. Many Argentineans lost with the crisis. The poor were particularly affected through job loss, which constitute their main (if not only) source of income (see also Chapter 4). Many holders of peso-denominated bank accounts had their assets depreciated due to devaluation; although holders of small dollar-denominated bank accounts had their assets protected through the conversion of their assets from dollar into pesos using parity rate, holders of larger accounts lost. Those who avoided losses altogether were the ones who managed to send their financial resources abroad before the crisis erupted. Presumably the wealthiest and well connected were those who did so.

Thus, although there is no clear statistical evidence on the impact of the crises in Brazil and Argentina on income distribution, it seems that such an impact was negative. While the poor were affected negatively through job losses, the rich managed to protect their assets through a combination of holding of domestic financial assets and capital flight (in the case of Brazil) and capital flight (in the case of Argentina).

During 2002, Brazil again suffered a major currency devaluation, caused by the markets' reaction to the likelihood that a left-wing candidate could win Brazil's presidential elections. But the domestic financial system was able to withstand the devaluation shock. At the same time, output did not suffer a major contraction, despite the increase in interest rates the authorities promoted at the time to combat the currency crisis.

The key reason behind the resilience of Brazil's financial system to the devaluation is the fact that financial institutions and their customers were fairly well hedged against exchange rate risk, with far less currency mismatches than in Argentina. The fact that in Brazil dollar-denominated bank accounts are not permitted also contributed to the smaller currency mismatch between assets and liabilities held by the banking system. Another key factor that explains why the banking system was able to withstand sharp devaluation is that the government did not default on its public debt, as in Argentina. If the Brazilian government had defaulted on its public debt, this would have had a major impact on the country's financial system, as the system is the main creditor of Brazil's government.

Default was avoided to an important extent because, unlike Argentina, Brazil benefited from a large loan package from the IMF, of US$30 billion dollars in the second half of 2002. These resources were more than sufficient for the country to meet its external financial obligations over 2003. The package may not have immediately eliminated uncertainty regarding Brazil's ability to overcome its problems, but at least stopped the situation from deteriorating further, and helped make the elected president commit himself to prudent macroeconomic policies. The continued demonstration of commitment to prudent macroeconomic policies by the new president helped to gradually rebuild the markets' confidence (see also Chapter 4). Had the country not reached an agreement with the IMF just before the presidential elections, the confidence crisis would have probably deteriorated even further, leading the country to a virtual collapse. It could have even affected the electoral process and the timetable of government transition, as has happened in Argentina in the past.

The non-collapse of the banking system in Brazil helps to explain why the economic recession the country experienced in 2002 and 2003 was much milder than in Argentina. In Argentina, the collapse of the banking system caused a sharp fall in domestic demand and acute shortage of working capital to the productive sectors.

Thus, two key factors help explain why more recently Brazil has suffered economically and socially much less than Argentina from the sharp devaluation which hit both countries. First, at the crucial time when markets were betting against Brazil, the country's authorities reached agreement with the IMF over a massive loan package, which helped stop the situation from deteriorating further. This helped the government in avoiding default on its public debt, thereby maintaining the country's banking system intact. Second, Brazil had the appropriate mechanisms in place, such as hedging practices which, together with a deposit system in which only domestic currency denominated bank accounts were permitted, helped the financial system and economy at large withstand the devaluation shock.

Avoiding major economic contractions caused by financial shocks is of crucial importance, because, as Lustig (2000) puts it,

> macroeconomic crises, with the exception of wars, are the single most important cause of large increases in income (or consumption) poverty. They are frequently accompanied by rising income inequality as well … the impact of economic contraction tends to disproportionately reverse previous gains in poverty reduction (p. 3).

Given these effects, Lustig (2000) discusses a number of macro policy measures that a country could adopt to avoid crises from occurring, or at least to mitigate their poverty and inequality effects. These are strengthening financial regulation and supervision, capital controls and counter-cyclical fiscal policy, including the adoption of stabilisation funds.

Strengthening financial regulation and supervision is a very positive initiative; it is particularly important that efforts are made to reduce the vulnerability of the financial system to volatility in key macroeconomic variables, particularly the exchange rate, through ensuring the system does not face major currency mismatches. As the Brazilian case demonstrates, this is key in reducing the likelihood of a banking crisis. However, as will be argued below, too much emphasis on strengthening the financial system may make it more difficult to pursue the objectives of growth and poverty reduction.

Given all the problems associated with capital flows (e.g. undesirable pressures on the exchange rate, the costs associated with attempts to combat it, their volatile behaviour, the crises they cause and their impact on the real economic and social variables), the literature has amply discussed the Chilean experience with capital controls. These controls were used with the purpose of reducing the levels of capital inflows, and to lengthen their maturity as well, the latter aimed at reducing the country's vulnerability to the volatility of short-term flows.[17] These controls, adopted in June 1991, took the form of unremunerated reserve requirement (URR). Initially, the URR was of 20 per cent on foreign debts with maturity of more than one year, to be deposited at the Central Bank during one year. Later, the URR was increased to 30 per cent.[18]

Restrictions on capital inflows in Chile led to a number of achievements. First, there is widespread consensus that the URR helped change the structure of capital inflows maturity towards longer-term flows and against short-term flows (de Gregorio *et al.*, 2000; Gallego *et al.*, 1999; Ariyoshyi *et al.*, 2000). Second, and perhaps most important, due to a debt structure biased towards the long term, Chile survived better the effects of the Asian crisis, having experienced only very mild volatility in the exchange and interest rates, and relatively small loss of international reserves. Finally, there is also some evidence that capital restrictions also contributed to reducing the overall level of net inflows (Gallego *et al.*, 1999).

Finally, the adoption of counter-cyclical elements such as stabilisation funds as Chile's Cooper Compensation Fund and Colombia's Oil Stabilisation Fund could be considered for adoption by other Latin American countries, especially the smaller ones, to be used during economic downturns. A further line of action could be adopting fiscal rules that have an in-built counter-cyclical element, like the Chilean ones, discussed below.

Macroeconomic issues concerning countries that did not attract different forms of private capital flows

The issues facing the smaller Latin American economies are somewhat different. Despite financial liberalisation, which in most cases has included the opening of the capital account, these countries have experienced less private capital inflows and therefore less of the instability caused by their volatile behaviour. As a consequence, these countries remained dependent on official flows, which they need to meet their external financing needs, in most cases quite large due to their high external debt stocks.

Macro-management problems of the sort confronted by the larger economies that received private flows seem less dramatic for these countries, although similar problems were not totally absent in some cases. For example, currency appreciation may have been the case for countries like El Salvador, due to excessive capital inflows caused by a combination of official flows, work remittances, capital repatriation and FDI.

On the whole, official flows provided by the international financial institutions predominate as the main source of external finance for these countries. They usually come with a string of conditionalities, such as the requirement to pursue tight fiscal and monetary policies.

These policies have been important during these countries' stabilisation efforts, especially in Bolivia in the mid-1980s, and Nicaragua in first half of the 1990s. However, once stabilisation was achieved, these countries experienced only modest economic growth over time (see Table 3.4). Their main problem is therefore how to enhance growth performance. Time has shown that providing a stable macroeconomic environment is not a sufficient condition. Although it seems clear more needs to be done, these countries' governments lack instruments to promote growth.

Table 3.4 GDP growth in Latin America (selected countries) (annual rates %)

	1995	1996	1997	1998	1999	2000	2001	2002	2003[1]
Bolivia	4.7	4.5	4.9	5.0	0.3	2.3	1.6	2.7	2.5
El Salvador	6.2	1.8	4.2	3.8	3.4	2.0	1.7	2.1	2.0
Guatemala	5.0	3.0	4.4	5.1	3.9	3.4	2.6	2.2	2.4
Honduras	3.7	3.7	4.9	3.3	−1.5	5.6	2.7	2.4	3.0
Nicaragua	6.0	6.6	4.0	3.1	6.9	4.4	3.1	0.7	2.3

Source: ECLAC 2003.

Note
1 Preliminary estimates.

That is one major problem these countries face. In the first three years of the twenty-first century, growth in most of these countries was even lower, due to the weakening of the international economy (see Table 3.4). Given the prudent monetary and fiscal policies their governments are pursuing, they have few macroeconomic instruments left to stimulate domestic demand, even when the economy is under recession with unutilised productive capacity.

Thus, these governments face at least two problems: one is how to enhance long-term growth, and the other is how to stimulate domestic demand to counteract economic slowdown, sometimes caused by external factors, such as world economic recession.

A third, and perhaps even more serious macroeconomic management problem, is how to deal with unexpected external shocks, such as a sudden and sharp decline in the terms of trade. The third problem differs from the second for its intensity, for being far more disruptive, and for the kind of solution needed to address it. These economies' capacity to absorb such shocks is very small and they have very few instruments to cope with them and/or with their consequences, which usually take the form of sharp income and output decline and higher unemployment. The poor are especially vulnerable to such shocks given their lack of assets (physical, natural, financial), which could be used to endure these shocks (World Development Report 2001, chapter 2).

How to address these problems?

To deal with short-term issues – i.e. how to stimulate domestic demand – innovative policy ideas are needed. In the past governments of developed and developing countries have used fiscal and monetary instruments to stimulate domestic demand during economic downturns. However, in Latin

America these instruments have more recently worked in a pro-cyclical way, partly due to government commitment to maintaining price stability through prudent policies, but also due to pressures from the international organisations and the international financial markets to tighten these policies even further during recessions.

In the case of fiscal policy, an ECLAC report shows that, in the 1990s, of 16 cases in which Latin American countries were in the upswing phase of a business cycle, 14 countries were simultaneously experiencing a public sector deficit above its own historical average (ECLAC, 2002: 144). That is, fiscal policy in Latin America has been pro-cyclical, with fiscal deficits increasing during phases of economic expansion, and decreasing during recessions.

A few Latin American countries are taking important steps to address pro-cyclicality, which could serve as lessons for other countries. For instance, Chile has adopted a counter-cyclical element in its fiscal policy framework. In this framework, a structural fiscal surplus of 1 per cent should be met. The structural fiscal balance is the difference between the actual fiscal balance and the cyclical component of the balance. Having a structural fiscal target rather than actual target implies that the government will be able to increase public expenditure during the downswing phase of the business cycle, and decrease it during the upswing phase (Fiess, 2002). This mechanism gives the government room for a fiscal policy that can be used to stimulate demand and counteract the negative poverty effects associated with economic recession. This is a rule-based policy, which therefore does not undermine government credibility (ECLAC, 2002).

The importance of correcting for the pro-cyclicality of fiscal policy is that this policy tends to accentuate volatility and harm the poor (Fiess, 2002). According to Ferranti *et al.* (2000),[19] social expenditures, and in particular targeted expenditure, tend to fall during the downswing of the business cycle (by 2 per cent for each 1 per cent fall in output).

As regards growth, the required strategy to enhance it should be the one that has a distributive impact (i.e. pro-poor growth), given these countries' current levels of poverty and inequality. There is broad consensus today that a pro-poor growth strategy should focus on promoting growth in those sectors in which the poor are concentrated or with strong linkages with such sectors (Alarcon, 2001). In the smaller Latin American economies, the poor are mainly concentrated in rural areas (at least in relative terms). The rural poor should therefore be provided with conditions that enable them to produce and generate incomes. These conditions include the provision of rural infrastructure, support services (e.g. micro-credit) and access by the poor to productive assets (Alarcon, 2001; Griffin and Brenner, 2001; McKinley, 2001). In addition, to further enhance the capacity of the poor more generally to produce and generate income, public social expenditure on health and education should be increased.

Data presented and discussed in Stallings and Peres (2000: chapter 5) show that in Latin America social expenditure on health and especially on education was very progressive in the 1990s, in the sense that they reached mostly the poor, thus showing that in Latin American it can be an effective policy in a poverty reduction strategy. In addition, the data for the same period show that social expenditure more generally (i.e. that includes social security) had a major redistributive impact over the period. Thus, social expenditures can alleviate quickly both income poverty – through the provision of social security – and non-income poverty through contributing to people's improved health. In addition, it can enhance long-term growth through improving the human capabilities of the poor, and improve distribution among households.

To be consistent with this growth strategy, macroeconomic policies should be capable of promoting simultaneously two types of public investment: investment in infrastructure and human capital. This represents a challenge for Latin American countries, however, as their governments face budgetary constraints to promote such policies. Moreover, they would have to overcome their past tendency of using public capital investment as a variable of adjustment when facing pressures to cut public expenditures. Indeed, public capital investment has historically shown to be very sensitive to adjustment policies Latin American countries have adopted in response to balance of payments problems (ECLAC, 2002).

Other macroeconomic policies that should be adopted to support a pro-growth strategy include moderate (rather than high) domestic interest rates and competitive exchange rates. As regards the latter, it is important to note that those Latin American countries that have dollarised their economies (e.g. El Salvador) have lost the ability to adjust their economies to shocks thereby making them more vulnerable to macro volatility, especially in the real variables (see the above discussion on Argentina).

At the micro level, the provision of credit can play a key role in enhancing the productive and earning capacity of the poor. In addition, they can encourage an increase in savings by the poor by opening up to them new investment opportunities. As Griffin (2001: 39) puts it, '[p]eople restrict their consumption not in order to save but in order to finance a desired investment'.

A country's domestic financial system should be the main credit provider to the poor. However, Latin American governments are at present adopting reforms in their financial sectors, which are not being conducive to more credit to the poorest segments of the population.

The purpose of these reforms has been to strengthen their financial systems and to make them more robust to international financial instability. These reforms have included the adoption of prudential regulation and supervision, and the increased internationalisation of the banking system. Although these measures are very important in ensuring the stability of the financial system, they are not being designed in ways to support growth, and even less pro-poor growth. For example, due to the need to meet capital adequacy levels, selective credit policies in support of specific groups or sectors which otherwise would not have access to credit, have been drastically reduced or even totally eliminated. International banks, which are increasingly dominating the domestic markets, tend in turn to adopt cherry-picking strategies, which means lending to foreign companies and big domestic companies (Gottschalk, 2001).

Domestic banks are the ones that still lend to small- and medium-size domestic companies, but to the extent that they have to comply with strict capital requirements, they will reduce lending to SMEs. In addition, as these banks are encouraged to adopt more sophisticated risk assessment systems, they may face constraints to lend to poor customers, as these customers are unlikely to be able to provide the information banks need to feed their new assessment systems. In addition, in response to pressures to gain efficiency, these banks have been closing their agencies in areas of lower population density, which tend to be the rural ones where the poor are concentrated. The overall trend is therefore of less, rather than more, credit to the poor – and the SMEs, which are important employment-generating sources.

In view of the current situation and future trends, thought should be put on new and creative institutional mechanisms to support credit to the poor and to job-generating sectors. Both public and private mechanisms should be considered for that purpose. Support from the international financial institutions for promoting such mechanisms should be encouraged.

To what extent do the poverty reduction strategies proposed in the Poverty Reduction Strategy Papers (PRSPs) Latin American countries have prepared address these issues? More generally, what role is macroeconomic management given in these strategies?

The PRSPs in Bolivia, Honduras and Nicaragua

A first, very positive aspect, in these strategies is the recognition that growth can play a very important role in reducing poverty, and that in fact growth and poverty reduction are two complementary policy objectives that can be pursued simultaneously.

A second positive aspect is that these strategies in turn recognise it is important to promote public capital investment. In addition, given that the poor are concentrated in rural areas in these countries, these strategies emphasise the importance of directing public investment towards the rural sector. At the same time, these strategies correctly emphasise the need to increase public social expenditure, particularly on health and education. These two elements – public investment in the rural sector and social expenditure on health and education – are stressed in the PRSPs because, it is believed, they can contribute to poverty reduction through increasing the capacity of the poor to produce and generate income.

However, important gaps in policies, particularly at the macro level, can be identified in these strategies.

First, at a more general level, growth and poverty reduction can indeed be seen as complementary, with growth being instrumental to poverty reduction, and poverty reduction in turn reinforcing growth. However, strictly at the budgetary level, there is a policy conflict on how to allocate public resources between capital expenditure and social expenditure. This conflict is not sufficiently acknowledged in the PRSPs, but it is important to do so, given the gap between the resources needed to meet the very ambitious targets set in these strategies, and the resources that are in reality available for that purpose, which are very limited. It is positive, though, that the PRSPs see growth as important, among other reasons, for permitting an increase in the absolute levels of social expenditure over time.

Second, the PRSPs suggest the adoption of macroeconomic policies such as prudent monetary and fiscal policies, under the reasoning these can ensure macroeconomic stability, a key condition for growth. This, however, is very timid advice for a strategy that has as its main objectives to enhance growth and be effective in reducing poverty. Recent growth performance in Latin American countries has been fairly poor despite stability, which means that stability alone will not automatically lead to higher growth. This means that macroeconomic policies should be designed in ways that can support stability, growth and poverty reduction at the same time.

Third, although the PRSPs acknowledge that Latin American economies are highly vulnerable to such shocks as terms of trade, financial shocks and natural disasters, they do not indicate what macroeconomic policies could be adopted to reduce this vulnerability or to cope with the volatility that shocks may generate domestically. These economies have very few mechanisms that can be activated when these events occur. Having these mechanisms in place is crucial in a poverty reduction strategy, given that macroeconomic volatility that results from shocks harms particularly the poor and the vulnerable in the short term, and, through discouraging investment, future growth in the long term. In acknowledging vulnerability to shocks, the PRSPs focus on having safety networks in place. But nothing is proposed in terms of having macroeconomic instruments embedded in a macroeconomic policy framework, which can be used mainly for preventive purposes.

Finally, the PRSPs do not sufficiently emphasise the positive role micro-credit can have in poverty reduction, nor do they identify how financing mechanisms can be provided. The focus is on strengthening the domestic financial systems, but, as seen above, this emphasis on financial strengthening may reduce rather than increase credit to the poor. Bolivia's PRSP is the only one of the three here analysed that clearly acknowledges the role micro-finance can play in reducing poverty, and that identifies what institutions and mechanisms should be promoted or created in order to ensure the poor have access to finance.

Inequality, and macroeconomic policies and performance

This section discusses how inequality may work as a constraint to macro-economic management and macroeconomic performance. It will examine in particular how inequality may affect fiscal and monetary policies, inflation, and the economic cycle.

Fiscal policy

The first possible constraint of inequality on the conduct of fiscal policy may work through political channels. The possible effects are controversial, however. For example, some academics argue that in a country where the income level of the median voter is much lower than the average income level, there will be a political demand through the voting process for fiscal redistribution (Persson and Guido, 1994; Alesina and Rodrik, 1994). This pressure may in turn lead to higher taxes, needed to finance higher levels of expenditures. To the extent higher taxes are distortionary, they may create inefficiency and therefore lower growth.

Others believe that the opposite may happen. That is, higher inequality may lead to lower rather than higher tax rates. This is because the rich are more capable of influencing the design of the tax system through the political system. Interestingly, as the reasoning goes, lower taxes may affect economic growth negatively, if the country is below its optimal tax level (Furman and Stiglitz, 1998).

Thus, two possible sequencing of events may arise from inequality: higher taxes and lower growth, and lower taxes and lower growth. Both cases imply pressures on the government for pursuing a fiscal policy that may not be optimal or even feasible, depending on the circumstances it faces.

Gradstein (2002) further argues that in unequal societies voters tend to support systems of fiscal redistribution that are based on discretion rather than on rules. This may constitute a major constraint for policy makers, if their wish is to adopt a rules-based fiscal system rather than a discretion-based system under the belief that the latter may undermine credibility in government policies, thereby affecting investment and growth negatively.

Many countries in Latin America have low tax rates as a proportion of the GDP; in some cases this clearly reflects structural deficiencies in the tax systems associated with their relatively low stage of development. However, political lobbying on the part of the elite may also partly explain low tax capacity. In richer countries like Argentina, this seems clearly the case. This gives some support to Furman and Stiglitz (1998) hypothesis that inequality may lead to lower, rather than higher tax rates.

Monetary policy and inflation

Inequality may also affect public expenditure through political channels without affecting tax rates (Al-Marhubi, 1997). If this is the case, the result may be higher public expenditure without concomitant tax increases. This may cause a fiscal imbalance. If the gap between revenue collections and expenditures is financed through monetary expansion, this may result in higher inflation levels. Al-Marhubi (1997) provides empirical evidence, which shows that countries with higher inequality have higher inflation levels, even after controlling for other factors, such as degree of openness and central bank independence and political instability.

The literature also suggests that inequality can lead to political polarisation, creating deadlocks that work as an impediment to the adoption of stabilisation programmes (Kaminsky and Pereira, 1996, among others, cited by Al-Marhubi, 1997). As seen earlier, the rich minority may not feel so much the need for stabilisation, as they are normally better able to protect their incomes and assets from inflation through access to various mechanisms, such as remunerated bank accounts and indexed financial instruments. The same argument, but in reverse, is that of Bruno (1993): where consensus exists due to higher equity, the chances to implement macroeconomic stabilisation successfully will be higher.

In Latin America, it is possible to find examples of countries that fit well with both situations, of excessive public expenditure leading to higher inflation, and lack of political consensus needed to combat high inflation with effectiveness. In Peru, public expenditures were at excessively high levels in the second half of the 1980s due to the wish to undertake a non-sustainable economic programme. And in Argentina and Brazil, defeating high and chronic inflation in the 1980s and early 1990s through an effective stabilisation plan was hard due to lack of political support to the stability objective.

Economic cycle

According to Furman and Stiglitz (1998), countries in which inequality is higher will face higher economic volatility as well. Demand would be the channel linking inequality and volatility. Starting with an initial shock – for example higher unemployment – the income of the poor households would fall. Due to their lack of assets (physical, financial) to rely on during the shock, their demand would fall as well and probably very sharply given their high propensity to consume. Given that unemployment tends to affect the poor disproportionately and that they constitute the majority of the population in a country where inequality is high, aggregate demand would be strongly affected. Under this reasoning, the higher the inequality – of incomes and assets – the higher the degree of volatility the country is subject to. Of course, lack of social security mechanisms that can work as automatic stabilisers aggravate the problem.

Conclusions

We have seen, first, that in Latin America high inflation may have hurt the poor and increased inequality in the 1970s and 1980s through various mechanisms, and that these poverty and inequality effects may have been magnified where initial levels of inequality were present. Partly as a result of better macroeconomic policies, high inflation was defeated in the Latin American region in the 1990s, bringing about immediate gains for the poorest.

In the 1990s, many Latin American countries liberalised their economies; those countries that received large amounts of private capital flows, and that had defeated high inflation, continued, however, to face macroeconomic problems which, although different from those related to price instability, were equally, if not more, challenging. During times of capital surges, they had to avoid currency appreciation and combat excess liquidity, with limited success, however. During times of capital scarcity, they had to fight investors' expectations through pushing up interest rates and cutting public expenditures, thus aggravating economic downturns and harming the most vulnerable. Those countries that did not witness large surges and reversals of private capital faced the challenges of how to enhance growth, cope with external shocks (trade, natural disasters) and combat alarming poverty.

Whilst the first group of countries has been vulnerable mainly to financial shocks associated with volatile capital flows, the second group has been vulnerable to shocks such as falling terms of trade. In both cases, the consequences of these shocks have been a high degree of volatility in key macroeconomic variables, such as output, employment, wages and real exchange rate. Both groups of countries have failed to deal adequately with these shocks, due mainly to lack of instruments to prevent them, and/or to mitigate their effects. For example, none of the countries that are of main concern here has had counter-cyclical instruments in their arsenal of policies to deal with the negative social consequences of deep economic downturns, or other instruments in place that could have avoided these downturns happening in the first place.

The inability to appropriately respond to external shocks resulted in major setbacks in the region's fight against poverty and inequality. In many countries, advances in poverty and inequality reduction in the first half of the 1990s have been reversed since then due to different sorts of shocks that have hit these countries. At the same time, the high levels of inequality across the continent may have worked as a further constraint to macro-economic policies, may have increased volatility effects of shocks, and contributed to aggravating inequality even further.

Unfortunately, those countries that in the recent past have designed poverty reduction strategy programmes have not sufficiently addressed these problems. These programmes, presented through Poverty Reduction Strategy Papers (PRSPs), have proposed a macroeconomic framework that provides little instruments for dealing with macroeconomic volatility, which has been an important deterrent to poverty reduction in these countries.

The way forward for these countries is not to reinvent macroeconomics; rather, it is to adopt those policies that have proved successful in other countries facing similar circumstances. Some of these policies have at present been considered for adoption even by developed countries. For example EU countries are questioning the growth and stability pact, and therefore aiming for counter-cyclical elements in their fiscal policy framework, because they feel they need more flexibility to cope with economic downturns. Other countries have implemented unconventional policies successfully within the Latin American region, such as Chile's capital controls and stabilisation funds.

Latin American countries may face constraints from the international financial markets, as well as lack of support and/or encouragement from the Bretton Woods institutions, for the adoption of such policies. In face of that, these countries need to make the case with international organisations such as the IMF and the World Bank on the appropriateness of such policies, in order to have their support for their adoption. The support of such organisations is important because they can provide technical assistance for the successful implementation of such policies, but even more important because they can legitimise the use of these policies in the eyes of the markets and rating agencies, which today are very reluctant to accept anything different from the strictly conventional.

Of course, in certain areas more research is needed. For example, no work has been done on how to conciliate the quest for strong domestic financial systems with, for example, the need to provide finance needed to enhance the earning capabilities of the poor. Also, more ideas are needed on innovative financing mechanisms, for example that involves public–private partnerships, which can benefit the poor.

Notes

1 See Hanmer *et al.* (1999), who state that, with no improvement in income inequality, Latin America will have to pursue growth rates at levels much higher than the current ones in order to halve poverty by 2015.
2 The first part of this section draws mainly on and Romer and Romer (1999).
3 See Collier and Dehn (2001) for evidence on the asymmetric impact of economic volatility on growth; and the IMF (2003) on the asymmetric impact of volatility on poverty.
4 According to Romer and Romer (1999), other channels include disrupted financial markets and higher effective tax rates on capital.
5 The effects of inflation variability on growth have also been tested, with mixed results (see Barro, 1996; Gottschalk, 1999).
6 See Gottschalk (1999) for empirical evidence supporting a non-linear relationship between inflation and growth for Brazil over the 1950–94 period.
7 Khan and Senhadji (2001) using new econometric techniques find that the threshold may actually be significantly lower – at 11–12 per cent for developing countries.
8 Honduras has been the only exception, in that inflation during most of the 1990s was higher than in the 1980s, when it was at one digit level.
9 According to Stallings and Peres (2000), the end of hyperinflation in Latin America in the 1990s had positive distribution effects.
10 Non-tradable goods refer to the set of products that are not traded internationally. This may be due to their intrinsic characteristics. For example, they are not transportable, or even if they are, it is not profitable for to do so.
11 Countries using fixed exchange rate regimes as an instrument to combat high inflation initially experienced real exchange rate appreciation due to residual inflation, which is domestic inflation caused by an increase in the domestic prices of non-tradable goods.
12 Monetary expansion means an increase in the quantity of money in the economic system. This may be a problem to the extent that too much money may cause a generalised price increase (i.e. inflation), due to excess demand. Excess liquidity is an expression for too much money in the economy. When the economy faces a situation of excess liquidity, the country's monetary authorities (i.e. the Central Bank) mop up the excess of money with the use of sterilisation instruments. These can take the form of Central Bank borrowing from commercial banks and Central Bank security sales in the open market, among others.
13 Quasi-fiscal costs refer to costs related to Central Bank (and other public financial institutions) operations, such as sterilisation.
14 See Gottschalk (2000).

15 See Furman and Stiglitz (1998) for a discussion on the effects of interest rate movements for bond holders and workers.
16 The factors that caused economic contraction in Argentina from mid-1998 onwards were actually somewhat more varied, not being limited to scarcity of foreign private capital flows. Argentina also suffered from the appreciation of the dollar and from devaluation in Brazil (Ocampo, 2002).
17 Although less well-known, Colombia also adopted similar types of capital controls with the same purposes.
18 In September 1998, when the problem Latin American countries were facing became that of not of excessive flows, but insufficient flows, the URR was brought down to 0 per cent.
19 Cited by Fiess (2002).

Bibliography

Al-Marhubi, F. (1997) 'A note on the link between income inequality and inflation', *Economics Letters*, 55, 317–19.

Alarcon, D. (2001) 'National Poverty Reduction Strategies of Chile, Costa Rica and Mexico: Summary and Findings', in T. McKinley (ed.) *Macroeconomic Policy, Growth and Poverty Reduction*, New York: Palgrave.

Alesina, A. and Rodrik, D. (1994) 'Distributive Politics and Economic Growth', *Quarterly Journal of Economics*, 109(2), 465–90.

Ariyoshi, A., Habermeier, K., Laurens, B. and Otker-Robe, I. (2000) 'Capital Controls: Country Experiences with Their Use and Liberalization', IMF Occasional Paper no. 190, 17 May. Washington, DC: IMF.

Barro, R. (1996) *Determinants of Economic Growth: A Cross-Country Empirical Study*, Cambridge, MA: The MIT Press.

Bruno, M. (1993) *Crisis, Stabilisation, and Economic Reform: Therapy by Consensus*, Oxford: Clarendon Press.

Bulir, A. (2001) 'Income Inequality: Does Inflation Matter?', IMF Staff Papers, 48:1, 139–59.

Collier, P. and Dehn, J. (2001) 'Aid, Shocks and Growth', World Bank Working Paper 2688. Washington, DC: World Bank.

Dornbusch, R. (1997) 'Brazil's Incomplete Stabilization and Reform', Brookings Papers on Economic Activity, 1, 367–404.

ECLAC (2002) 'Globalisation and Development', study prepared by the ECLAC secretariat for the twenty-ninth session of the Commission, May, Brasilia.

Fiess, N. (2002) 'Chile's new fiscal rule', mimeo, April.

Fischer, S. (1993) 'The Role of Macroeconomic Factors in Growth', *Journal of Monetary Economics*, 2, 485–512.

Furman, J. and Stiglitz, J. (1998) 'Economic Consequences of Income Inequality', Federal Reserve Bank of Kansas City Papers and Proceedings, 221–63.

Gallego, F., Hernández, L. and Schmidt-Hebbel, K. (1999) 'Capital Controls in Chile: Effective? Efficient?', Working Paper of Central Bank of Chile n. 59, December.

Goldfajn, I. (2003) 'The Swings in Capital Flows and the Brazilian Crisis', in S. Griffith-Jones, R. Gottschalk and J. Cailloux (eds) *International Capital Flows in Calm and Turbulent Times*, Ann Arbor, MI: University of Michigan Press.

Gottschalk, R. (1999) 'Essays on Investment, Growth and Inflation in Brazil 1950–1998', DPhil Thesis, University of Sussex, Brighton.

—— (2000) 'Sequencing Trade and Capital Account Liberalization: The Experience of Brazil in the 1990s', UNCTAD/UNDP Occasional Paper, 132, UN, Geneva, September.

—— (2001) 'A Brazilian Perspective on Reform of the International Financial Architecture', report prepared for DFID, July.

Gradstein, M. (2002) 'Rules, Stability, and Growth', *Journal of Development Economics*, 67, 471–84.

De Gregorio, J., Edwards, S. and Valdés, R.O. (2000) 'Controls on Capital Inflows: Do They Work?', *Journal of Development Economics*, 63(1), October, 59–83.

Griffin, K. (2001) 'Macroeconomic Reform and Employment: An Investment-Led Strategy of Structural Adjustment in Sub-Saharan Africa', in T. McKinley (ed.) *Macroeconomic Policy, Growth and Poverty Reduction*, New York: Palgrave.

Griffin, K. and Brenner, M.D. (2001) 'Domestic Resource Mobilization and Enterprise Development in Sub-Saharan Africa', in T. McKinley (ed.) *Macroeconomic Policy, Growth and Poverty Reduction*, New York: Palgrave.

Griffith-Jones, S. (2003) 'Capital Flows to Emerging Markets: Does the Emperor Have Clothes?', in R. Ffrench-Davis and S. Griffith-Jones (eds) *From Capital Surges to Drought: Seeking Stability for Emerging Economies*, New York: Palgrave Macmillan in association with WIDER.

Hanmer, L., Jong, N.D., Kurian, R. and Mooij, J. (1999) 'Are the DAC targets achievable?, Poverty and Human Development in the Year 2015', *Journal of International Development*, 11(4), 547–63.

Institute of International Finance (IIF) (2004) 'Capital Flows to Emerging Market Economies', Institute of International Finance, pdf document, April.

International Monetary Fund (IMF) (2003) 'Fund Assistance for Countries Facing Exogenous Shocks'. Document prepared for the members of the Executive Board, SM/03/288, August.

Khan, M. and Senhadji, A. (2001) 'Threshold Effects in the Relationship Between Inflation and Growth', IMF Staff Papers, 48:1.

Lustig, N. (2000) 'Crises and the Poor: Socially Responsible Macroeconomics', Sustainable Development Department Technical Papers Series, Washington, DC: IADB, February.

Kaminsky, G. and Pereira, A. (1998) ' The debt crisis: lessons from the 1980s for the 1990s', *Journal of Development Economics*, 50(1), 1–24

Kormendi, R.C. and Meguire, P.G. (1985) 'Macroeconomic Determinants of Growth: Cross-Country Evidence', *Journal of Monetary Economics*, 16, 141–63.

McKinley, T. (2001) 'The Macroeconomic Implications of Focusing on Poverty Reduction', in T. McKinley (ed.) *Macroeconomic Policy, Growth and Poverty Reduction*, New York: Palgrave.

Ocampo, J.A. (2002) 'The Lessons of the Argentine Crisis', mimeo, Santiago de Chile, Chile: ECLAC.

Persson, T. and Guido, T. (1994) 'Is inequality Harmful for Growth?', *American Economic Review*, 84(3), 600–21.

Romer, C. and Romer, D. (1999) 'Monetary Policy and the Well-Being of the Poor', Federal Reserve Bank of Kansas City Papers and Proceedings, 159–201.

Smyth, D.J. (1994) 'Inflation and Growth', *Journal of Macroeconomics*, 16, 261–70.

Stallings, B. and Peres, W. (2000) *Growth, Employment and Equity: The Impact of Reforms in Latin America and The Caribbean*, Washington, DC: ECLAC and Brookings Institution Press.

World Bank (2001) *World Bank Development Report*, Washington, DC: World Bank.

4   Inequality in Latin America

What role for the international community?

Stephany Griffith-Jones and
Jenny Kimmis

Introduction

Latin American countries have carried out important market reforms, mainly in the 1990s. The reforms included trade and capital account liberalisation. It was hoped these reforms would lead to sustained growth and poverty reduction.

In the first half of the 1990s, the liberalisation of the capital account and changes in the international capital markets led to large surges of capital flows to Latin America (Ffrench-Davis and Griffith-Jones, 1995). However, from the mid-1990s and especially from 1997 until 2002, a sharp reversal of capital flows to the region took place. The capital flow reversals led to major crises in the region, which were developmentally very costly. As indicated in the previous chapter, and as will be argued here further below, financial crises have caused major setbacks in the region's fight against poverty, as well as increases in inequality. As regards inequality, which is the focus of this book, recent empirical work has shown that inequality trends have been upwards in the majority of Latin American countries (which the statistics and the analyses provided elsewhere in this book confirm), and that capital account liberalization and financial crises have been key factors behind this upward movement (Cornia, 2004).

Therefore, an essential pre-condition for the reforms carried out in Latin America to help recover growth and reduce poverty is that changes take place on the international side that lead to higher and more stable private and public flows, so as to sustain – and not undermine – growth in the region. This would also imply having fewer crises and helping to manage them better if they occurred. To achieve better distribution, also a key policy objective, it will be necessary to adopt other policies, such as greater investment in human capital, tax reforms and asset redistribution.

Bearing the above in mind, the objectives of this chapter are to analyse financial crisis episodes that have occurred in Latin America in the recent past, assess their impact on growth, poverty and inequality, and provide a discussion on the role the international financial community has played in these crises. The aim is to draw lessons for the international financial institutions on what role they should play in helping prevent future crises in the region and, when they occur, reduce their economic, social and distributional costs.

The remainder of this chapter has two broad sections. The first will discuss the financial crises of Mexico and Argentina, with a brief reference to Brazil's crisis, with a focus on the role the international financial institutions, and the IMF in particular, have played in these crises. It will be seen that whilst in Mexico they helped the country overcome the crisis fairly rapidly and therefore avoid major poverty and distributional effects in Argentina their reluctance in providing timely and sizeable financial support to the country when it was facing external financing difficulties resulted in a deep and prolonged financial crisis, with extremely negative growth, poverty and distributional effects. Drawing on the crisis episodes in the three countries under examination, the final section will conclude and put forward a number of proposals on what the international financial community should do to help countries prevent crises and, if crises do occur, manage them better so that their economic, social and distributional costs can be minimised; also, on policies they can adopt to improve equality both in the short and long run, and more broadly the role they can play in encouraging more stable capital flows in support of sustained growth and development.

The Mexican, Argentine and Brazilian crises

The Mexican crisis of 1994/5

The US–IMF led rescue package put together in early 1995 to halt the Mexican peso crisis is widely recognised as having been one of the more successful rescues of recent years. This is particularly true in terms of Mexico's rapid return to international capital markets, and is also largely true in terms of stemming currency volatility and depreciation, as well as limiting contagion to other countries both within the region and beyond. The handling of Mexico's 1995 crisis was not, however, without problems. The rescue package was hastily put together and the scale of financing necessary was severely under-estimated initially. It is also evident that the policy mix adopted to achieve stabilisation took insufficient account of the likely negative impact on the domestic economy, and particularly the social fall out.

The way in which the Mexican crisis unwound, and the response of the international community, raises a number of important issues that are of relevance to other countries in the region, as well as to the ongoing debate on how to better prevent and manage crises.

With commitments totalling nearly US$50 billion, the US–IMF led package for Mexico in 1995 was the largest that had ever been seen for a country experiencing a currency crisis. It was not only large in financial terms, but was also ambitious in its objectives – the aim of the package was to resolve Mexico's liquidity problems by providing enough money to cover the total outstanding short-term debt the Mexican government had with the private sector. In order to understand why this was necessary, as well as why the international community was willing to rescue Mexico, a brief overview of the crisis is useful.

The crisis and the rescue packages

In December 1994, dwindling international reserves and pressure on the Mexican currency forced the government to abandon the currency band and float the peso. The devaluation caused a huge loss of confidence in financial markets. At the time, Mexico had very high levels of foreign currency denominated debt, including US$17 billion in short-term instruments (Tesobonos) owed to foreign investors. Fears that Mexico would default on its debt sent the market into panic and put the peso under increased pressure. As investors wanted to exit the market, Mexico was unable to roll over the short-term debt as it came due – a classic case of self-fulfilling prophesy (Griffith-Jones, 1997).

In order to prevent financial collapse in Mexico, it soon became clear that a rescue package would have to be large enough to assure investors that Mexico would not be forced to default on its debt. However, it would take a number of attempts before a financial assistance package from the international community was sufficiently large to stem the downward slide of the peso.

As the institutional framework for currency support from the US and Canada was already in place in the North American Framework Agreement (NAFA),[1] swap lines could be activated relatively quickly. However, markets soon realised that taken together these swap lines and Mexico's international reserves were insufficient to cover the short-term debt falling due in 1995 (Lustig, 1996).

The first rescue package of US$18 billion was put together in early January 1995, consisting principally of an expansion of the swap facilities with the USA and Canada, together with assistance from other countries – but without the involvement of the IMF. However, it soon became apparent that this was going to be insufficient to quell market panic and the pressure on the Mexican currency continued. The first stand-by arrangement with the IMF (for US$7.8

billion) was announced in late January, but again failed to convince the markets. Finally, at the end of January a rescue package of US$48.8 billion was put together with commitments from the USA ($20 bn), the IMF ($17.8 bn), Canada ($1 bn) and the BIS ($10 bn).[2] Mexico was also able to borrow US$3 billion from the World Bank and the IADB.

In broad terms, there was agreement between the Mexican authorities and the IMF on the need for austerity measures to help stabilise markets. This would have been a contributory factor in the relatively rapid agreement of a stand-by arrangement for Mexico in late January. However, the US Treasury did press the Mexican government to follow a macroeconomic policy mix, centred on high short-term interest rates to stabilise the peso, that the latter did not favour. The Mexican authorities, worried that high domestic interest rates would have negative impacts on the already weak banking system (and the real economy), would have had a preference for lower interest rates even if it was at the expense of a weaker peso (Lustig, 1996). The jury is still out on the relative merits of these approaches.

Reasons for the support for Mexico

In Mexico in 1995, the international community, and particularly the US government, gave unprecedented support to help an emerging market country facing a liquidity crisis. This rapid and large support was key in limiting the length of the Mexican crisis and the contagion effects spilling out from it.

There are a number of reasons for this. First, and perhaps most critically, Mexico had enjoyed good relations with the US in the years immediately preceding the crisis, particularly as a result of NAFTA. Second, Mexico had been a model reformer. Failing to support Mexico when it faced a crisis could have sent a strong message to other developing country governments that were following market-oriented reforms that their efforts would not necessarily be rewarded. Third, the international community recognised the dangers of contagion to other markets, particularly in Latin America, and was keen to prevent it. Finally, the role of the market over-reaction in the crisis, as compared with the domestic policy mistakes, was widely acknowledged.

The success and failure of the rescue

The announcement of the US$48.8 billion rescue package at the end of January 1995 did succeed in stopping the downward slide of the peso, and the currency market became much more stable following the announcement of the government's economic programme in March of the same year.

As noted above, the rescue package was also extremely successful when measured by the speed with which Mexico was able to return to international capital markets. A Mexican development bank managed to borrow in the international markets in April of 1995, and Mexico continued to raise money over the following months on increasingly better terms and maturities. The rescue package for Mexico was also largely successful in stemming contagion from the Mexican crisis (or Tequila effect).

The rescue package did not, however, manage to prevent a major recession in Mexico nor did it prevent significant increases in poverty and important losses to human capital. In 1995, output in Mexico fell by nearly 7 per cent. This represented the worst recession for the country since the Great Depression (Lustig, 1996). During 1995, unemployment doubled to almost 7 per cent and real wages contracted by around 15 per cent. Social expenditure in Mexico decreased as a percentage of GDP from 9 per cent in 1994 to 6.8 per cent in 1995 (Lustig, 2000).

Through such channels – rising unemployment, falls in real wages, and cut-backs in social expenditure – financial and economic crises often have devastating impacts on the living standards of poor people, and Mexico in 1995 was no exception. The incidence of poverty in Mexico rose from 36 per cent in 1994 to 43 per cent in 1996 (World Bank, 2001). Crises tend to have a negative impact not only on income poverty, but they also lead to a deterioration (or a slower improvement) of social indicators. As a result of the crisis, infant and pre-school mortality caused by nutritional deficiency rose in Mexico in 1995. The rate of growth of total primary enrolment in Mexico fell from 0.44 per cent in 1994 to 0.35 per cent in 1995 (World Bank, 2001). The deterioration in social indicators represents a reduction in human capital that can have both immediate and long-term negative impacts on poverty and inequality.

While inequality as measured by the Gini coefficient reportedly did not worsen in Mexico as a result of the crisis, this may not show the full picture. For example, the figure for school enrolment growth is a national average and therefore probably reflects a reduction among the more vulnerable sections of society. Clearly, the failure to participate in primary education represents an irreversible deterioration in human capital that perpetuates inequalities by limiting the capacity of poor people to escape from poverty.

Lessons from the Mexican experience

While some elements of the Mexican experience are clearly peculiar to that country's situation, and particularly its close relationship with the USA, there are also useful lessons that can be drawn from the international community's response to the crisis in Mexico. First, focusing on what the international community got 'right' in Mexico some general recommendations about crisis management can be made. Key among these would be the importance of preparedness; rapid arrangement and disbursement of funds; sufficient amount of funds; medium-term repayment terms; and national 'ownership' of macroeconomic policy response.

On the issue of preparedness, the Mexican case has both positive and negative aspects. On the one hand, the existence of pre-agreed swap facilities with the USA and Canada meant that these could be rapidly activated when the currency came under pressure. On the other hand, all parties failed to recognise initially that the amount of financing needed to stem market panic was going to be significantly larger than the swap arrangements allowed for. Clearly, an earlier announcement of larger levels of financing would have been more successful in halting market panic and may well have limited the negative impact on the real economy and therefore on poverty and inequality.

Turning to what the international community could have done better in Mexico, first there should have been a more careful consideration of the contractionary effect of the policy mix chosen to achieve stabilisation and a more open attitude to possible alternatives. Second, there should have been more mechanisms put in place to compensate vulnerable members of society from the negative impact of the austerity measures.

While there were clearly a number of domestic problems that contributed to the crisis, the experience of Mexico also highlighted the key role played by international financial markets in precipitating crises in emerging market countries. While the impulse of private sector lenders and investors to exit a market when financial difficulties loom may well be rational at the micro level, the aggregate effect can be devastating. Market panic can, as was the case in Mexico, become more central to the crisis than any problem with economic fundamentals.

As a result of the Mexican and subsequent crises, important policy lessons have been drawn for emerging market countries. Key among these are the need for a gradual approach in liberalising the capital account, and the importance of avoiding reliance on large levels of foreign currency denominated short-term debt (particularly *vis-à-vis* levels of international reserves). Lessons on how to limit the negative impact of market behaviour, however, have been less clearly drawn. Increasing support over the last few years for a mechanism for 'bailing-in' the private sector during crises has culminated in the IMF proposal for a Sovereign Debt Restructuring Mechanism (SDRM). There are also a range of proposals designed to encourage stable private capital flows to developing countries that should be considered. Some of these proposals will be discussed in the final section of this chapter.

The Argentine crisis of 2001/2

In contrast to the Mexican case, the response of the international community to the crisis in Argentina has been woefully inadequate. When the Argentine economy was hit by serious financial disturbances during 2001, the IMF failed to offer support and the country continued to fall further into financial, economic, political and social crisis. This response to the crisis in Argentina was based on heightened concerns about 'moral hazard' problems and a belief, mistaken as subsequent events have shown, that contagion to other economies would be avoided.

The unravelling of the Argentine crisis, and the response of the international community, again raise a number of important issues of relevance to other Latin American countries as well as to efforts to reform the international financial architecture.

The background to the crisis

The crisis in Argentina has its antecedents in both domestic and international factors. The major factor on the domestic side was the convertibility regime, which despite its success in bringing down inflation and restoring credibility in the country's financial system, had made Argentina vulnerable to sudden changes in the external financing environment (see also Chapter 3).

The convertibility regime, adopted by Argentina in the early 1990s, had been effective in restoring the country's monetary and financial system and bringing about economic recovery. However, the convertibility system also resulted in a high dependency on volatile international capital flows, and a tendency towards an overvalued exchange rate that made exports non-competitive (Ocampo, 2002). The lack of economic policy flexibility meant adjustment following shocks came at greater cost in terms of foregone output and employment. The inherent difficulties of convertibility were already exposed during the Mexican crisis, when the Argentine economy was the most severely affected by contagion, but on that occasion the convertibility regime survived.

Following the Asian crisis of 1998, the external financing environment for Latin American countries became very difficult, with capital flows being scarce, expensive and extremely volatile. For Argentina, this already difficult situation was made even worse by the appreciation of the US currency and the Brazilian devaluation in 1999, when the overvaluation of the Argentine peso was further exposed. In 2001, the events of 11 September increased risk aversion among international investors leading to further falls in capital inflows to Argentina and other emerging markets.

Despite the considerable costs to the economy of an overvalued currency, the Argentine authorities were reluctant to abandon convertibility because of the high exit costs (Ocampo, 2002). Clearly, in the aftermath of the Asian crisis there were a number of external factors that contributed to putting the convertibility regime under intense pressure. One lesson from the Argentine experience is that economic systems, of which the exchange rate regime is a central part, need to be flexible enough to cope with shocks and accommodate necessary adjustments. Throughout the 1998–2001 period, and of course earlier, the IMF supported economic policy in Argentina and did not suggest that the country should change or abandon the convertibility regime.

The crisis and the response of the international community

During 2001, economic activity in Argentina collapsed, the level of bank deposits fell dramatically, and international reserves were sharply reduced. Following failed attempts to save the convertibility regime by making it more flexible, the Argentine authorities were forced to introduce restrictions on deposit withdrawals, declare a moratorium on public debt and introduce exchange controls. Then in January 2002, the Argentine peso was devalued and the currency effectively collapsed.

Argentina proved to be extremely vulnerable to the sharp cycles in international capital flows to emerging market economies that result in massive capital inflows during good times, followed by massive withdrawals of capital when difficulties begin to show. Successful reforms introduced in Argentina in the early 1990s, and particularly the convertibility regime, had raised investors' expectations and attracted high levels of international capital flows to the country. Following the Asian crisis, however, investors' perceptions of risk in emerging markets changed dramatically and capital flows dried up. Clearly, there were also domestic problems within Argentina concerning the management of economic policy. When the Argentine economy hit difficulties in 2001, the markets lost confidence in the sustainability of the country's debt servicing capacity and withdrew further. As was the case in the Mexican peso crisis, the financial markets helped to create the very situation they feared.

In stark contrast to Mexico in 1995, however, the international community failed to come to Argentina's rescue. As the crisis in Argentina deepened, the IMF not only failed to provide additional financial resources to help the country, but actually suspended lending under the stand-by arrangement that was already in place. The suspension of IMF lending to Argentina in December 2001 increased concern in the international financial markets and triggered a further deepening of the crisis.

Difficult negotiations between the IMF and Argentina have continued thereafter. Progress in reaching an agreement has proved extremely difficult by the IMF adding new conditions to granting a loan, once the Argentine government had fulfilled previous requirements. The unusual decision of the Argentine authorities, in November 2001, to default on a loan repayment to the World Bank was widely recognised as a signal of the country's intense frustration over failed negotiations with the IMF.[3]

The actions of the IMF in Argentina appear to be the polar opposite of how the Fund should respond during crises. First, as the sustainability of the convertibility regime became increasingly doubtful, particularly in the post-1998 period, the IMF should have discussed far more alternatives with the Argentine authorities. Second, as the Fund supported Argentine economic policy in the years immediately preceding the crisis, they certainly should have supported the country through the crisis. To cut Argentina loose at the very time when it most needed assistance was not only irresponsible, but also goes against the purpose of the Fund to maintain output and employment as laid down in the Articles of Agreement.

The IMF's response to the crisis in Argentina stems, in part, from increased concerns over the 'moral hazard' problem. The main argument being that large rescue packages lead to excessive 'moral hazard', implying that borrowers and especially lenders will behave more irresponsibly when they believe they will be 'bailed out' should a crisis occur. The issue of debtor moral hazard has been dismissed by many, as no country would opt for policies that they believe will lead to a crisis. Added to that, in the case of Argentina the IMF had endorsed economic policy in the pre-crisis period. The problem of creditor moral hazard has also been over-stated; the problem in recent years has been a capital flow drought, rather than the 'irrational exuberance' of international investors in emerging markets that was sometimes seen in the early 1990s.

The response to the crisis was also partly due to the international community's belief that the crisis could be contained within Argentina, or that contagion was no longer an issue. However, accumulated experience from many previous crisis episodes showed that contagion to other markets is a problem. This has again happened in the case of Argentina, with negative impacts being transmitted to other countries in the region – including low-income countries such as Bolivia – through trade linkages and lower flow of external capital. Brazil was clearly threatened by contagion from Argentina. In Uruguay the Argentine crisis sparked a run on bank deposits, with the banking system suffering considerably and with very negative effects on the economy.

In the case of both Brazil and Uruguay, the IMF has provided assistance. The experience of Brazil, where the Fund rapidly put together a fairly large package with reasonable conditions attached, suggests that the IMF may have learnt some of the lessons from the mishandling of the crisis in Argentina (see below).

The economic and social impact of the crisis

The recession in Argentina worsened dramatically as a result of the financial and economic crisis. In 2001, GDP fell by 4.5 per cent and, in 2002, by 11 per cent. Investment fell to nearly half its former level. 2002 saw a 70 per cent fall in the peso, and inflation ran at around 40 per cent during 2002. The limits imposed on bank withdrawals caused steep falls in consumer spending and credit availability, and seriously damaged consumer confidence.

Economic contraction forced thousands of companies out of business. As a result, demand for labour dwindled, leading to heavy job losses and a steep fall in real wages. Unemployment went up to 22 per cent during the crisis, bringing the number of workers either unemployed or in part-time jobs to some 5.6 million. Real monthly wages declined by 18 per cent over the course of a year (CEPR, 2002).

Poverty in Argentina rose sharply as a result of the crisis. In the year to May 2002, the number of poor people in Argentina had risen by 6.15 million to a staggering 19 million – or 53 per cent of the total population (INDEC, 2002). Of the 19 million people in poverty, 9 million were living in extreme poverty – representing an increase of 4.5 million in one year. Children were particularly hard hit by the crisis, with reports of child deaths in the Tucuman and other provinces[4] and malnutrition and hunger in various provinces and in the suburbs of Buenos Aries (CEPR, 2002). Poverty levels in Argentina had never before risen so much in such a short space of time. Inequality, measured by the GINI coefficient, increased from 0.49 to 0.53 between May 1999 and May 2002 (Perry and Serven, 2003).

The main reasons for the sharp increase in poverty in Argentina were increases in unemployment and in less secure employment, the fall in wages and the steep increases in the price of basic goods. The economy-wide crisis also resulted in a high degree of social unrest and political instability, which further undermined human security in the country.

Lessons from the Argentine experience

As was the case with the Mexican experience, the crisis in Argentina raises a number of important issues concerning both the behaviour of international financial markets in emerging economies and the response of the international community to financial and economic crises.

First, the Argentine crisis has again highlighted the devastating impact of volatility in financial flows to emerging market countries. Sharp cycles of under-estimation of risk, with corresponding capital inflows, and over-estimation of risk, bringing capital withdrawals, are extremely destabilising and very costly to developing countries (Ocampo, 2002). Changing market perceptions, for example over the sustainability of debt servicing as has been the case in Argentina, can easily become self-fulfilling prophecies.

The IMF has an important role to play in correcting these market failures, and providing stability during times of financial disturbance. The crisis in Argentina has highlighted the devastating consequences when the IMF abandons a country experiencing difficulties. In the years immediately preceding the crisis, the Fund should have been advising the Argentine government on alternative policies to allow the economy to respond with more flexibility to shocks. In 2001, when the country was hit by crisis, the IMF should have continued to provide financial assistance and even increased lending, as well as being more supportive of a coherent policy package.

It is also essential that the international community in general, and the IMF in particular, adopts a more flexible approach to the policy mix that can be applied to achieve stabilisation in different crisis situations. Pursuing fiscal adjustment through further expenditure cuts during crises serves only to deepen recession which not only worsens the economic outlook, but also results in further increases in poverty and inequality. As outlined in the lessons from the Mexican crisis, it is also important that mechanisms be put in place that can help protect the most vulnerable members of society from the negative impact of austerity measures.

Brazil and its lessons

In the case of Brazil, the response of the IMF has been far more positive. As market pressure built up in 2002, this led to a sharp decline in the value of the real (the Brazilian domestic currency), and to an absurd increase in the risk premium on Brazilian sovereign bonds, both putting a lot of pressure on the Brazilian Balance of Payments. Significantly, in mid-2002, the IMF granted a large loan package of US$30 billion. This IMF package had several positive aspects. First, it was large enough to allow Brazil to meet its external obligations during 2002 and 2003. Second, IMF lending was complemented by fairly large loans from the IADB and the World Bank. Third, the conditionality was relatively well focused making it fairly easy for the new government to comply with (even though it did limit its ability to deliver on increased spending to reduce poverty). Indeed, the new President – as well as other candidates – supported, even before the elections, the fiscal target agreed by the Cardoso government, of a 3.75 per cent primary surplus (this target was later increased to 4.25 per cent).

Although the IMF loan did not immediately significantly improve market perceptions, which was disappointing given its scale and features, it stopped a further deterioration, and, as mentioned above, encouraged the new

President to commit to prudent macroeconomic policies, which time has shown led to renewed market confidence. As pointed out in Chapter 3, without the IMF package market perceptions would have deteriorated further, threatening economic collapse and possibly even the timetable of government transition. In the next section, we will discuss how the official sector can try to help encourage a more positive reaction from financial markets, in Brazil and similar situations.

Conclusions and policy recommendations

Macroeconomic crises have been one of the major causes of lower growth and increases in poverty, as well as inequality, in Latin America in recent years. Crises affect not only the current living standards of the poor, but also cause irreversible damage to human capital that can seriously undermine their capacity to grow out of poverty. Even when economic recovery after crises is accompanied by fairly rapid improvements in poverty rates, as was the case with the Mexican crisis of 1995, the damage to the human capital of poor people has more long-term negative effects. Crises and excessive macroeconomic volatility also discourage capital investment in Latin America, which damages the outlook for future growth and poverty reduction.

In order to achieve real gains in poverty reduction and equality in Latin America, improvements are needed in crisis avoidance and crisis response policies. This section will put forward a range of policy proposals that could contribute to better crisis avoidance and crisis response, as well as policies designed to encourage more and more stable private capital flows to Latin America.

The role of the IMF in crisis avoidance and crisis response

The IMF has a central role in fostering stability in the international financial system, as well as an institutional commitment to poverty reduction. As the principal provider of emergency liquidity assistance during episodes of financial disturbance, the Fund plays a crucial role in both preventing and containing crises. The experience of past crises, including those in Mexico and Argentina outlined in this chapter, shows how important it is to achieving poverty reduction and improved equity that the IMF continues to disburse large loans to prevent and contain crises. This sub-section will begin by looking at the key issues surrounding IMF liquidity provision, before putting the case for the mainstreaming of social considerations in the design of IMF policy.

IMF liquidity provision[5]

During the 1990s, capital account liberalisation and the large scale of private capital flows greatly increased the need for official liquidity to deal with sudden and large reversals of flows. Among the key lessons learnt from the crises in Latin American and other regions, one has been that the provision of emergency financing may need to be large-scale, should be able to be disbursed rapidly, and should be available to countries that may suffer contagion effects. As a result of the East Asian and other large crises, IMF resources were significantly enhanced. This facilitated the provision of fairly large financial packages to assist in the management and containment of crises.

However, there are still a number of problems around the provision of emergency financing and crisis management. As the case study on Argentina has shown, one of the most serious problems is a reduced willingness by the international community to provide large-scale financing to countries in crisis. This unwillingness to lend contributed to both trigger and deepen the crisis in Argentina (even if it did not cause it). It seems important, from the perspective of both crisis avoidance and management, that the IMF continues to disburse large loans to avoid crises occurring, deepening, and spreading through contagion. The response to the crisis in Brazil, where the IMF has provided large-scale emergency lending in a timely manner, seems an encouraging sign and a good example of how the Fund should respond.

With the enhancement of IMF resources following the Asian crisis, two new facilities were established. The creation of the Supplementary Reserve Facility (SRF) facilitated the provision of fairly large, more expensive, relatively short-term loans to countries hit by crises. The SRF provides financial assistance for exceptional balance of payments difficulties due to a large short-term financing need resulting from a sudden and disruptive loss of market confidence reflected in pressure on the member's capital account and reserves. The SRF was useful in providing large loans to countries like South Korea and Brazil, once they were hit by major crises.

Reportedly, several of the G-7 countries wish to establish limits on the scale of lending through the SRF. However, such limits would diminish the effectiveness of the SRF in restoring market confidence and could thus imply deeper crises in individual countries, as well as more risk of contagion in other countries; both could have very negative effects on growth, poverty reduction and inequality in the affected countries.

The second facility created after the East Asian crisis was a preventive one, the Contingent Credit Line (CCL). As the IMF defined it, the CCL was created as 'a precautionary line of defence readily available against future balance of payments problems that might arise from international financial contagion'. To qualify, the increased pressure on a country's capital account and international reserves must thus result from a sudden loss of confidence among investors triggered by external factors.

The CCL was thus a potentially very important and positive step because it could significantly reduce the chances of a country entering into a crisis, by providing contingency lending agreed in advance. However, despite a modification in the terms and conditions of the CCL designed to make it more attractive to borrowers, no country applied to use it during the time it was in place. The key problem was that of the perceived stigma attached. Developing countries with 'good' policies feared that applying for a CCL could be counter-productive and reduce – rather than strengthen, as was the intention – confidence of the markets in that country (Griffith-Jones and Ocampo, 2002).

The CCL, which was eliminated by the Fund Board in late 2003, could be reintroduced in a modified way as to make it more attractive and to diminish any potential stigma. One option would be that all countries that had been favourably evaluated by the IMF in their annual Article IV consultations could automatically qualify for the new CCL. Therefore, a country would have a right to draw on the CCL, should the need arise. This would imply that quite a large number of countries – including the developed ones – would qualify for the CCL (even though few would use it), thus eliminating the stigma on its use. Automatic access to the new CCL could be seen as a sign of strength, rather than as a sign of possible future weakness. The fact that countries could have access to the CCL would hopefully diminish the likelihood both of crises and therefore of the need for countries to draw on it.

Mainstreaming the social implications of macroeconomic policy

Crises clearly have a negative impact on growth, poverty reduction and inequality. A second, and closely related, issue is how the crisis response impacts on growth and the living standards of poor people. Concerns over the social impacts of the policy conditions of the IMF required during some recent crises, most notably the crises in East Asia, highlighted the need for changes in the conditionality that traditionally accompanies rescue packages as well as the importance of strong social safety nets.

Three key issues that have been raised in relation to IMF conditionality are the importance of country 'ownership' of adjustment programmes, the need for a more flexible attitude towards the policy mix adopted to achieve stabilisation, and the need to limit the scope of IMF conditionality.[6] The first two of these issues, 'ownership' and flexibility, are closely related as negotiations between the Fund and national governments often involve disagreements over the exact nature of the adjustment programme. It seems very important that the IMF, in its country programmes, allow governments the fiscal policy space to pursue expansionary policies to counteract economic contraction during crises. This, in turn, would provide space to continue with existing, and implement new, social protection measures. The IMF should also play a role in helping to persuade financial markets to accept a less contractionary fiscal stance during crises.

One important lesson from the recent crises in Latin America and elsewhere has been that in order to limit the negative impact on living standards, it is essential that the social implications of programmes be mainstreamed into the design of macroeconomic policy.

The last few years have seen a significant shift in the approach of both the IMF and the World Bank regarding non-economic issues in their policies and programmes. The major changes began with the launch of the Comprehensive Development Framework (CDF) by the World Bank in January 1999. The CDF is basically a tool for deciding development priorities that emphasises the interdependence of all elements of development: economic, financial, social, structural, human, environmental and governance. The CDF process entails co-ordination between governments, donors, the IFIs and private and civil society stakeholders to deliver a long-term, joined-up, poverty-focused development programme. The CDF approach was made operational in the Bank's activities in the poorest countries through the introduction of the PRGF later that same year.

At the Bank–Fund annual meetings in 1999, the IMF announced that poverty reduction was to be adopted as the institution's new priority. In his address to the IMF Board of Governors, outgoing Managing Director Michel Camdessus, said:

> A vital interrelationship exists between growth and social development. This linkage has been too loose in our programmes so far…[s]trong social policies that address poverty at its roots lay the foundation for sustained economic growth.
>
> (Camdessus, 28.09.99)

The immediate result of this new approach was the transformation of the ESAF into the Poverty Reduction and Growth Facility (PRGF). Under the PRGF, poverty reduction was to be the key objective of IMF and World Bank programmes in poor countries. Poverty Reduction Strategy Papers (PRSPs) are produced by national governments, in a transparent way with the participation of civil society. PRSPs are then considered by the Boards of the IMF and the World Bank as the basis for concessional lending and debt relief under the enhanced Heavily Indebted Poor Countries (HIPC). The dominance of the IMF in ESAF programmes has been replaced with a more co-ordinated approach involving the World Bank and other actors. Most importantly, in an approach that mirrors the CDF, macroeconomic, structural and social reforms in poor countries should be coherent and poverty-focused.

A strong focus on poverty reduction and social equity in IMF and World Bank programmes in poor countries was clearly a necessary and welcome step. The extent to which this has been achieved in practice is still a matter of some debate. Many international NGOs have asserted that the move to the PRGF was little more than a change in acronyms. Many have observed that the PRGF approach has failed to align macroeconomic issues and poverty issues, and that macroeconomic frameworks in Bank-Fund programmes have not changed significantly since its introduction.[7]

Despite pressure from civil society groups and donors, until recently there has been no method of systematically evaluating the poverty and social impact of policy reforms introduced as part of the PRGF. The World Bank is now working to assist PRSP countries with ex-ante poverty and social impact analysis (PSIA) of macroeconomic and structural policy reforms. This would facilitate a better understanding of the trade-offs in alternative policy packages being considered as part of a PRSP. In 2002, the Bank produced a draft guidance manual for poverty and social impact analysis (PSIA) and began a series of PSIA case studies.

Middle-income countries appear to have been left out of the equation. While the CDF was envisaged as an approach that would encompass the IFI's programmes in all countries, it has been somewhat eclipsed by the PRGF, which is limited to HIPC countries. Poverty reduction and improvements in social equity are as central to achieving sustained economic growth in middle-income countries, which comprise the majority of Latin American countries, as they are in the poorest countries. This should be acknowledged by the IFIs, and should influence their decision making on both whether to lend to middle-income countries and what conditions to attach to such lending. IMF programmes in middle-income countries would benefit from increased national ownership and a stronger recognition of the country's poverty reduction and growth priorities. Poverty and social impact analysis (PSIA) should also be rolled out to IMF-led programmes in middle-income countries.

Past experience of IMF activities in developing countries indicates that it would be very useful for the IMF to consult with a wider group of stakeholders during the design of lending agreements and rescue packages. A PSIA unit within the IMF could provide the political motivation for support for alternative strategies that could be more effective, for example in response to macroeconomic crises. This could provide the basis for the IMF to consult systematically with independent experts, who would be able to offer a wider variety of experience and insights. Some examples of alternative strategies that could be considered would include: the level of fiscal deficit required to achieve stabilisation; the policy mix adopted to achieve fiscal stabilisation and the consequences for growth and poverty of alternative strategies such as raising taxes, cutting expenditure, etc.; pro-poor considerations in the reform of domestic financial systems; and the adoption of counter-cyclical fiscal policy.[8]

Recent crisis episodes have also illustrated the need for strong social safety nets to manage the social repercussions of financial disturbances in developing countries. Social safety nets are made up of policies and programmes that provide emergency income support and access to basic social services to the poor during financial and economic crises. They are important in mitigating both the immediate and the long-term negative impact of crises; preventing more people from slipping into poverty, and helping individuals and households cope with the consequences of crises without undermining human capital. Social safety nets can include mechanisms such as: unemployment insurance, income support, public works programmes, price subsidies, nutrition programmes, social service fee waivers and micro-finance programmes.

Analyses of social safety nets undertaken since the Asian crisis have drawn a number of conclusions. Key among these:

- they should be part of permanent social protection schemes, so they can respond quickly to the needs of vulnerable people during crises;
- a combination of various programmes, with different target groups, is most effective;
- they should be country-owned and designed, and principally financed domestically in normal times.

It is difficult for governments to fund sufficiently large social safety nets in times of crisis, as government revenues often decline at a time the needs of vulnerable people are increasing. For this reason, the international community should also be willing to provide assistance to developing countries with financing social safety nets during economic shocks. Appropriate mechanisms should be designed, and resources allocated, for this purpose.

The role of the MDBs, the World Bank and the IADB in Latin America

Increased lending

The multilateral development banks (MDBs) have a number of important roles to play, both in low-income and middle-income countries (in Latin America, as well as in the rest of the developing world). The essential role of MDBs in low-income countries has been widely recognised; it becomes even more essential: (a) when examining low-income countries' external financial needs in a context of meeting the Millennium Development Goals, especially as regards poverty reduction; (b) in the small proportion of private flows going to low-income countries during the 1990s (see Griffith-Jones and Ocampo, 2002); and (c) in the further decline of private flows to low-income countries post-Asian crisis. Indeed, it is a paradox that when middle-income countries have crises and lose access to private flows, there is a negative trickle-down, with low-income countries automatically also having their access to private flows sharply reduced.

The MDBs also need to play an important role in providing lending to middle-income countries, as well as helping catalyse private flows to them (US Treasury, 2000; Gurría and Volcker 2001, Gurría *et al.*, 2002). There are a number of reasons why MDBs should continue – and even increase – their role in lending to middle-income countries. First, as the report of the Commission led by Gurría and Volcker (2001) emphasised, access by emerging markets, especially those of Latin America, has become '*unreliable, limited and costly*'. This is particularly true in the years following the Asian crisis, when private flows experienced a strong decline.

The problem of volatility both of availability and cost of private funds as well as their rapid reversals has contributed in a major way to a slow down in growth and poverty reduction in the Latin American region since the Asian crisis. Lower growth, caused by declining private flows, and even more crises *tend to hurt the poor most*, through lost jobs and income and interrupted education for children.

Therefore, MDB lending to middle-income countries when private flows fall and especially when these dry up or reverse, is crucial to protect growth as well as poverty reduction programmes. More specifically, MDB lending can assist in maintaining adequate public spending in health and education as well as funding social safety nets during crises. Furthermore, when the MDBs maintain or, far better, significantly increase lending during difficult times, they may help rebuild market confidence in the country affected, as well as reduce the risk of contagion.

Besides their crucial role in providing financing when private flows fall or reverse sharply, MDBs also have other important roles in middle-income countries in more 'normal' times. First, long-term MDB loans can finance investment in sectors where long-term social returns are significantly higher than short-term private returns (such as investments in health, education and infrastructure), and therefore where the private sector does not wish to invest and where national governments may not have sufficient own resources to fund. Second, MDBs – and especially the IADB in the case of Latin America – have an important role in funding provision of global and regional public goods, such as regional infrastructure. Third, MDBs need to play an important role in capacity building, institutional development (including promoting international codes and standards) and intellectually diverse knowledge brokering (see Stiglitz, 1999; see also Griffith-Jones and Ocampo, 2002; Gilbert *et al.*, 1999).

An important reason why MDBs should lend to middle-income countries is that this lending indirectly supports lending to poorer countries. Indeed, avoiding a crisis in Brazil not only provides a stable growing export market for poor countries like, for example, Bolivia, it also increases the prospect that countries like Bolivia will be able in the future to attract more private flows, and – more immediately – reduces significantly the likelihood of large capital flight from Bolivia that a crisis in Brazil would spark off. In the case of some multilaterals like the World Bank and the IADB, net income ('profits') originated in lending to middle-income countries is transferred to their soft window, so lending to middle-income countries indirectly supports highly concessional lending for the poorest countries.

Given all the functions that MDBs have to perform, an important issue that the international community has not devoted sufficient attention to, is that fulfilling these functions appropriately (so as to support growth and poverty reduction) may require an increase in resources available to the MDBs, complemented by a more active use of existing resources and mechanisms for such lending as well as of catalytic mechanisms such as guarantees and co-financing to encourage private flows (discussed below). Indeed, the current scale of MDB lending to middle-income countries (at only 8.4 per cent of private flows, excluding FDI to these countries in the 1990–9 period[9]), though valuable, is insufficient to perform appropriately and on sufficiently large scale, the counter-cyclical role, which is so essential for attempts to sustain growth and social spending in difficult times.

Given that crises have unfortunately become so frequent, it may be advisable to formalise more emergency loans and make them regular World Bank and IADB products. Their features should include the possibility of additional resources – beyond ordinary lending – and include features such as accelerated repayment if economies recover.

Besides creating new and improving existing mechanisms, and ensuring sufficient resources for appropriate MDB lending, it is also important that these institutions also play a bigger role in helping catalyse private flows. We now turn to this in some detail.

Expanding the catalytic role

A key policy challenge for the World Bank and the IADB, as well as more broadly for the official international community, is how to help catalyse private flows to Latin America in times of serious drought of such private flows, and how to provide additional counter-cyclical lending to compensate for sharp reversals of private flows. This is crucial because, without such measures, Latin America will continue to be the victim of boom-bust patterns of capital flows, leading to very frequent and developmentally very costly crises. These crises also tend to worsen income distribution as they tend to hurt the poor most, through lost jobs and income and interrupted education for children, as well as through worse health care. Besides their tremendous costs in terms of lower growth and higher poverty levels, crises, and the resulting focus on managing the short term also inhibit any possibility for LAC governments to design long-term development strategies which focus on crucial strategic issues, such as improving income distribution.

A particular source of concern is the fact that there may be cases, as in Brazil in the second half of 2002, where the official community has provided a large package (see above) and yet private actors are unwilling to lend/ invest even though fundamentals are basically sound. It is therefore urgent to find new mechanisms that would hopefully catalyse private flows to the region.

A number of mechanisms can be designed or improved to help catalyse private flows. These include: (1) guarantees and co-funding; and (2) influencing socially responsible investment (SRI) so as to encourage SRI investors to channel long-term flows to support pro-poor growth in developing countries. We will concentrate more here on guarantees, with a fairly brief reference to SRI.

(1) GUARANTEES

Two types of private credit flows dry up in difficult periods: one is trade credit, typically granted by commercial banks, the other is long-term lending. The drying up of short-term trade credit lines (both for exports and imports) is particularly problematic. A sharp decline or lack of short-term credit for exports is especially damaging for countries trying to avoid crises (e.g. Brazil, in the second half of 2002) or in crises (e.g. Argentina, during 2002). In both cases, there has been a significant depreciation of the currency, which increases the competitiveness of the country's exports. However, lack of export credit seriously undermines the ability of significantly increasing exports which is crucial both for kick-starting growth and avoiding or containing crises.[10]

It is therefore very encouraging that the IADB is exploring the creation of guarantee mechanisms, that would be specifically tailored to encourage trade finance, provided by commercial banks. Such guarantees would be *particularly effective* for countries experiencing difficulties with access to trade credit, but not in crisis (e.g. Brazil, in late 2002), a country that had seen trade credit cut quite significantly. It seems worthwhile to attempt to develop guarantees carefully focused on specific risks (e.g. country risk) and not cover standard commercial risk. This could help provide greater leverage to the public resources contributed by the IADB. However, guarantees should not be too restrictive of the type of risk they cover, as this could defeat their purpose – if they did not lead to a restoration of access to private credit lines. Should guarantees of the IADB or other institutions, like the World Bank, not prove successful in helping restore private credit lines, the option of allowing institutions like the IADB to grant trade credit in special circumstances may need to be evaluated. It is important to stress that either guarantees for – or provision of – trade credits should basically be temporary, for periods when countries lose access to such private financing. Once full access is restored, either guarantees or credit provision by an institution like IADB become unnecessary. However, the mechanism should stay in place, to be available if and when a similar problem occurs in the future.

As regards more long-term private loans, either via bank lending or via bonds, there is a need to review, improve and enhance existing guarantee mechanisms for lending to both the public and private sector in Latin America. It is important, for example, to understand why some existing guarantee mechanisms (which have a number of positive features) to catalyse private flows were never used, in the case of the IADB, and were so scarcely used in the case of the World Bank facility – in the recent period, only for Argentina and Colombia. Were there possibly too many restrictions? Was the process of approval of guarantees too cumbersome? Were guarantees too expensive? How could these be structured better to provide more leverage to the World Bank and IADB and to make their use more attractive to borrowers and lenders?

Clearly, greater flexibility is needed to make procedures more agile. Also, creative ways need to be found, or expanded further, to guarantee only those risks that the markets do not want to cover (e.g. possibly covering only country risk, as suggested above for guarantees for trade credit). It is also possible to cover only initial maturities and then rolling over the guarantee once these initial payments have been made.

Alternatively, in some cases private actors may be willing to lend for early maturities, and institutions like the IADB or World Bank may need to guarantee later maturities or provide co-financing for later maturities. This is particularly appropriate for infrastructure investments, which have high initial sunk costs and very long gestation periods before the project becomes profitable (see Gurría and Volcker, 2001; Griffith-Jones, 1993). Through these or similar mechanisms, it may be possible to achieve higher rating (lower spreads and/or access to markets where there would have been none) for tranches without the IADB or World Bank guarantees. If successful, this will facilitate leverage of resources. At present, guarantees are expensive – as they are typically valued like loans; a review of their pricing also seems important.

Another issue to examine is whether national export credit agencies (ECAs) of developed countries could not play a larger role in helping sustain/catalyse private flows in times of crisis. Reportedly, ECAs are already somewhat less pro-cyclical than private lenders for three reasons: (1) they tend to fund more long-term projects, which implies that their time horizon is longer than that of banks and bond holders; (2) they reschedule collectively via the Paris Club, which apparently gives them more leverage and means to recover unpaid debt; and (3) they have somewhat higher risk tolerance. ECAs use broadly the same indicators as external credit agencies, but by taking a longer view, tend to interpret these somewhat differently. Nevertheless, there seems to be increasingly fairly small differences between ECAs' assessment of risk and that of rating agencies, thus diminishing the counter-cyclical role of ECA guarantees (Griffith-Jones and Spratt, 2001). Furthermore, at present, the level of guarantees provided by the major ECAs is relatively small and seems to be decreasing. Finally, ECAs do not provide guarantees for short-term trade credit, either for exports or imports.

An important question is whether ECAs could not: (a) increase the scale of their guarantee operations for lending to Latin American countries; and (b) increase the counter-cyclicality of the level of guarantees. The justification for the latter would be that private lenders are prone to boom-bust patterns, which are often more determined by changing global preferences for risk aversion and/or to contagion between developing countries, and not so much determined by countries' fundamentals. ECAs could therefore be more active in providing guarantees, when private lenders are less willing to lend; this would encourage higher levels of private lending. Once the private flows recovered, the ECA could try to sell those guarantees in a secondary market. Thus, the greater counter-cyclicality of guarantees would not need to increase, by itself, the level of guarantees (though it might increase somewhat their riskiness).

It may also be useful to explore whether different ECAs could not co-ordinate amongst themselves to provide more counter-cyclical financing. Mechanisms like expanding re-insurance amongst ECAs could be useful to diversify risk, although admittedly this may be made somewhat difficult by the fact that ECAs also compete amongst each other.

(2) SOCIALLY RESPONSIBLE INVESTMENT (SRI)

As regards other mechanisms to encourage private flows, an area clearly insufficiently explored is SRI. Traditionally, SRI tends to have a negative slant, implying restrictions on investing in undesirable activities, such as those that employ child labour, do not meet environmental standards, do not meet labour standards, etc. These restrictions may in fact discourage investment in developing countries, as the existence of low wages and lower environmental standards is part of underdevelopment. A recent example of this is when the large US pension fund, Calpers, introduced a number of restrictions on their investment (e.g. minimum labour standards), which led to their withdrawal from several major developing countries.

A new definition of SRI could imply that one of its central aims is to support *long-term* private flows to developing countries that *help fund pro-poor growth*. Crucially, this would encourage more long-term and therefore less volatile flows, which is important, both for growth and income redistribution, as stable private flows allow for higher growth. It could also encourage pro-poor and thus more equitable patterns of growth. In turn, this would provide a firmer basis for improved labour standards, both because incomes, and especially wages would be higher and because SRI foreign investors by being present and engaged in developing countries, could have a positive influence on those aspects.

A change in the approach towards SRI from a negative 'anti-bad' things to a pro-poor growth in developing countries emphasis, potentially could have a positive impact on increasing private flows to Latin America and making them more stable. In particular, pension funds could potentially provide more stable flows as their liabilities are on average very long term. It should also be emphasised that if a pension fund invests part of its portfolio in Latin American equities (and other developing regions), there is fairly clear evidence that return/risk ratio will be, in the long term, higher than if it invests purely in developed countries (see, for example, Kimmis *et al.*, 2002). Thus, SRI investment in developing countries could also be a more profitable investment.

Notes

1 Under NAFA, the three NAFTA countries agreed to provide mutual currency support.
2 The terms of the loans available from the BIS were too short term, so the loans were never used.
3 *Financial Times*, 14/11/02.
4 *The Guardian*, 25/11/02
5 This section draws on Griffith-Jones and Ocampo (2002).
6 At the time of the Asian crisis, IMF conditionality was widely perceived as being too far-reaching and intrusive. The IMF has since accepted the need for conditionality to be streamlined.
7 See Gottschalk (2005) for a comprehensive analysis of the macroeconomic content of various PRSPs.
8 For a discussion on alternative macroeconomic policies, see Chapter 3.
9 Source Griffith-Jones and Ocampo (2002), based on World Bank data.
10 A similar problem emerged in East Asia, during and immediately after the 1997/98 crisis.

Bibliography

Camdessus, M. (1999) Address to the Board of Governors of the Fund, 28 September 1999. Online. Available HTTP: <http://www.imf.org/external/np/speeches/1999/092899.htm> (accessed October 2003).
CEPR (Centre for Economic and Policy Research) (2002) 'Argentina Since Default, the IMF and the Depression'. Briefing Paper.
Cornia, G.A. (ed.) (2004) 'Inequality, Growth, and Poverty in an Era of Liberalization and Globalization', UNU-WIDER Studies in Development Economics, UNU-WIDER and UNDP, Oxford University Press.
Financial Times 'Argentina Defaults on Loan Payments', 14 November 2002.
Ffrench-Davis, R. and Griffith-Jones, S. (eds) (1995) *Coping with Capital Surges: The Return of Finance to Latin America*, Boulder, CO: IDRC/Lynne Reinner.
Gilbert, C., Powell, A. and Vines, D. (1999) 'Positioning the World Bank', *Economic Journal*, 109 (November), 598–634.
Gottschalk, R. (2004) 'The Macroeconomic Content of the PRSPs: Assessing the Need for a more Flexible Macroeconomic Policy Framework', *Development Policy Review*, 23(4), 419–42.
Griffith-Jones, S. (1993) 'Guarantees for Large Infrastructure Projects', Luxembourg: European Commission.
—— (1997) 'Causes and Lessons of the Mexican Peso Crisis', Helsinki: World Institute for Development Economics Research.
Griffith-Jones, S. and Ocampo, J.A. (2002) 'What Progress on International Financial Reform? Why so Limited?', mimeo, Brighton: Institute of Development Studies.
Griffith-Jones, S. and Spratt, S. (2001) 'Will the Proposed new Basel Capital Accord Have a Net Negative Effect on Developing Countries?', mimeo, Brighton: Institute of Development Studies.
The Guardian 'Child hunger deaths shock Argentina', 25 November 2002.

Gurría, J.A. *et al.* (2002) *The Challenge of Being Relevant, the Future Role of the IDB*. Report of the External Advisory Group.

Gurría, J.A. and Volcker, P. (co-chairmen) (2001) 'The Role of the Multilateral Development Banks in Emerging Market Economies', Carnegie Endowment for International Peace, EMP Financial Advisors LLC, and the Inter-American Dialogue, Washington, DC.

INDEC (2002) Report on the Social Situation in Argentina.

Institute of Development Studies, University of Sussex (2000) 'A Foresight and Policy Study of the Multilateral Development Banks', Brighton.

Kimmis, J., Gottschalk, R., Armendariz, E. and Griffith-Jones, S. (2002) 'UK Pension Fund Investment and Developing Country Assets', mimeo, Brighton: Institute of Development Studies.

Lustig, N. (2000) 'Crises and the Poor: Socially Responsible Macroeconomics', Sustainable Development Department Technical Paper Series, Washington DC: Inter-American Development Bank, February.

Lustig, N. (1996) 'Mexico in Crisis, the US to the Rescue: The Financial Assistance Packages of 1982 and 1995', Brookings Discussion Papers, Washington DC: The Brookings Institution, June.

Ocampo, J.A. (2002) 'The Lessons of the Argentine Crisis', unpublished paper, Economic Commission for Latin America and the Caribbean.

Perry, G. and Serven, L. (2003) 'The Anatomy of a Multiple Crisis: Why Was Argentina Special and What Can We Learn From it', World Bank Working Paper no. 3081, Washington, DC: World Bank.

Stiglitz, J.A. (1999) 'The World Bank at the Millennium', *Economic Journal*, 109 (November), 577–97.

United States Department of the Treasury (2000) 'Response to the Report of the International Financial Institutions Advisory Commission', 8 June.

World Bank (2001) World Development Report 2000/2001, Washington DC.

5   Inequality and trade in Latin America

David Evans

Introduction

Income inequality is an important aspect in the process of development and growth of a country. Inequality affects democracy, governance, poverty and economic growth. This chapter is concerned with the impact of trade policies and trade policy reform on income distribution in a group of Latin American countries: Argentina, Brazil, Colombia, Bolivia, Peru, Nicaragua, Honduras, Guatemala, El Salvador, Chile and Mexico. These we refer to in summary as the target Latin American countries.

Disentangling the impact of trade on income inequality is difficult when many features of the target Latin American economies – structural, economic policies, social and political factors – affect the distribution of income. This chapter sketches a framework for assessing how trade policy reform has an impact on the distribution of income, distinguishing between short-run and medium- and long-run effects. In particular, the framework chosen is designed to highlight the interplay between theoretical and empirical aspects which help to make clear the linkages between trade policy reform and economic inequality in Latin America. In the short run, macroeconomic variables such as the real exchange rate can have an important impact on the distribution of income and economic growth. In the medium and long run, structural features of the economy such as factor endowments, the pattern of trade, trade policies, labour market institutions and a variety of mechanisms that influence the rate of technical change are of particular importance. All of the above need to be examined from an economy-wide perspective, and in the context of trading partner policies that have important implications for the target Latin American countries. Often, a more detailed sectoral approach is also needed to understand better how important sectors link into the wider framework.

Typically, trade policy reform can be pursued through a variety of institutional mechanisms. First, major trade policy reforms are often carried out unilaterally under World Bank Structural Adjustment Programmes

(SAPs) or under the auspices of the World Trade Organisation (WTO). Secondly, through trade policy changes aimed at creating regional integration through Regional Trade Agreements (RTAs) such as Free Trade Areas (FTA), Customs Unions (CU), or regional integration through Open Regionalism (OR). Finally, major trade policy reform may take place as a part of the General Agreement on Tariffs and Trade (GATT) and World Trade Organisation (WTO) rounds, where a global round of trade policy reform takes place. In this chapter, when looking at trade policy reform in the target Latin American countries, some attempt will be made to disentangle the different levels of reform, or proposed future reform. However, even when full information is available on the layers of unilateral, regional and global tariff reform, the impacts on inequality and growth by institutional initiatives can only be imperfectly disentangled from the historical experience.

Surprisingly, relatively little is known about the impact of trade policy on inequality. The required historical datasets are notoriously difficult to assemble and are incomplete even in recent datasets where the mapping between household and factor incomes is often weak and incomplete. Also, measuring the impact on price of trade control measures across sectors and over time is difficult and incomplete in the target Latin American countries. The same can be said about measures of income inequality. In the trade literature, comparative static studies have dominated for a long time and the methodological and empirical basis of dynamic studies is not well developed. All types of methodologies suffer from the incompleteness of the database, and the incompleteness of the available analytical frameworks from which researchers can choose. Modelling approaches to separating the impact of trade policy reform from other influences affecting the historical patterns of growth and income distribution are limited both by the modelling approaches themselves as well as the empirical difficulties described.

In this chapter, the approach adopted is to assemble in an accessible form as much as possible the structural and other data typically needed to explore the relationship between trade policy and income distribution in the long run, and in the short and medium run. These datasets will be used to illustrate some of the empirical linkages where useful observations can be made. Often, in the absence of well-specified linkages between trade policy, inequality and growth, the findings should be couched in terms of potential changes rather than actual changes predicted by the study.

The main findings of this chapter are that the historical impact of trade reform in the target countries has been associated with a rise in the household income inequality, and that these processes have continued from the latter part of the 1980s until the present time. However, the data requirements to definitively establish this result are extremely demanding and are not readily available at the present time. There is some evidence from the 1990s that real exchange rates have not been appropriate, which appears to have affected many of the target countries negatively. Possible future trade policy reform in the northern markets for the target Latin American country exports is likely to yield large welfare gains and stimulate productivity change, but the impact of these reforms on income distribution is uncertain. The key policy message is that rapid accumulation of skills is likely to improve the prospects for economic growth and eventually reverse the adverse income distribution consequence of trade policy reform.

The chapter is organised as follows. The following section, 'Analytical framework' describes a framework for exploring the links between trade reform and income inequality. The third section, 'Analysing the inpact of trade policy reform on income inequality in target Latin American countries' attempts to analyse empirically the impact of trade on income distribution in the target Latin American countries, drawing on the framework outlined in 'Analysing framework'. The data presented are stylised, capturing only a part of the picture. The interpretation of such stylised data reveals some insights as well as the complexity of the theoretical and empirical issues that need to be taken into account when arriving at an historical perspective on trade policy reform and inequality in Latin America. The section will in addition analyse the impacts of trade reforms taking into account the macroeconomic adjustment, or its absence, which is expected to take place in parallel in support of the reforms. Finally, the chapter summarises the findings, drawing together the strong results, indicating the areas of ambiguity, and suggesting areas that may be of particular importance for future research.

Analytical framework[1]

Income inequality and the gains from trade

In the long run, trade policy reform is normally associated with improvements in economic welfare. Households and consumers gain from access to consumer goods at lower prices and efficient economic activities gain from access to world as well as domestic markets. Thus, traditional static gains from trade can be summarised in terms of increased welfare for consumers due to more product variety and lower prices, and also as a result of increased efficiency in the allocation of resources in more competitive and efficient industries. In addition, trade can bring about dynamic gains in terms of knowledge acquisition, and increased efficiency from specialisation and growth. The impact of the improved gains from trade is not, however, necessarily evenly distributed across households and individuals. Usually, there will be some who gain and others who lose, and among those who gain there will be some who gain more than others, and the impacts will vary depending on whether a long-, medium- or short-run perspective is taken. Therefore, trade policy reform can have important effects on income distribution.

Recently, there has been an increased concern in the trade literature on the impact of trade reform on poverty. This literature is informative because it makes explicit the diversity of channels through which trade affects both inequality and poverty. It is important to separate poverty and inequality effects because inequality is typically a relative concept, whereas poverty can be measured in absolute or in relative terms (see, for example, McCulloch *et al.*, 2001). Thus, if trade reform raises overall income and growth, then absolute poverty levels may be reduced over time. This positive effect on absolute poverty levels may, however, also be associated with increased income inequality, if, for example, the result is an increase in relative income of more highly skilled workers. For the most part, this chapter focuses on trade policy reform and inequality with only brief reference to poverty issues.

Trade and trade policy reform affects income distribution through a variety of channels in the short, medium and long run. Short run in this context refers to periods of 1–3 years, medium run 3–5 years and long run over 5 years. The key differences in the way that the identified channels operate can be reduced to the speed of adjustment of commodity, factor markets and foreign exchange markets, and of inducement mechanisms that affect technical change and growth. Typically, in the short run, commodity markets adjust to trade policy reforms faster than factor markets and foreign exchange markets can over-react in one way or another. In the medium run, foreign exchange markets may be less subject to speculative influence and factor markets are likely to be more fully adjusted to the trade policy reforms. It is only in the long run that full factor market adjustment will take place and that inducement mechanisms affecting technical change and growth will be operative. The following sub-section attempts to identify these channels in more detail, in order to establish a framework that will show the link between trade and income inequality.

Linking trade policy reform to inequality in detail

Short-run channels

PRICE TRANSMISSION – IMPORT SIDE

Increased openness to trade for a small country is about adopting international prices. The movement to international prices affects consumption and production, but since the price effect of trade policy measures is almost never uniform across sectors, the relative impact on sectors will not be the same. Regarding consumption, we may expect an overall increase in consumer welfare. International competition will lower prices in protected import-competing sectors and the households whose incomes depend on these sectors will see their incomes reduced. However, trade policy reform affects prices of imported goods, and the effectiveness of the price transmission in the economy depends on the competitive structure of the economy, the government marketing institutions such as marketing boards and the domain of trade. Frequently, price formation in domestic markets is not competitive, especially in relation to the distribution of products. Concentration of ownership in the means of transport and distribution of goods can lead to significant inequality directly and indirectly. Small producers may lose out when it comes to selecting goods for market. Ultimately, the effects of price changes on household income distribution on the import side will be transmitted through the induced effects on the production structure and associated changes in the functional distribution of income.

PRICE TRANSMISSION – EXPORT SIDE

Trade policy reform works on the export side through two principal mechanisms. The removal of export taxes or subsidies on exports will directly affect the domestic price of exports, bringing them closer to international prices, but the changes to achieve this will vary across sectors. The removal of tariffs or subsidies on traded inputs used in the export sector will indirectly have an effect, again in a non-uniform fashion. Since exportables usually form a small percentage of the household consumer bundle, the greatest effect of trade policy reform on the export side is on producers of exports, who benefit from any tariff cuts on importable inputs but who may lose from any removal of export subsidies. The ultimate effect of trade policy reform on household income distribution on the export side depends on induced changes in the production structure and changes in the functional distribution of income. There are notable exceptions where trade policy reform on the export side may have a great impact on domestic consumers, such as the case of the removal of export taxes on oil in Venezuela.

PRICE TRANSMISSION – EXCHANGE RATES

In the short run, exchange rates are subject to multiple determinants. Macroeconomic adjustment to trade policy reform normally requires a devaluation of the real exchange rate – that is, a rise in the price of tradable goods relative to non-tradable. This is required since the short-run effect of the trade policy reform is to lower the domestic price of importables, leading to an excess demand for foreign exchange at the initial exchange rate. When trade policy reform takes place in the context of multiple forces affecting the exchange rate, for example short-run speculative capital movements, the desired devaluation of the real exchange rate may not take place. A real exchange rate appreciation at the same time as trade policy reform may happen instead, and this will tend to work against the adjustment process and the desired medium- and long-run real exchange rate depreciation, increasing the short-run harm to households earning income from import competing production, and lessening benefits to income-earning from export production.

RELATIVE DEMAND AND REMUNERATION OF FACTORS OF PRODUCTION

Trade liberalisation affects the border prices of inputs purchased by firms or of commodities that compete with the output of domestic firms. Border price change transmitted to firms from trade policy reform will have an impact on the profits, wages and rental incomes that are ultimately received by households, but the transmission process may not be immediate. The effects on the sources of income will depend on a variety of factors. Domestic and international firms may respond initially to increased import competition by allowing excess capacity to develop. Import competing firms may be slow to shed labour in the face of increased import competition and slow to react to improved cost conditions for exports. Resource-based economic activity (farming and mining), where rental income can cushion adverse short-run effects, may take longer to adjust to new cost conditions than manufacturing or service firms. Some factor that is fixed and immobile in the short run is usually behind sluggish adjustment to short-run impacts of trade policy reform. Existing plant may be immobile or it may have a fixed use. Existing infrastructure may be inappropriate for new patterns of import competing and expand production. Land and other natural resources are another example of resources that are immobile in the short run. Labour market rigidities are also another consideration that may slow down factor adjustment to the trade policy reform in the short run.

Medium-run channels

SPECIALISATION AND ENDOWMENT EFFECTS

Through the effects of increased openness to trade on commodity prices, the returns to factors of production also change and the allocation of factors of production in the medium run shift resources towards the sectors where the economy has a comparative advantage. This specialisation following trade policy liberalisation can be motivated by differences in technology and/or differences in resource endowments or by the differences in the institutional conditions affecting the determination of wages and profits in capital and labour markets.

In a complex world of many economic activities with many differing levels of tariffs and other price distorting influences, the association between trade policy reform and comparative advantage needs to be qualified. The principle of comparative advantage determines what a country will produce and trade at world prices in the absence of market distortions. Typically, trade policy reform at a particular time only removes part of a complex structure of trade control measures. Whilst the result will tend to induce a trade pattern that utilises a country's comparative advantage better, the impact on different sectors will be uneven because the height of the initial distortions and the structure of production varies between sectors. Typical market rigidities that affect the adjustment process in the medium run include factor immobility between sectors and factor market institutions that influence the return to factors.

Trade policy reform, macroeconomic adjustment and income inequality in the medium run

In the short run, it was argued that trade policy reform would lower the domestic prices of import substitutes and create an excess demand for imports. Restoration of macroeconomic equilibrium normally requires a depreciation of the real exchange rate, or a rise in the price of tradables relative to non-tradables. When this adjustment process is carried out smoothly, the arguments concerning short-run macro adjustments carry over to the medium run. However, it is not unusual for the exchange rate adjustment process to be held back, even in the medium run, for example, by pegging the exchange rate or by sustained high interest rates that induce a capital inflow. Thus, a disequilibrium exchange rate appreciation that may result in the short run and may carry over to the medium run. At various stages in the post-war period, this has happened in many Latin American countries, and exchange rate effects can dominate the price effects of trade policy reform in the medium run whereby the exchange rate can be overvalued for several years before the inevitable collapse and devaluation occurs (see also discussion in Chapter 3). Sometimes, even in the medium run, it is difficult to disentangle the impact of trade policy reform that requires real exchange rate depreciation arising from the combined effects of a nominal exchange rigidity with domestic inflation or an unsustainable capital inflow that may lead to a real exchange rate appreciation in the medium run.

In addition, exchange rate volatility usually has a negative impact on the amount of trade. Countries with more stable currencies tend to have larger trade flows if other things are kept constant. In this case, exchange rate volatility affects the gains from trade as well as the short and medium-run effects on income distribution. One possible response to exchange rate volatility is to transfer factors of production to the non-tradable sector.

A final important remark on the link between macro policies, trade and income inequality is the sequencing of capital account liberalisation. In addition to the effect of capital account liberalisation on trade through the effect of capital inflows on the exchange rate, capital account liberalisation can affect the allocation of resources from trade. If financial reform is carried out while some industries are still protected, capital inflows have an incentive to be allocated in protected industries in order to capture protection rents. This offsets the allocation of resources that would result from trade reform and improves the return in the factors more abundant in protected industries. Conversely, if capital account liberalisation is carried out after trade has been liberalised, the sector allocation of capital inflows will be in line with comparative advantage.

Long-run channels

International trade theory has been traditionally concerned with the long run. Technological differences that affect comparative advantage are usually associated with Classical Political Economy, especially with Adam Smith and David Ricardo. Smith was concerned with the division of labour through the extension of the size of the market. Ricardo really had two theories of trade. He developed his theory of comparative advantage in a static context where factors were immobile between countries and technical differences between countries governed comparative advantage. Ricardo also had a dynamic theory of trade in which a combination of differences in technology and endowments of land governed comparative advantage. It is now generally accepted that the relative availability or endowment of factors of production in an economy can have powerful effects on the prices of goods, the distribution of income and the determinants of comparative advantage. This is often associated with Heckscher and Ohlin, or the H–O theory of comparative advantage. The mechanism works by noting that a relatively abundant factor will give an economy an advantage in exporting goods that are intensive in that factor. When a factor is relatively scarce, the price of goods intensively using that factor will be high and the economy will have a comparative disadvantage and the product will be imported. Trade policy operates by creating an incentive to produce the good with a comparative disadvantage, thus rewarding the factor used intensively in producing that good and harming the factor used intensively in export production. Trade openness, by lowering the domestic price of import goods, lowers the rewards to factors used intensively in import-competing production and raises rewards to those factors used intensively in export production. The final impact on inequality is determined once the pattern of household ownership of factors is known. Thus, the H–O theory provides a powerful insight into the analysis of the impact of trade policy reform on factor prices, particularly in the medium and long run. When comparative advantage is determined by technological differences (the Ricardian case) as well as by differences in factor endowments, the H–O propositions about the impact of trade policy reform on factor prices still hold.

Economists have long been ambivalent about the H–O theory. The postwar theoretical version of the theory switched between two-commodity two-factor versions of the model with labour combining with land or labour combining with capital. In careful hands in theoretical discourse and in the classroom, the standard 2×2 H–O labour–land or labour–capital model proved extremely useful. However, it obviously does not apply to the real world. Ohlin himself was quite aware of this, and proposed extending the classical division of factors into labour, land and capital to a nine-factor version of his model for empirical studies. For empirical application of his theory, he had three types of labour, five types of natural resources and capital, the latter expressed as a sum of money (see Evans, 1989, p. 90). Such a fine disaggregation of factors is rarely found in empirical work on trade, but is now regularly built into to the datasets used in a new generation of computable general equilibrium (CGE) models of the global economy or for individual countries.[2]

Leaving out induced technological change and growth for the moment, the final impact of any particular reform of trade control measures on income distribution in the medium run will ultimately depend on the sectoral pattern of the reforms, the endowments of key factors especially natural resources, human and physical capital, and on market institutions that may influence factor returns outside flexible market responses governed by factor supply and demand. To a greater or lesser extent, unskilled wages are institutionally determined in the medium run and even in the long run in Latin America. Similarly, returns to capital are strongly influenced by the international rate of profit. To the extent that labour market institutions influence payments for unskilled labour and international returns to capital govern the rate of return on capital, the endowments of these factors only influence the returns to remaining types of labour and natural resources. Thus, a useful stylised H–O model suggests that both factor endowments and institutions combine to determine comparative advantage and influence the impact of trade policy reform on the income distribution. Since key institutions may not change markedly in the medium or long run, this boils down to considering endowments of one or two types of skilled labour and natural resources as the key factor endowments that determine comparative advantage along H–O lines and institutions that may determine the returns to unskilled labour and capital combine to determine the impact of trade policy reform on income distribution. Of course, the real world can never be reduced to a simplistic application of the above but, as will be readily apparent in the following section, 'Analysing the impact of trade policy reform on income inequality in target Latin American countries', the stylised H–O framework is a useful starting point.

Some recent theories on international trade emphasise the role of sector-specific factors, economies of scale and choice of varieties of goods leading to two-way intra-trade flows. These theories are particularly relevant for trade between developed economies, but have some application in developing economies as well. In this case, the effects of trade policy reform can be more sector specific than in the factor endowments case, affecting mainly the returns of the sector specific factor. Such effects can arise in developing countries when the liberalisation of trade control measures reverses import substituting industrialisation policies, with a sharply reduced return to immobile specific factors occurring as a result.

Factor price adjustments may vary greatly between types of factors. In capital markets, if the rate of profit is flexible and set by domestic competition, then price changes caused by trade liberalisation will be reflected in profit changes, affecting the amount of capital employed. When the rate of profit is set by internationally mobile capital, price changes caused by trade policy reform may influence the amount of capital employed but not the rate of profit. In labour markets, when wages are fully flexible and the level of employment stays constant, price changes caused by trade policy reform will cause changes in wages but not in the level of employment. However, when there is a large pool of unemployed – or labour surplus – price changes induced by trade policy reform will cause changes in the level of employment but not in the wage rate.

TARIFF REVENUE AND SPENDING

Trade policy reform will affect government receipts of tariff revenue and therefore the capacity of governments to finance government expenditure. In countries where tariffs are an important source of government revenue, government accounts will have to be rebalanced. This can be done by an increase in government revenue, increasing other forms of direct or indirect taxes, or by cutting expenditure. In the case of increasing other forms of taxation, the distributional effect will depend on whether the new taxes are direct or indirect (see, for example, Ebrill *et al.* (1999)). A progressive increase in direct taxation, increasing taxes more than proportionally for higher income households, may improve income distribution compared with the case of high tariffs, where the burden of the tariffs lies partly in higher prices for all households. On the other hand, if the revenue from tariffs is replaced by other indirect taxes, the distributional tariffs could be neutral or regressive depending on which are the goods that carry the tax. Nevertheless, if the reduction in tariff revenue is compensated with a reduction in government expenditure, the impact on income distribution can be negative if this expenditure was directed towards the poorest households.

PRODUCTIVITY AND TECHNOLOGY TRANSFER

Long-run productivity improvements can be transmitted through trade. For example, international trade in intermediate inputs can provide important learning effects that increase productivity for the using sectors. Competition through openness to international trade can also induce productivity effects in the tradable sectors, benefiting most the factors employed intensively in those sectors. Technical change can also be biased towards factors that are intensively employed in any sector. Both biased and neutral technical change can have important effects on factor returns.

LONG-TERM GROWTH AND VOLATILITY

Although there is little conclusive evidence on the link between trade reform and growth, the evidence seems to suggest that trade openness does not harm long-run growth. The long-run impact of trade on income distribution through long-term growth will depend on how income growth trickles down in the economy. The impact on income inequality will then depend on existing macro policies and labour market conditions, factor endowments and specific labour market conditions such as wage bargaining and levels of unemployment. A strand of the trade literature in the Lewis and Prebisch-Singer tradition suggests that surplus labour affecting the poorest unskilled labour in primary exporting developing countries, may contribute to declining terms of trade for developing country primary products in the long run. More recently, this argument has been extended to developing countries with surplus unskilled labour exporting low-skill manufactured products. Thus, trade policy reform that leaves unchanged the surplus labour conditions will not lead to an improvement in the terms of trade. Further, it has been suggested in the Prebisch-Singer tradition that more open economies are more volatile, also with adverse income distribution consequences. One potential explanation of the vulnerability argument is that if trade increases specialisation in primary sectors, the economy will be more vulnerable to shocks in those sectors than a diversified and industrialised country. More recent work on poverty profiles over time suggests that vulnerability to income fluctuations over time is much greater for the poorest than for those better off poor families who are able to recover faster from income shocks over time (see also Chapter 3).

Trade policy reform, macroeconomic adjustment and income inequality

Factor accumulation, factor movements and technical change compete with trade policy reform, to influence the long-run real exchange rate. Failure to adjust the real exchange rate was a characteristic of the period of import substitution industrialisation in many of the target countries at various stages in the period 1960 to 2000. Import controls were often used to protect domestic producers from international competition in the context of an overvalued real exchange rate in the short and medium run, which sometimes extended into the long run. The combined effect of such exchange rate overvaluation and import controls usually led to low growth and a host of other undesirable consequences. Macroeconomic adjustment for trade policy reform in this context must deal with the initial overvaluation of the real exchange rate, often large, as well as the real exchange rate depreciation required to restore macroeconomic equilibrium after the trade policy reform. In the import control case, exporters are taxed by the overvalued exchange rate and protection of importable producer and consumer goods whilst import-competing sectors receive protection according to the private sector rents generated by the system of import controls. Reform increases returns to exporters, lowers protection to import competing sectors, especially the high returns to importers who are able to obtain import licences, and in so far as import controls are replaced by tariffs, government revenue may increase.

Unilateral, regional and multilateral liberalisation

Trade policy reform is usually in a long-run context, though its impact is felt in the short and medium run as well, as already discussed. To date, concern has been with unilateral or single country trade policy reform, often carried out as a part of Structural Adjustment Programmes or SAPs, or under the auspices of the World Trade Organisation or WTO. In the wider context of multilateral trade policy reform, the bargaining process is greatly complicated by the sheer number of countries involved. As far as our discussion of the income distribution impacts for single countries is concerned, there is not a great deal of additional complication in moving from a unilateral to a multilateral context except on the export side, as lowering or removing trade barriers in export markets effectively increases export prices with favourable income consequences for exporters. On the import side, for price-takers on the world market as in the case of our target Latin American countries, import prices will be lowered only to the extent that exporters to the target countries have lower costs from the multilateral trade policy reforms impacting on their home producers. Since most tariffs are on final goods rather than producer goods, these effects are likely to be small. The study of the welfare and income distribution effects of trade policy reform is greatly complicated when regional integration is involved because the liberalisation takes place only between member countries and third countries are excluded. In this case, when regional integration involves increased trade that exploits comparative advantage there will be some gains from trade creation. However, some increased trade with regional integration may be against comparative advantage leading to losses from trade diversion. In essence, trade creation exploits comparative advantage and trade diversion involves comparative *disadvantage.* The final welfare impact of regional integration depends on the balance between the two effects. The effects on factor income distribution will depend again on which factors of production enjoy an increase in their relative demand. Adding up the welfare impact and income distribution consequences of regional integration is complex because only partial trade policy liberalisation is involved. Normally this can only be done with the assistance of an economic policy model.[3]

Analysing the impact of trade policy reform on income inequality in target Latin American countries

The analysis of the impact of trade policy reform on income distribution proceeds in two parts. The approach is largely descriptive with the ad hoc application of theory developed in the previous section to assist in interpreting the data.

The following sub-section analyses the long-run historical impact of trade policy reform on income inequality in the target Latin American countries in a global context. Trade policy reform in the target countries is treated as if it is carried out in a unilateral context. It links trade policy reform with the pattern of trade and impacts on income distribution using a stylised H–O model that combines institutional determination of the returns to unskilled labour and capital, with endowments of skilled labour and natural resources determining skilled wages and resource rents in a similar manner to the simpler 2×2 H–O framework. This analysis is then extended to consider patterns of factor endowments and accumulation in the target Latin American countries in a global context over the period 1960 to 2000, providing the background for analysing the relationship between factor endowments, factor accumulation, trade policy reform and the historical pattern of income distribution. The sub-section 'Skill and resource endowments: Latin America in a global perpsective' switches to medium- and short-run analysis of the period from the late 1980s to 2000 in a multilateral and regional context, including an analysis of 1997 data on trade flows, economic structure and tariffs rates.

The effects of trade policy reform and factor accumulation on inequality in the long run

In a country with scarce labour compared with natural resources such as land and minerals, exporting resource-intensive products and importing labour-intensive products, trade policy may be used to foster industrialisation through the protection of labour-intensive import-competing manufactured production. In this case, the tariff protection will raise wages and lower resource rents. If households are roughly divided into those who receive income only from labour and those who receive income only from resource rents, tariff protection will tend to improve income equality. Historically, this argument has been used on redistributive grounds, for example in Australia in the pre-war period. It has also been linked to the early stages of industrialisation in much of Latin America. For developing countries with abundant labour and scarce natural resources, the argument reverses: high tariff protection on resource-intensive imports will raise resource rents, lower wages and increase inequality. In this two-factor context, it is possible to map from changes in the functional distribution of income to changes in household distribution of income. Generally speaking, lowering tariffs will improve income equality by raising unskilled wages and lowering resource rents.

The stylised H–O model discussed in the previous section is a version of the empirical model developed by Wood (1994, 1997) but without the institutional determination of unskilled wages and profits. In fact the analysis of comparative advantage in the Wood and the stylised H–O model with institutional determination of skilled wages and the rate of profit are essentially the same. Wood's key argument is that it is the relative endowments of skills or skilled labour relative to natural resources that is the critical factor for determining comparative advantage and the pattern of trade. Typically, there are thousands of primary and manufactured commodities that enter into world trade but any one country will only produce a narrower sub-set, some with complete and some with incomplete specialisation.[4] When manufacturing goods are skill intensive compared with primary products that are resource intensive, then the Wood model and the stylised H–O model predict that the share of manufactured commodities in total exports will increase when endowments of skilled labour are higher relative to natural resources as skilled labour accumulates in a single country when international prices and domestic trade policy are unchanged. In the short run, the accumulation of skilled labour lowers skilled wages relative to resource rents, lowers the relative price of manufactured commodities compared with resource-based commodities and manufacturing exports expand relative to resource-intensive products. In the medium and long run, the accumulation of skilled labour relative to resources at constant world prices, constant trade policy and constant technology, the long-run equilibrium will restore the skilled wage to resource rents to their initial values and the relative price of manufactures and resource-based products will restore their relationship with world prices with unchanged trade policies but manufactured commodities will have a higher share of total exports. Wood's empirical work is confined to testing the predictions of the pattern of trade in manufactured and resource-based commodities from the endowments of skilled labour and resources.

The key to the development of the argument about the impact of trade policy reform on income distribution is the observation that the channels of transmission through which the Wood and stylised H–O models of comparative advantage work are the same as for the analysis of the impact of factor accumulation or trade policy reform on income distribution. However, the data demands for the analysis of comparative advantage and the pattern of trade are very much less than that required for the analysis of the impact of factor accumulation and trade policy reform on income distribution. The argument is developed first by looking at the comparative advantage side of the Wood and stylised H–O model, then at the income distribution side, for the impact of different scenarios involving factor accumulation and trade policy reform on skilled wages and resource rents. The argument then turns to an analysis of the implications of the different scenarios for income distribution.

The greater complexity of the analysis of income distribution in the stylised H–O model compared with the analysis of comparative advantage and the pattern of trade can be seen from an example. If a country has a small endowment of skilled labour compared with natural resources and is importing skill-intensive products and exporting resource-intensive products, using capital and unskilled labour as well, lowering tariff protection will lower skilled wages and raise resource rents. In this respect, the lowering tariff protection is likely to increase income inequality, but even in this simplified and stylised account, there are other important changes to be taken into account. The returns to capital and unskilled labour are taken to be institutionally unchanged; but the amount of capital and unskilled labour employed will change but in a direction dependent on the use of unskilled labour and capital in the manufactured and resource commodities. The impact of the lower tariff protection on the functional income distribution will depend on the initial employment of unskilled and skilled labour, resources and capital, the changes in skilled wages and resource rents, and changes in the employment of unskilled labour and capital. The final effect on the distribution of income at the household level will depend on how the functional income changes map into changes in household income and cannot be predicted without detailed empirical analysis. If the country exports relatively skill-intensive products, lowering tariff protection will raise skilled wages and lower resource rents and the final outcome on the distribution of household income can only be determined once impacts on the demand for unskilled labour and capital, the initial shares of unskilled and skilled labour, resources and capital in total income, and the mapping from the functional to household income is known. In both cases, the impact of lowering tariffs on income inequality does not automatically follow even in the simplified example. It is only the direction of change of resource rents and skilled wages that can be inferred from knowledge of factor endowments and changes in trade policy.

Skill and resource endowments: Latin America in a global perspective

Figure 5.1 summarises the evolution of endowments of skilled labour and natural resources in the target Latin American countries in the global economy by Wood and Mayer (1999), abstracting from the role of physical capital, unskilled labour and technical change. Endowments of skills or skilled labour are proxied by the average years of schooling, and resource endowments by land area per 100 workers. The chart shows the change in factor endowments in Latin American countries and their main northern trade partners in five-year intervals from 1960 to 2000.

Extensive regression analysis by Wood and Mayer found that the relative endowments of skilled labour and natural resources, as proxied in Figure 5.1, are a good predictor of the composition of trade measured by the ratio of primary exports to total exports, or primary exports to manufactured and service exports. That is, there is strong empirical support for a theory of comparative advantage as measured by the endowments of skill and natural resources, and the pattern of endowments shown in Figure 5.1 can be used as a good predictor of comparative advantage and the pattern of trade.

Further inspection of Figure 5.1 reveals a wide dispersion of the endowment ratios in the target Latin American countries. This picture is clarified in Table 5.1 where the Latin American target countries are ranked by skill/resource endowment ratios for 1960.

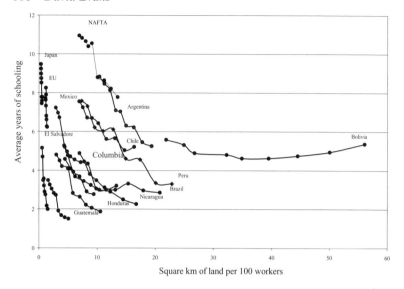

Figure 5.1 Skills and resources in Latin American countries 1960–2000

Source: The dataset was kindly provided by Adrian Wood and aggregated as shown. Schooling and adult population data are from Barro and Lee database at www.cid.harvard.edu/ciddata/ciddata.html. Land data is from World Bank, World Development Indicators.

Notes
Average years of schooling and 'workers' refer to all adults (over 15). All series are in 5-year intervals and begin in 1960 (lower right) and end in 2000 (upper left).

The striking result from Table 5.1 is that, with the exception of Bolivia, all of the target Latin American countries have rates of increase in years of schooling relative to natural resources that are greater than their main trading partners in the North. The resultant impact on the resource endowment ratios compared with their trading partners is shown in Table 5.2.

Thus, in 1960, only El Salvador has a higher skill/resource endowment ratio than NAFTA. The remaining 10 target Latin American countries have lower skill/resource endowment ratios compared with all their principal northern trading partners. By 2000, the position is slightly altered in that Honduras, Guatemala, Mexico and El Salvador all have higher skill/resource endowment ratios compared with NAFTA.[5] Compared with the EU, Honduras, Guatemala, Mexico all have a lower skill/resource endowment ratio and only El Salvador is higher. As for 1960, Japan has a higher skill/resource endowment ratio compared with all of the target Latin American countries. Thus, with the exception of El Salvador, in 1960 all of the target countries had lower skill/resource endowments than NAFTA, EU and Japan. By 2000, Honduras, Guatemala, Mexico and El Salvador have higher skill/

Table 5.1 Growth of schooling and land per 100 workers 1960–2000

Country	Land sq. km per 100 workers			Average years of schooling			Difference
	1960	2000	growth % pa	1960	2000	growth % pa	Growth % pa
Bolivia	56.08	21.84	−2.33	5.37	5.58	0.10	2.43
Nicaragua	16.77	4.46	−3.26	2.26	4.58	1.78	5.04
Brazil	20.79	6.97	−2.70	2.85	4.88	1.35	4.05
Peru	22.83	7.33	−2.80	3.30	7.58	2.10	4.90
Honduras	10.57	2.96	−3.13	1.87	4.80	2.38	5.52
Colombia	13.33	4.33	−2.77	3.20	5.27	1.26	4.03
Argentina	19.39	10.40	−1.54	5.25	8.83	1.31	2.85
Mexico	9.42	2.88	−2.92	2.76	7.23	2.44	5.36
Guatemala	5.09	1.56	−2.91	1.50	3.49	2.13	5.04
Chile	16.40	6.92	−2.14	5.21	7.55	0.93	3.07
NAFTA	13.55	6.92	−1.67	7.78	10.95	0.86	2.52
El Salvador	1.50	0.54	−2.54	1.99	5.15	2.41	4.95
EU	1.39	1.19	−0.39	6.22	8.25	0.71	1.10
Japan	0.58	0.35	−1.22	7.78	9.47	0.49	1.71

Source: The dataset was kindly provided by Adrian Wood and aggregated as shown. Schooling and adult population data are from Barro and Lee database at www.cid.harvard.edu/ciddata/ciddata.html. Land data is from World Bank, World Development Indicators.

Note
Average years of schooling and 'workers' refer to all adults (over 15).

Table 5.2 Endowment ratio target Latin American countries

	Ratio years of schooling/land per 100 workers		
	1960		2000
Bolivia	0.10	Bolivia	0.26
Nicaragua	0.13	Brazil	0.70
Brazil	0.14	Argentina	0.85
Peru	0.14	Nicaragua	1.03
Honduras	0.18	Peru	1.03
Colombia	0.24	Chile	1.09
Argentina	0.27	Colombia	1.22
Mexico	0.29	NAFTA	1.58
Guatemala	0.29	Honduras	1.62
Chile	0.32	Guatemala	2.24
NAFTA	0.57	Mexico	2.51
El Salvador	1.33	EU	6.93
EU	4.46	El Salvador	9.61
Japan	13.52	Japan	26.86

Source: The dataset was kindly provided by Adrian Wood and aggregated as shown. Schooling and adult population data are from Barro and Lee database at www.cid.harvard.edu/ciddata/ ciddata.html. Land data is from World Bank, World Development Indicators.

Note
Average years of schooling and 'workers' refer to all adults (over 15).

resource endowment ratios compared with NAFTA. With the exception of El Salvador, all target countries in 2000 have lower skill/resource endowment ratios compared with the EU and all target countries have a lower skill/ resource endowment ratio that Japan. Thus, by 2000, the Wood and the stylised H–O model predict that Honduras, Guatemala, Mexico and El Salvador are likely to have predominantly skill intensive manufactures in their exports for some or all of their Northern trading partners. This implied change in the pattern of comparative advantage in the target countries ultimately has important implications for the impact of trade policy reform on the distribution of income.

For the predominantly resource-based exporting countries, trade policy reform will tend to increase resource rents relative to skilled wages, inducing a shift in the pattern of trade towards resource-based products. This is the historical pattern in the target countries. Where some trade policy barriers remain but where some skill-based exports have developed as a result of skill accumulation as in the cases of Honduras, Guatemala, Mexico and El

Salvador, trade policy reform will tend to increase skilled wages and lower resource rents and induce an increase share of skill-based exports. Therefore, with the possible exception of El Salvador in the early part of the period 1960–2000, with the likely exception of Honduras, Guatemala, Mexico and El Salvador in the latter part of the period 1960–2000, trade policy reform in the target Latin American countries is likely to have had downward pressure on relative skilled wage/resource rent ratio. If the changes in the demand for unskilled labour and capital are relatively low, if the share of skilled labour in total income is relatively low and if the share of resource rents high, trade policy reform may have ultimately contributed to a worsening of the house-hold distribution of income in the earlier part of the 1960–2000 period. For some of the target countries, trade policy reform at the end of the period 1960–2000 may increase the skilled wage/resource rent ratio. When such factor price changes dominate the effects of any change in demand for unskilled labour or capital, household income distribution may also worsen, but for different reasons. If the share of skilled wages in total income is significant and the share of resource rents low, further trade policy reform that increases skilled wages relative to resource endowments may worsen household income distribution because of the implied increase in the skilled/unskilled wage ratio.

The above findings have to be qualified when technical change is taken into account. Historically, as argued in the development literature variously by Prebisch, Singer and Lewis and others, technical change in Latin American countries was likely to have been concentrated in the resource-based export sectors, thus increasing resource-based exports and increasing resource rents compared with unskilled and skilled wages. More recently, Taylor (2000) found from an examination of 27 cases of economic reforms among our target countries that go as far back as 1976, that in 21 cases the skilled/unskilled wage ratio increases, and that the rate of technical change is faster in traded good sectors compared with non-traded. This observed rise in the skilled/unskilled wage ratio cannot be attributed to trade policy reform when resource-based exports dominate skill-based manufactures, but it could be attributed to trade policy reform when skill-based manufactures dominate exports (see above). The rise in the skilled/unskilled wage ratio could also arise from an underlying shift in the bias of technical change from resource-based commodities as historically observed to skill-based commodities as the accumulation of skill leads to skill-based manufactured exports dominating resource-based exports. If the traded sector has a higher skilled to unskilled labour ratio than the non-traded sector, then the Taylor observation about biased technical change in favour of the tradable sectors also holds for skill-intensive sectors compared with unskilled labour-intensive sectors. A similar point is made by Wood (1997), who suggests that increased wage differentials in Latin America may be the result of new technology biased against unskilled workers. Thus the observed increase in the skilled/unskilled wage ratio could be explained by the observed bias in technical change. This explanation of the rise in skilled/unskilled wages is in addition to the case of trade policy reform increasing the skilled/unskilled wage ratio when skilled manufactured exports dominate resource-based exports (see above).

In addition, Wood (1997) suggested an indirect mechanism that is closely related to the biased-technical-change argument in the more skill-intensive sectors. The incorporation of China into the world market as a chief low-skill competitor during the 1980s has indirectly affected the target Latin American countries by further shifting their comparative advantage towards higher-skilled manufactures. Once the shift to a skill-based rather than resource-based comparative advantage has happened, the response of further trade policy reform is likely to increase skilled wages relative to resource rents.

So far the argument has been that unskilled wages are fixed institutionally and do not vary over time. This argument is likely to be undermined when growth is rapid enough to increase the demand for unskilled labour and to put upward pressure on unskilled labour. Similarly, where there is a strong distinction between domestic and foreign (FDI) capital markets, it may be appropriate to treat the return to domestic capital as endogenous and only the returns to FDI as being determined internationally in the long run. To the extent that the unskilled wage rate and the return on domestic capital becomes endogenously determined along with the skilled wage rate and resource rents, the estimation of the impact of trade policy reform on income distribution is even more complicated than in the stylised H–O model with institutions and endowments determining factor prices.

The evolution of inequality in historical context

Reform of the historically high levels of tariff protection observed in the 1960s began with Chile in 1973–4 and moved on to other target Latin American countries, namely Bolivia, El Salvador, Guatemala and Mexico. In the late 1980s and early 1990s, Honduras, Peru, Argentina, Brazil and Colombia experienced rapid trade policy reform. Over the period from the early 1970s to the latter part of the 1990s, the historically high levels of trade protection were reversed in all of the target Latin American countries. What was the likely impact of trade policy reform on income distribution?

The daunting list of data requirements for linking trade policy reform to income distribution were set out in the previous section. All that can be done with available data is to look for an association between the accumulation of skilled labour and resources, trade policy reform in the target countries described above, and the final outcome on the distribution of household income. The overall pattern of factor accumulation has already been presented in Tables 5.1 and 5.2. In Table 5.3, factor endowments and factor accumulation are linked with timing of trade policy reform in the target countries as set out in Table 5.3.

In Table 5.3, for each 10-year period from 1960 onwards, the endowment ratios and Gini coefficients are shown for each of the target Latin American countries and the direction of change in the Gini coefficients from 1960 to 2000 and for the sub-periods 1960–80 and 1980–2000. Over the whole period, it can be seen from Table 5.3 that, for the 11 countries where comparisons are possible, income distribution worsened in seven cases namely Argentina, Bolivia, Brazil, Chile, El Salvador, Guatemala and Nicaragua. Income distribution improved in the four other cases, namely for Colombia, Honduras, Mexico and Peru. However, a strikingly different story is found by examining the sub-periods. For the period 1960–80, with the exception of Chile, trade policy was practically unchanged. In four cases where it was possible to compare Gini coefficients, income inequality increased, whilst in four cases it improved. This mixed finding is quite consistent with the observation that the rapid accumulation of skilled labour could lead to improved income distribution because of a higher share of skilled wages in total income. However, from 1980–2000, major changes in trade policy reform took place in the target countries, except for Chile whose trade policy reforms were implemented quickly in the 1970s. In all of the target countries, income distribution worsens over the period when trade policy reforms were being implemented. These findings do not conclusively link trade policy reform to rising inequality, but the findings are consistent with the stylised H–O model discussed. This finding is also reached by Cornia (2004), who also suggests that trade liberalisation may have contributed to rising inequality in the target Latin American countries after 1980.

It would be tempting to link the above finding, that trade policy reform has increased income inequality, with trade policy reform increasing poverty. As discussed above (see 'Income inequality and the gains from trade'), increased inequality is measured over the whole range of household income, whereas rising or falling levels of poverty covers only the lower range of households. Thus in recent research on trade policy reform and poverty based on 1997 data, trade policy reform lessens poverty in Brazil, Chile and Columbia whilst it increases poverty in Peru (see Hertel *et al.* (2003, Table 9)).

Table 5.3a Historical patterns of factor endowments and inequality in the target Latin American countries, 1960–80

	1960 Endowments	Gini	1970 Endowments	Gini	1980 Endowments	Gini	1960–80 Change in Gini
Argentina	0.27	42.0	0.38	44.0	0.50	n/a	Increase
Bolivia	0.10	n/a	0.11	53.0	0.13	n/a	n/a
Brazil	0.14	53.0	0.22	57.6	0.28	57.8	Increase
Chile	0.32	n/a	0.43	46.0	0.63	53.0	Increase
Colombia	0.24	62.0	0.31	52.0	0.62	55.0	Decrease
El Salvador	1.33	54.6	2.50	46.5	3.72	48.4	Decrease
Guatemala	0.29	42.3	0.44	n/a	0.93	49.7	Increase
Honduras	0.18	n/a	0.27	61.9	0.48	n/a	n/a
Mexico	0.29	55.1	0.53	58.0	0.96	50.0	Decrease
Nicaragua	0.13	n/a	0.24	n/a	0.36	n/a	n/a
Peru	0.14	61.0	0.26	55.0	0.48	49.3	Decrease

Table 5.3b Historical patterns of factor endowments and inequality in the target Latin American countries, 1980–2000

	1980 Endowments	Gini	1990 Endowments	Gini	2000 Endowments	Gini	1980–2000 Change Gini	1960–2000 Change Gini
Argentina	0.50	n/a	0.67	43.1	0.85	49.0	Increase	Increase
Bolivia	0.13	n/a	0.18	55.0	0.26	60.0	Increase	Increase
Brazil	0.28	57.8	0.44	57.0	0.70	59.0	Increase	Increase
Chile	0.63	53.0	0.81	54.7	1.09	56.4	Increase	Increase
Colombia	0.62	55.0	0.87	57.0	1.22	56.0	Increase	Decrease
El Salvador	3.72	48.4	4.82	n/a	9.61	55.0	Increase	Increase
Guatemala	0.93	49.7	1.40	60.0	2.24	56.0	Increase	Increase
Honduras	0.48	n/a	1.07	54.0	1.62	58.0	Increase	Decrease
Mexico	0.96	50.0	1.91	53.1	2.51	54.0	Increase	Decrease
Nicaragua	0.36	n/a	0.59	57.0	1.03	60.0	Increase	Increase
Peru	0.48	49.3	0.65	46.0	1.03	50.5	Increase	Decrease

Source: Endowments: years of schooling/sq. km of land per 100 workers from dataset used in Figure 5.1. Gini coefficients from World Income Inequality Database, WIDER (2000).

Notes
Gini coefficient estimates as near as possible to the end of each 10-year period were chosen. For the most part they were based on gross income of persons or households and were graded 'OK' in the tables. Change in Gini coefficients estimated for shorter time periods where data missing.

Recent experience: medium- and short-run impacts of trade policies on income inequality

Introduction to medium- and short-run impacts

A statistical picture of the trade structure and pattern of protection in import and export markets for most of the target Latin American countries for 1997 is provided in Table 5.4.

Table 5.4 Structural features of key Latin American countries in 1997

	Share of total exports	Share of total imports	Exports to gross output	Imports to gross output	Average import tariff
Argentina					
Primary agriculture and fishing	17.6	2.2	10.4	1.5	7.9
Minerals	7.8	1.5	26.4	6.0	1.0
Food, beverages and tobacco	26.7	3.0	9.8	1.3	15.9
Textiles, clothing, leather	5.4	4.1	3.8	3.3	18.7
Motor vehicles and capital goods	14.1	44.2	7.7	28.3	15.8
Other manuf.	16.6	29.3	4.0	8.2	11.7
Utilities	0.2	0.8	0.1	0.5	0.0
Services	11.5	15.0	2.2	3.3	0.0
Total	100.0	100.0	5.2	6.1	11.9
Brazil					
Primary agriculture and fishing	11.4	4.2	5.8	3.0	7.9
Minerals	6.2	6.6	18.7	28.0	4.2
Food, beverages and tobacco	14.0	3.8	6.3	2.4	16.6
Textiles, clothing, leather	6.1	3.1	4.6	3.3	18.2
Motor vehicles and capital goods	20.5	36.6	9.4	23.5	19.2
Other manuf.	28.6	23.5	5.6	6.5	9.9
Utilities	0.1	2.8	0.1	1.8	0.0
Services	13.1	19.6	1.2	2.5	0.0
Total	100.0	100.0	3.8	5.4	11.2
Chile					
Primary agriculture and fishing	8.8	1.9	13.9	3.4	11.1
Minerals	13.3	7.0	46.6	27.8	11.1
Food, beverages and tobacco	14.9	4.7	17.0	6.1	11.1
Textiles, clothing, leather	1.5	7.1	5.6	29.4	11.1
Motor vehicles and capital goods	2.2	39.3	15.1	305.7	10.9
Other manuf.	44.2	26.2	34.1	22.8	11.0
Utilities	0.1	0.1	0.1	0.2	0.0
Services	15.1	13.8	5.0	5.1	0.0
Total	100.0	100.0	13.7	15.5	9.4
Columbia					
Primary agriculture and fishing	21.6	4.8	20.8	5.3	11.7
Minerals	20.8	0.2	51.4	0.7	5.4
Food, beverages and tobacco	6.0	5.1	4.4	4.3	18.2
Textiles, clothing, leather	6.2	3.8	16.2	11.6	17.4

	Share of total exports	Share of total imports	Exports to gross output	Imports to gross output	Average import tariff
Motor vehicles and capital goods	3.3	36.9	10.6	138.3	11.9
Other manuf.	16.7	29.5	12.4	25.6	9.9
Utilities	0.1	0.1	0.1	0.2	0.0
Services	25.2	19.6	4.8	4.3	0.1
Total	100.0	100.0	9.1	10.6	9.5
Mexico					
Primary agriculture and fishing	3.2	4.0	7.5	8.3	17.1
Minerals	9.6	0.6	43.1	2.3	3.9
Food, beverages and tobacco	2.5	3.2	4.6	5.0	31.6
Textiles, clothing, leather	7.1	5.2	28.0	17.9	4.7
Motor vehicles and capital goods	51.5	47.8	69.4	57.0	2.6
Other manuf.	16.1	28.3	16.0	24.9	2.5
Utilities	0.1	0.2	0.1	0.4	0.0
Services	9.9	10.8	4.4	4.2	0.0
Total	100.0	100.0	17.1	15.1	3.9
Peru					
Primary agriculture and fishing	7.0	5.5	5.9	5.6	14.8
Minerals	15.4	6.6	48.8	25.0	11.7
Food, beverages and tobacco	19.9	8.1	12.3	6.0	15.2
Textiles, clothing, leather	7.7	2.7	8.7	3.7	16.5
Motor vehicles and capital goods	1.0	32.1	1.0	39.1	12.2
Other manuf.	30.0	27.6	13.7	15.1	12.0
Utilities	0.1	0.1	0.1	0.1	7.3
Services	19.0	17.3	3.7	4.1	9.3
Total	100.0	100.0	7.2	8.7	12.1
Central America and Caribbean (includes El Salvador, Guatemala, Honduras and Nicaragua)					
Primary agriculture and fishing	13.2	3.4	26.5	10.3	9.3
Minerals	1.8	5.5	30.7	141.1	4.4
Food, beverages and tobacco	11.3	7.5	22.5	22.3	17.9
Textiles, clothing, leather	20.8	11.9	49.3	42.0	19.5
Motor vehicles and capital goods	8.8	35.0	36.5	216.1	10.9
Other manuf.	20.6	26.4	29.9	57.1	9.0
Utilities	0.3	0.4	0.9	1.8	7.6
Services	23.1	9.8	13.1	8.4	3.0
Total	100.0	100.0	22.1	33.0	10.7
Rest of Andean (includes Bolivia together with Ecuador and Venezuela)					
Primary agriculture and fishing	24.7	3.8	30.7	5.4	9.2
Minerals	26.7	0.1	58.2	0.3	6.2
Food, beverages and tobacco	22.5	7.1	24.8	9.0	17.8
Textiles, clothing, leather	1.8	5.4	4.7	16.1	12.5
Motor vehicles and capital goods	2.2	32.2	5.8	96.8	10.7
Other manuf.	12.3	40.5	11.7	44.2	9.0
Utilities	0.1	0.1	0.2	0.1	6.5
Services	9.8	10.8	4.0	5.0	9.4
Total	100.0	100.0	14.2	16.3	10.4

Source: GTAP dataset 1997.

Table 5.4 suggests that in 1997 average import tariffs were around 10 per cent in all the countries with the exception of Mexico, which had a much lower import tariff. In addition, import tariff protection was biased in most countries towards 'food, beverages and tobacco' and 'textiles, clothing and leather'. Exceptions to this were Mexico, which had a very low tariff on 'textiles, clothing and leather', and Chile, where the tariff structure was much more uniform than other target Latin American countries. The tariff equivalent of trade control measures in the primary sectors are lower than in manufactures except in Chile, where they are similar to the manufacturing sectors, in Mexico where high protection of 'primary agriculture and fishing' reflects the special treatment of Mexican corn in NAFTA, and in Peru where protection of 'primary agriculture and fishing' is similar to the manufacturing sectors. The structure of imports is similar in all target Latin American countries, with motor vehicles and capital goods having the largest share of imports in all cases except the aggregate group 'rest of Andean' which includes Bolivia. The structure of exports, however, differs quite significantly between countries. Argentina, Brazil and Mexico export mainly manufactures and capital goods. Colombia also has a relatively strong export base in manufactures. Further trade reform in these countries is likely to increase output of skilled intensive manufactures and increase the skilled wage/resource rent ratio. In the case of Chile, Table 5.4 suggests a strong export base in manufactures, but a significant share of exports of 'other manuf.' is processed minerals rather than higher value added components of manufactured exports.

Another group of countries – the Andean countries and Peru – has an export structure based more on primary products, minerals and food production. If further trade openness increases specialisation in these sectors, it may be expected that there will be an increase in the returns on resource rents relative to skilled wages and therefore an increase in income inequality. For the Central American countries, textiles and other manufactures are the main source of exports and the effects of trade policy reform on income inequality are likely to be ambiguous.

As regards trade barriers, three striking characteristics of the present pattern of protection can be found. First, barriers to trade in primary products are low relative to protection on manufactured products in the target countries. Second, there remain substantial trade policy barriers to processed agricultural product imports or 'food, beverages and tobacco', for lower-skill manufactured imports or 'textiles, clothing and leather', and for higher-skilled products from 'Motor Vehicles and Capital Goods'. The final column of Table 5.4 shows the aggregate trade barriers. Whilst it is true that the measured tariff equivalents of the trade barriers for 1997 may not reflect all of the special concessions arising from the cross-cutting web of regional trade agreements, the overall pattern probably captures the central realities of trade policy barriers as they existed at the end of the 1990s in the target countries. Finally, there are substantial trade policy barriers facing the target countries in their export markets, principally in North America (not shown in Table 5.4), chiefly in agricultural and processed agricultural products. Multilateral reform that further opened manufacturing trade in the target countries and reduced barriers to agricultural-based products in their export markets is likely to have similar effects on increasing resource rents relative to skilled and unskilled wages as occurred in the 1980s and 1990s. Such an outcome is likely to further increase inequality as already observed over the 1980s and 1990s. Brazil and Mexico and possibly Argentina, where skill-based manufactured exports are more important, are different in that trade policy reform may increase the skilled wage/resource rent ratio, and increase inequality as well because of the relatively high share of skilled wages in total income.

If the analysis in previous sections has been oversimplified, it is immediately apparent from Table 5.4 that estimating the income distribution consequences of regional integration is likely to be even more complex and the impacts on income distribution are likely to be very difficult to pin down. However, Azevedo (2001) found that the welfare benefits from MERCOSUR were much less significant than for unilateral trade policy reform. This suggests that any income distribution consequences for regional integration are likely to be low compared with the income consequences of unilateral trade policy reform.

Trade reform, income inequality and macroeconomic factors from the late 1980s to 2000

For the purpose of analysing the interaction between trade policy reform and macroeconomic adjustment, one way to look at trade policy reform across the 11 countries is to place them in three groups according to the average height of tariff. Roughly speaking, average tariffs of over 20 per cent are taken as 'high', greater than 10 per cent but less than 20 per cent are taken as 'medium' and less than 10 per cent are taken as 'low'. Inspection of Table 5.5 reveals a very incomplete coverage. However, it is possible to interpolate the index of trade policy reform shown in Table 5.5 approximately by setting a score of 0.85 on the tariff index as roughly equivalent to an average tariff of 20 per cent and 0.90 as roughly equivalent to 10 per cent. If this is done, we can infer that the differences between the end of the 1980s and 1990s are striking. At the end of the 1980s, eight out of 11 of the target Latin American countries had 'high' tariffs. Mexico had 'medium' tariffs, and Chile had 'low' tariffs. By the end of the 1990s, the position had reversed.

Table 5.5 Trade policy reform index for targeted Latin American countries

Year	Arg	Bol	Bra	Chi	Col	El Sal	Gua	Hon	Mex	Per
1987	>20%	<10%	>20%	<10%	>20%	>20%	>20%	>20%	10%–20%	>20%
1988	>20%	<10%	>20%	<10%	>20%	10%–20%	>20%	>20%	<10%	>20%
1989	>20%	<10%	>20%	<10%	>20%	10%–20%	10%–20%	>20%	<10%	>20%
1990	10%–20%	<10%	>20%	<10%	10%–20%	10%–20%	10%–20%	>20%	<10%	>20%
1991	<10%	<10%	>20%	<10%	10%–20%	<10%	10%–20%	>20%	<10%	>20%
1992	<10%	<10%	10%–20%	<10%	<10%	<10%	<10%	>20%	<10%	<10%
1993	<10%	<10%	<10%	<10%	<10%	<10%	<10%	>20%	<10%	<10%
1994	<10%	<10%	<10%	<10%	<10%	<10%	<10%	10%–20%	<10%	<10%
1995	<10%	<10%	<10%	<10%	<10%	<10%	<10%	10%–20%	<10%	<10%

Source: An index of trade policy reform was obtained privately in a paper by Morley *et al.* (1999: Tables A1, A2 and A3). This was transformed into the table above by setting a score of less than 0.85 on the tariff index as equivalent to an average tariff of greater than 20%, between 0.85 and 0.90 as 10%–20%, and more than 0.90 as equivalent to less than 10%.

Nine countries had 'low' tariffs. This detailed estimation of the extent of trade policy form in the 1980s and 1990s corroborates the cruder informal estimates of trade policy reform used in discussing Table 5.4.

There were dramatic changes in average tariffs prior to 1987. These were continued from the end of the 1987 to 2000. As already noted in the second section of this chapter, 'Analytical framework', substantial macroeconomic adjustment is required for the trade policy reforms to be successful, principally the devaluation of the real exchange rate in the short to medium run to restore macroeconomic equilibrium and to facilitate the shift of resources from import-competing production and non-tradables to export production. To the extent that other macroeconomic changes occur simultaneously, such as capital inflows, an opposite appreciation of the real exchange rate will happen. The estimated real exchange rate changes for the target countries from 1987 to 1999 are shown in Table 5.6.

The first striking characteristic of the real exchange rate changes from the end of the 1980s to the end of the 1990s shown in Table 5.6 is the strong short-run fluctuations exhibited. In several cases, the short-run changes are around 25 per cent; and in the cases of Brazil and Argentina, the fluctuation is over 50 per cent. Second, from the point of view of trade policy reform alone, depreciation of the real exchange rate in the medium to long run, roughly from the end of the 1980s to the end of the 1990s, would be desirable. This happened in a clear way only in Bolivia and Honduras. In nearly all other countries, the real exchange appreciated during most of the 1990s.

Chapters 3 and 4 in this book attribute the real exchange rate appreciation to increased private capital flows in the 1990s (see Chapter 3, Table 3.2). Such cases of real exchange rate appreciation, when combined with trade policy reform, means that resource allocation on the import side would have been stronger and the export response weaker, than if there had been a real exchange rate depreciation. When capital flows are volatile, real exchange rate appreciation followed by depreciation may produce a macro economic environment inimical to successful trade policy reform. Overvaluation of the real exchange rate over the medium run, held up by monetary policy, followed by a collapse of the real exchange rate as in Argentina (see discussions in Chapters 3 and 4), also gives the wrong macro signals for adjustment to trade policy reform. In short, countries with strong or volatile capital inflows may have inappropriate macro policies for accompanying successful adjustment to trade policy reform. Only those very few Latin American countries, with no change or exchange rate depreciation, were closer to an accommodating macro adjustment associated with trade policy reform.

As previously argued, the combined short- and medium-run effects of trade policy reform and exchange rate adjustment on income inequality can

Table 5.6 Real exchange rate for targeted Latin American countries[1] (index 1995 = 100)

Year	Arg	Bol	Bra	Chi	Col	El Sal	Gua	Hon	Mex	Nic	Per
1987	187	64	126	n/a	115	128	103	55	114	109	166
1988	208	66	114	n/a	117	114	106	55	91	105	226
1989	281	69	87	n/a	121	100	108	52	86	130	144
1990	166	83	82	n/a	133	129	125	90	82	80	116
1991	121	84	99	113	134	126	112	94	75	84	97
1992	104	88	117	109	133	125	111	93	69	85	94
1993	95	93	112	111	125	114	112	102	66	82	106
1994	95	98	112	107	102	107	107	113	68	95	100
1995	100	100	100	100	100	100	100	100	100	100	100
1996	102	94	94	97	93	93	96	102	89	102	99
1997	99	92	93	91	87	92	91	96	77	106	99
1998	97	88	97	94	94	91	92	88	78	105	101
1999	90	87	147	99	106	92	105	85	71	107	110

Source: ECLAC.

Notes
1 Real effective exchange rates. Downward movement indicates appreciation.

only be loosely associated. The available Gini coefficients for 1989–99 are shown in Table 5.7.

Table 5.7 shows that income inequality worsens from 1989–99 in all target countries with the exception of Columbia and Guatemala, although in the cases of Argentina, Chile, Honduras and Mexico the worsening of income distribution is only marginal. These findings are consistent with the apparent instability and incomplete real exchange rate adjustments observed. They are also consistent with the stronger link between trade policy reform and rising inequality found for the period 1980–2000. Cornia (2004) links the observed rise in inequality since the 1980s to financial liberalisation as well as to trade policy reform. To the extent that financial liberalisation may have contributed to the observed real exchange rate fluctuations from 1987, the above findings are consistent with Cornia's results.

Some findings from the secondary literature

To what extent are these findings confirmed by reference to the secondary literature on the effects of trade expansion and in particular trade policy reform on income distribution? The studies cited below work with a variety of different analytical frameworks and channels of transmission. As with the findings in this chapter, at best only a partial link between trade policy reform and inequality can be established because the frameworks used and data used are inevitably partial.

Broadly speaking, other studies support the hypothesis that trade expansion may increase income equality in developing countries in the long term. Calderon and Chong (2001) find that, for a sample of developing and developed countries, a 5 per cent increase in the volume of trade reduces the income inequality and the Gini coefficient by 1.2. The authors suggest, however, that increase in trade in primary products may be associated with increasing inequality, while the increase in manufactures trade is associated with lower inequality. Harrison (2002) focuses on the share of income by capital and labour. She finds that these shares are not constant over time and that the labour share is reduced with increasing trade flows. Savvides (1998) argues that among less developed countries, more open economies experienced increased income inequality during the late 1980s.

An interesting study of the impact of trade policy reform on inequality for the case of Latin America is by Morley (2001). By using the trade policy reform index shown in Table 5.6 in an econometric exercise, he finds that trade reform has increased income inequality.[6] Similarly, Cornia (2004) used econometric techniques to find an association between rising income inequality in Latin America, trade policy reform and financial liberalisation. Behrman *et al.* (2001) analyse the impact of trade and financial liberalisation

Table 5.7 Inequality in the target Latin American countries 1989–99

Year	Arg	Bol	Bra	Chi	Col	El Sal	Gua	Hon	Mex	Nic	Per
1989								0.57	0.53		
1990		0.55		0.55			0.60	0.54	0.53		
1991					0.57			0.50			0.46
1992			0.57	0.52				0.55	0.53		
1993		0.53	0.60		0.60			0.54		0.57	
1994				0.56					0.54		0.48
1995					0.57	0.51					
1996	0.48	0.53	0.59	0.56				0.53	0.53		
1997		0.59	0.59		0.58	0.52		0.59			
1998	0.49	0.59	0.59	0.56	0.57	0.56	0.56	0.59	0.54	0.60	0.51
1999		0.60	0.59		0.56	0.55		0.58			

Source: Chapter 2, Appendix B.

on income inequality in 17 Latin American countries between 1977 and 2000. The authors find that trade reform has a small but insignificant effect on improving income distribution, but a significant negative effect from financial liberalisation. Their finding on the impact of trade policy reform is at variance with the findings in the chapter, and the findings of Morley (2001) and Cornia (2004). The findings on financial liberalisation are interesting because they trace the impact on inequality to a fall in the cost of capital induced by financial liberalisation, which if sustained would impact on long-run comparative advantage.

Hanson and Harrison (1999) find for the case of Mexico that trade reform in the 1980s increased income inequality. The authors suggest that the potential explanation of this increase in inequality could be explained by the role of foreign direct investment (FDI), export orientation and technological change increasing the demand for high-skilled labour. Gindling and Robbins (2001) suggest that more rapid radical liberalisation in Chile explains the more rapid rise in relative demand for more skilled workers, which in turn increased returns to schooling and income inequality. Beyer, Rojas and Vergara (1999) also analyse the link between trade liberalisation and wage inequality in Chile. They find that inequality increased due to the reduction in the relative price of labour-intensive goods, which offset the equalising effect of the increased proportion of skilled workers.

Attanasio *et al.* (2002) analysed how trade reform affected income distribution in Colombia. The authors identified three main channels through which the income distribution was affected. The first channel has been by increasing the returns to college education, mainly due to skill-biased technological change. This technological change was not only induced by tariff reduction, but also by increase in competition and investment. The second channel is through changes in industry wages that hurt the sectors that had initially lower wages and a higher fraction of unskilled workers. The authors observe that the larger reduction in wage premiums is observed in the sector that experience larger liberalisation. The last channel that they observe is a transfer of the labour force towards the informal sector, which pays lower wages. They point out that the informal sector increases in size in the more liberalised sectors. The authors conclude that despite this clear effect of trade reform on income distribution, the magnitude of the impact is small.

Finally, Leamer *et al.* (1999) suggest that countries with natural resource-intensive sectors, particularly permanent agriculture, absorb capital that might otherwise flow to manufacturing. This depresses workers' incentive to accumulate skills, increases inequality and delays industrialisation.

Summary and policy recommendations

The main points in this chapter that are worth summarising are:

1   The exposition of the analytical framework in the second section of this chapter was designed to be comprehensive yet capable of strategic simplification for application in the third section 'Analysing the impact of trade policy reform on income inequality in target Latin American countries' to descriptive data analysis of trade policy reform and income distribution in the long, medium and short run. In the short run, trade policy reform affects income distribution through the adoption of international prices, which are lower than protected domestic prices, thereby affecting consumption and sources of income. Factor prices may also be affected in the short run, but the main effects are likely to come through only in the medium and long run. In the medium and long run, the impact of trade policy on inequality works through specialisation and endowment effects, productivity and technology transfer, tariff revenue and spending and long-term growth and volatility. In the long run, resource endowments, economic institutions, economic structure and trade barriers provide the basis for understanding the way in which trade policy reform is likely to affect income distribution. In this stylised framework, both institutions and resource endowments interact to determine comparative advantage. The stylised framework can also help to determine the impact of trade policy reform on factor prices, but a great deal of additional information is required to estimate the final impact of trade policy report on household income distribution.

2   The third section of this chapter was characterised by the assembly of a large amount of descriptive data on factor endowments, income distribution, trade patterns, and the level of and trend in trade protection. The data assembled and analytical methods aimed to provide policy makers with something akin to a partial kit for looking at trade policy and inequality issues in an empirical context using a simplified version of the analytical framework to help interpret the data. According to this framework, when countries with a low skill/resource ratio accumulate skills, they will expand skill-intensive manufactured exports which, as skills accumulation proceeds, will eventually dominate resource intensive exports. When resource-based exports dominate, trade policy reform will favour resource intensive exports and resource rents will increase relative to skilled wages and usually household income inequality will rise as well. When the accumulation of skills has reached the point when skill intensive manufactured exports dominate, trade policy reform will tend to increase the skilled wage/resource rent ratio

and the skilled wage/unskilled wage ratio. In this case, it is also likely that trade policy reform will increase household income inequality.

3   The results derived from the analysis were rich and diverse, but quickly pointed to the severe data limitations for the analysis of the impact of trade policy on income distribution, and the need for formalised research methods and greatly increased data to carry the argument forward. The main findings were that the target Latin American countries experienced worsening income distribution over the period 1980–2000 arising from trade policy reform in the long run. During the 1990s, it was also suggested that all but one of the target countries under analysis may have experienced adverse adjustment consequences from a lack of appropriate real exchange rate as trade policy reform proceeded.

The main policy suggestions, seen as necessary to make trade reforms supportive of better income distribution in Latin America, are threefold. First, it is important that Latin American countries grow out of their historical pattern of factor endowments through rapid accumulation of skilled labour, and that this is translated into high-skill export industries. This process may need the support of generic government policies targeted to assist skill and knowledge acquisition. The immediate effect of such trade policy reform and skill accumulation may be to increase household income inequality, but in so far as unskilled labour is able to acquire skills and the ownership patterns in the resource-based sectors are more egalitarian, this is less likely. Second, current efforts by developing countries to push for trade policy liberalisation in Northern markets in agricultural and agricultural processing sectors should continue, as this is likely to have large welfare effects (see Diao *et al*. 2002), even if the short- and medium-run effects are to worsen the distribution of household income before the accumulation of skills reverse these adverse effects in the long run. Finally, trade reforms to be successful have to be accompanied by sound macroeconomic policies, especially a stable and competitive exchange rate. This will contribute to long-term sustainability and success of reforms, both in terms of growth and to ensure a less traumatic transition period with adverse short-run income distribution consequences.

Acknowledgements

I would like to thank Xavier Cirera for assistance in researching material for this chapter and for producing early drafts of parts of section 2 and section 4. Arnab Acharya, Martin Greeley, Ricardo Gottschalk, Adrian Wood, and Sue Holloway made useful comments along the way. Rosalind Goodrich and Jeanne Grant provided excellent editorial assistance. I thank them all but implicate none.

Notes

1 The analytical framework developed in this section is an amalgam of that developed by McCulloch *et al.* (2001) and the SAM-based empirical and modelling framework used by the author in a recent article (Evans, 2003).
2 This is discussed in a Southern African context in Evans (2003).
3 For example, the study of MERCOSUR by Azevedo (2001).
4 For an estimate of the minimum number of commodities that enter world trade, see Evans (1989, p. 90).
5 Mexico is included in NAFTA and is shown separately as well. Relative to NAFTA, Mexico has a higher skill/resource endowment ratio. Ideally, Mexico should have been excluded from NAFTA but because Mexico is a small economy relative to the USA and Canada, the skill/resource endowment ratio for NAFTA would not be much influenced by the exclusion of Mexico from NAFTA. For the purposes of this analysis, NAFTA can be treated as if Mexico were not included.
6 It should be observed that this result is not statistically significant.

Bibliography

Attanasio, O., Goldberg, P.K. and Pavnik, N. (2002) 'Trade Reforms and Income Inequality in Colombia', Paper prepared for the 2002 IMF Conference on Macroeconomic Policies and Poverty Reduction, 14–15 March, Washington, DC.

Azevedo, A.F.Z. de (2001) 'The Economic Effects of Mercosur: An Empirical Analysis', DPhil Thesis, University of Sussex, Brighton, October.

Behrman, J., Birdsall, N. and Szekely, M. (2001) 'Pobreza, Desigualdad y Liberalizacion Comercial en America Latina', Working Paper 449, Washington, DC: Inter-American Development Bank.

Beyer, H., Rojas, P. and Vergara, R. (1999) 'Trade Liberalization and Wage Inequality', *Journal of Development Economics*, 59, 103–23.

Calderon, C. and Chong, A. (2001) 'External Sector and Income Inequality in Interdependent Economies Using a Dynamic Panel Data Approach', *Economics Letters*, 71, 225–31.

Cornia, G.A. (2004) 'Inequality, Growth, and Poverty: An Overview of Changes over the Last Two Decades', in G.A. Cornia (ed.) *Inequality, Growth, and Poverty in an Era of Liberalization and Globalization*, UNU-WIDER Studies in Development Economics, UNU-WIDER and UNDP, New York: Oxford University Press.

Diao, X., Díaz-Bonilla, E. and Robinson, S. (2002) 'Scenarios for Trade Integration in the Americas', TMD Discussion Paper no. 90, Washington, DC: IFPRI.

Ebrill, L., Stotsky, J. and Gropp, R. (1999) 'Revenue Implications of Trade Liberalization', Occasional Paper 42, Washington DC: IMF.

Evans, (H.) D. (1989) *Comparative Advantage and Growth: Trade and Development in Theory and Practice*, Hemel Hempstead: Harvester Wheatsheaf.

Evans, D. (2003) 'Trade Employment and Poverty in Southern Africa: The Analysis of Winners and Losers in Retrospect and Prospect', TIPS Working Paper 6–2003, Johannesburg.

Gindling, T.H. and Robbins, D. (2001) 'Patterns and Sources of Changing Income Inequality in Chile and Costa Rica During Structural Adjustment', *World Development* 29(4), 725–45.

Harrison, A. (2002) 'Has Globalization Eroded Labour's Share? Some Cross-Country Evidence', UC Berkeley mimeo.

Hanson, G. and Harrison, A. (1999) 'Who Gains from Trade Reform? Some Remaining Puzzles', *Journal of Development Economics*, 59(1), 125–54.

Hertel, T., Ivanic, M., Preckel, P.V. and Cranfield, J.A.L. (2003) 'Trade Liberalisatino and the Structure of Poverty in Developing Countries', GTAP Working Paper no. 25, Purdue University, West Lafayette, IN.

Leamer, E.E., Maul, H., Rodriguez, S. and Schott, P.K. (1999) 'Does Natural Resource Abundance Increase Latin American Income Inequality?', *Journal of Development Economics*, 59, 3–42.

McCulloch, N., Winters, L.A. and Cirera, X. (2001) *Trade Liberalisation and Poverty: A Handbook*, London: DFID and CEPR.

Morley, S. (2001) *The Income Distribution Problem in Latin America and the Caribbean*, Santiago de Chile: ECLAC.

Morley, S., Machado, R. and Pettinato, S. (1999) 'Indexes of Structural Reform in Latin America', Serie Reformas Económicas, No. 12, Santiago de Chile: ECLAC.

Savvides, A. (1998) 'Trade Policy and Income Inequality: New Evidence', *Economics Letters*, 61, 365–72.

Taylor, L. (2000) 'External Liberalization, Economic Performance and Distribution in Latin America and Elsewhere', UNU/WIDER Working Paper no. 215, Helsinki: UNU/WIDER.

WIDER, (2000) *World Income Inequality Database*, Helsinki: WIDER, United Nations University.

Wood, A. (1994) *North-South Trade, Employment, and Inequality: Changing Fortunes in a Skill-Driven World*, Oxford: Clarendon Press.

Wood, A. (1997) 'Openness and Wage Inequality in Developing Countries: The Latin American Challenge to East Asian Conventional Wisdom', *World Bank Economic Review*, 11(1), 33–57.

Wood, A. and Mayer, J. (1999) 'Africa's Export Structure in a Comparative Perspective', IDS and UNCTAD. Update of IDS monograph of same title, 1998, University of Sussex.

6 The political economy of inequality

The privatisation of utilities in Latin America

Arnab Acharya, Aaron Schneider and Cecilia Ugaz

Introduction

In severely unequal developing countries there are large numbers of poor, a small number of rich, and few in-between. This simple description, sadly, portrays much of Latin America. What is more difficult to describe is why policy makers have failed to do anything about it. Political economy theories of elections and policy making suggest that rational politicians in democratic systems should enact policies that appeal to the median voter. Given the skewed distribution of wealth in Latin America, the median voter is located closer to the vast majority of poor voters, i.e. policies targeted at the median voter should be pro-poor. Yet, in Latin America one can find some of the most regressive policies in the world (Weyland, 1996). This is especially the case when one examines reform of utilities sectors. Under state ownership, they were inefficient and often failed to reach the poor, and after privatisation, universal service provision remains elusive. What explains the regressive policy bias in public sector utilities, and more generally, and what can be done about it?

Utilities are especially important because they provide essential inputs for a decent standard of living. One of the defining features of poverty is lack of access to basic utility services. Recent privatisation of telecommunications, electricity, water and sanitation have changed the structure, ownership, access, and cost of public utilities in many Latin American countries. This chapter seeks to answer three questions about public utility privatisation. First, what political economy models can help us understand why policy makers failed to address the needs of the poor? Second, what have been the specific motivations and impacts of privatisation reforms, especially with respect to the poor? Third, what might be done to promote more pro-poor utility policy choices in the future?

The first section of the chapter is dedicated to a political economy understanding of reforms affecting the utilities sector. Why would Latin American policymakers, supposedly interested in winning elections, choose policies that would alienate poor voters? In turn, why would voters support them, as often happened? The tools from the emerging field of political economics, mostly incorporating game theory and standard economic analysis, are especially useful in situations in which there are multiple actors with potentially competing interests. Electoral politics and utility privatisation offer an opportunity to model the strategic decisions faced by voters and political representatives of different stripes. Representatives must choose from a range of utility policy options that vary from progressive to regressive and voters must choose whom to elect. In many Latin American countries, Rightist and Centrist parties offered regressive models of privatisation and voters elected them. We hypothesise that intra-partisan politics and a multidimensional issue space may be the best way to understand the policy maker and voter choices.

We then turn to empirical cases of public utility privatisation. Most South American countries embarked on privatisation in the early 1980s and 1990s. Close analysis of telecommunications, electricity and water and sanitation suggest some strikingly similar trends across countries. In Argentina, Bolivia and Peru, these sectors were dominated by state owned companies that provided poor service to a slim portion of the population. Privatisation brought in needed fiscal resources, and service was expanded, to cover poor areas. Coverage was not complete, however, and tariffs rose, significantly in some sectors. The main shortcoming in the post-privatisation utility sector has been weak regulation. We characterise these policy outcomes as regressive privatisation. The main motivation appears to have been macroeconomic stabilisation, and regulation has failed to prioritise pro-poor outcomes.

Based on the political economy models derived in the first section and the empirical cases of utility privatisation, we suggest a number of interventions that might reverse the scenario. In particular, political economy approaches help us understand the institutions and interactions required for more pro-poor outcomes. Applications to the example of utility privatisation suggest that the failure to enact pro-poor regulation can at least partly be traced to faulty incentives and institutions.

Privatisation

What explains the failure to address inequality in Latin America? We are most concerned here to address the period during the 1980s and 1990s when many governments privatised public utilities. During this period, drying up of international capital, rising interest payments, and weakening domestic capacity left most countries in Latin America with serious fiscal crisis. Over the course of the next decade, governments in most of the countries chose, or were forced, to adopt adjustment strategies. These strategies generally sought to cut spending, raise revenues, and shrink the roles and obligations of government.

Frequently, privatisation of public enterprises was a major emphasis of these adjustment strategies. Privatisation implied fiscal resources in the short term, as governments essentially exchanged public assets for liquid assets. For obvious reasons, the most profitable public companies fetched the highest prices, but even less profitable companies usually attracted some immediate inflow of cash to government. In cases of enterprises that were losing money, governments at times had to sanitise the enterprise before sale. This may even have implied a short-term cost, as debts, personnel obligations, or credit guarantees had to be offered.

In these cases, it was the longer-term benefit that was most important. By selling enterprises, governments eliminated future liabilities from these losing companies. The short-term cost of handing over the enterprises was balanced by the longer term fiscal gain of cutting losses. To some, this aspect of privatisation was attractive even in cases of profit-making enterprises. Removing government roles in direct provision and employment in the long term was favoured by some observers regardless of the profitability of enterprises.

Exclusive attention to these fiscal goals frequently resulted in a regressive privatisation regime. By regressive, what is meant is the redistributive impact of the privatisation process and the ensuing environment. A regressive privatisation process concentrates assets through the manner in which the sale occurs. Following privatisation, the subsequent environment allowed continued inequality in access, service and quality. Further, regressive privatisation allowed a continued price structure that favoured accumulation for the wealthy.

More progressive strategies of privatisation would prioritise the needs of the poor even as short-term fiscal goals were met. All privatisation necessarily brought immediate resources to the public sector. What differentiated progressive privatisation was the process of privatisation and the ensuing market structure. Progressive privatisation opened access to the utility sector, making it possible for multiple actors to realistically consider entering. In some cases, this included breaking apart monopolies to encourage competition. In other cases, natural monopolies were pre-served, but ownership was pulverised to spread the potential access to assets. Progressive privatisation also resulted in universal access and lower tariffs. Under progressive privatisation, utilities moved towards universal access and affordable tariffs.

A few notes about the distinction between progressive and regressive privatisation are appropriate. First, the distinction is more a continuum than a dichotomy. Most privatised utilities fell somewhere in-between progressive and regressive, and an attempt will be made below to offer an accurate portrayal of several cases. Second, it is also important to place privatised utilities in the correct context. Some observers would be unsurprised to find out that privatisation had regressive impacts. It is the nature of private ownership, they might suggest. To this objection, it is necessary to remember that publicly owned enterprises did not always perform progressively. Even where service was meant to be universal and tariffs low, many citizens found they were excluded. Difficulty of access could mean that citizens found themselves paying high black market prices for supposedly free services.

It is also important to remember the fiscal constraint facing many countries in Latin America. In many cases, not privatising at all was simply not an option. Utilities losing money were a drain on scarce resources. Even apparently profitable utilities often implied a drain on resources when one considered investments required to sustain and expand their services. This exacerbated an international context in which countries needed liquid assets in the short term to pay down debts that were rapidly exploding.

The key conclusion that emerges from the discussion below is that regressive privatisation results from political economy realities that distort policy making away from the interests of the poor. This does not directly address whether or not privatisation of utilities had to occur, though it suggests that a focus on regressive or progressive outcomes may be more important than private or public ownership.

Why regressive privatisation?

The choice of privatisation policy was not made in a vacuum, and this chapter looks at the actors and institutions that lead to policy choices. The political leaders who chose a regressive pattern of privatisation depended for their survival on the support of their parties and voters. If the vast majority of voters were poor, as is the case in Latin America, one would expect politicians to seek progressive patterns of privatisation that include strong state regulation of privately owned utilities. Why then, do we see a regressive pattern of privatisation? Put another way, why would politicians go against the wishes of the median voter, and why would voters let them get away with it? The current approach attempts to understand regressive privatisation in terms of an electoral game played by politicians, party activists and voters along multiple dimensions. Despite the large number of poor voters, policy outputs deviate from the preferences of median voters when it comes to distributive issues.

This is surprising given that political leaders seek votes. Indeed, some have even gone so far as to define political parties according to this goal.[1] In presidential systems in which a majority is required (i.e. almost all of Latin America), the surest way to win office is to appeal to the median voter.[2] If voter preferences were at least in part linked to their economic status, the median voter in Latin America would be poor and prefer progressive outcomes. Indeed, populist appeals to poor voters have consistently been a successful electoral strategy for politicians seeking office in Latin America (Collier and Collier, 1991). Why, then, do we see regressive policies as a successful electoral strategy of the Latin American Centre and Right?

Political economy of inequality

There are many accounts that can be given regarding the political economy of inequality. To understand the logic of political economy approaches, this chapter will review a series of literature that attempt to understand inequality. This literature focuses on socio-economic determinants, the difficulty of reform, the problems of intra-party conflict and the possibility of political competition along multiple issue spaces.

Most of the literature exploring political economy of distribution processes focuses on voting behaviours. For convenience, one can begin with the assumption that income is what is to be redistributed, although land or some other type of resource can be understood in the same way. The standard median voter model would predict that voters would vote for redistributive policies if the median voter's income were less than the mean income. Though the median voter in Latin America is generally poor, voters have not generally chosen the candidates offering the most progressive policies. Economics literature has offered four general strands to explain this paradox:

i   Voters think that too much taxation would generally decrease incentives to work and, therefore, many in a dynamic setting would end up suffering due to lack of increasing GDP which could trickle down to them (Meltzer and Richard, 1981).

ii   Voters think that their children or even they themselves can be high income earners and that they would suffer if there is too much income distribution (Piketty, 1995).

iii Voters believe that the rich person – indeed everyone – deserves their wealth. Studies show that voters do not hold this as a moral view, but a substantial number of voters may believe that hard work has large payoffs and have material interests that outweigh their sense of distributive justice (Piketty, 1995; Putterman, 1997).

iv   Voters care about distributive justice as long as their income is lower than the mean but also care about issues such as religion, race, cultural and ethnic identity, which influences strongly their voting patterns regarding distribution (Roemer, 1998). They may also have concerns over fiscal chaos, particularly if they actually experience it, and national security.

Yet another possibility is that voters, even if risk-neutral, will not seek changes because they will be unable to know their personal pay-off from reform. When reforms do not occur and there is bias toward the status quo, there may be little learning as to how to have the right, optimal level of reform. Thus if voters do not experience a pro-poor reform at some early stage, they may be reluctant to support reform-minded policy.

Many of the arguments in the theoretical economics literature have been developed in the context of democracies with high incomes. However, it is worth revisiting them briefly. Below we examine five sets of theories regarding why inequalities persist. The first focuses on economic factors. The second focuses on social factors. The third examines the interaction of these two with levels of participation. The fourth brings in intra-party stances to median voting model. The final discussion adds the possibility of political competition along multiple dimensions. Each confirms that the citizen with the median well-being is unlikely to gain the most politically advantageous situation.

Inequality through economic segregation

The first set of arguments relies on segregation and electoral participation. It is argued that citizens acquire human capital through neighbourhood and ethnic contacts. Empirical evidence verifies that better educated people come from specific neighbourhoods and that there is high correlation in types of profession between generations among ethnic groups. Further, higher earning ethnic groups usually tend to generate higher future income earners (Loury, 1981; Borjas, 1992, 1995). Bénabou (1993) and Piketty (1995) have used economic theory to explain empirical findings of voting patterns.

Bénabou (1993) starts off with the empirical finding that some environments facilitate acquisition of human capital. In a community where human capital is large, there is a local public good generated from combined high achievements of people in the community. This makes it cheaper to educate the next generation in comparison with regions where combined achievements in human capital are rather low. From a starting point of some inequality, the more human capital endowed community is more attractive to everyone. Thus, the land or property value within these communities rises as rents are bid up. These communities become more attractive but affordable only by people who can acquire large human capital and have higher skills.

146   *Arnab Acharya, Aaron Schneider and Cecilia Ugaz*

Such segregation reproduces and exacerbates inequality. The areas with greater public goods have large numbers of skilled workers and areas with lower public goods have large numbers of unskilled workers. Over time, the inequalities will get worse. The areas with skilled workers produce more skilled workers at a lower cost whereas areas with unskilled workers are unable to produce skilled workers or produce them at a high cost. There will be under-investment in skill production in the low-skilled area because the returns are lower.

In many parts of Latin America, of course, the segregation that occurs is not geographic, but social. Inequalities worsen over time, and citizens are painfully aware that human capital skills are poorly distributed. Still, attempts to spread human capital and skills receive surprisingly little support. The efficiency gains that could conceivably emerge do not appear to convince many to support reform. Among the well-off, this is perhaps not surprising. Why should they support reform? Among the vast majority, the less well-off, we should be surprised that they do not overwhelmingly favour a redistribution of human capital and skills.

Inequality through a status-quo bias

One way to understand the lack of mobilisation around redistribution is the fear of uncertainty. Although current arrangements are widely recognised as unsatisfactory, few are willing to 'rock the boat'. Instead, they prefer incremental and gradual modifications, rather than major changes in distribution.

To understand this pattern, Fernandez and Rodrik (1991) show that uncertainty about future benefits can create a status quo bias. *Ex-post* winners and losers as a result of a policy shift may not be able to identify themselves before the policy shift or reform actually takes place. Thus, *ex-ante* calculations discount the value of future benefits, and possible winners fail to support reform even if they are not risk averse. In the examples constructed the point is easily understood if we imagine that although some people are sure (or more sure) of how the possible outcome would affect them, there might be many who are not.

The poor, one might expect, are unlikely to be favourable towards reform more than other groups. One reason is that knowledge about future conditions probably depends on current socio-economic status. And further, it is they who are likely to face a degree of risk higher than others. These two factors suggest in particular that progressive reform will be difficult. Thus the main constituency for reform, the poor, are likely to discount the value of reform in the future.

If voters are unsure if they will win, they are less likely to support reform. A key corrective, of course, is to decrease uncertainty. The role of learning, gaining information based on prior events, could alter this calculus. If a reform has occurred in the past, it may provide information that allows people to better evaluate outcomes of future reforms. Thus, the 'unsure' categories would be smaller, and one might expect the poor majority to have a greater influence on policy. Of course, if pro-poor policies have never occurred, then the poor will have little information to recognise or support pro-poor reforms.

The politics of inequality: participation

The situations above imply that the poor are prevented from picking their preferred policy either by being segregated out of the political process or provided inadequate information. There are other reasons the poor majority may not get their preferred policy, however. For example, one set of theories explores the voting behaviour of the poor.

These models examine the interaction of socio-economic factors and political participation. They suggest that it may be less costly for the rich to participate in political processes. Data from the USA and Europe show that campaign contribution and volunteerism by the rich in the political processes is higher than it is for the poor. The well-off may through this process maintain policies that support ghettoisation, induce lower investment on goods that the poor may want, or limit other types of redistribution. For example, Bénabou (2000) shows that the decisive voter in such a model can be richer than the actual median income earner. Further, at least over a certain range, he shows the surprising result that popular support for redistributive policies decreases with inequality. In short, societies that begin at high levels of inequality will persist that way because either the poor do not vote or they are disenfranchised.

The interaction between levels of inequality and political influence has unusual implications for where we would expect to see redistribution. We might expect a U-shaped relation between wealth inequality and redistribution. At low levels and at high levels of inequality, redistribution is likely.

Suppose that the poorest in a population (P) do not vote, then the decisive voter using a median voter model is $\frac{P + \pi}{2}$ th voter.[3] This has been the case in many heterogeneous richer countries as there is a positive correlation between wealth and both political participation in terms of involvement in politics as well as in terms of casting votes. In heterogeneous populations, redistribution mainly helps the least well off. With very high levels of inequality, there is homogeneity among a large group of people, and even accounting for limited participation, the poor, numbering many, would press for redistribution. At more medium levels of inequality, the fall in participation of the poor is enough to weaken the pressure for redistribution, and the political influence of the rich is decisive. Redistribution falls. In extremely egalitarian societies, however, the portion of the population that does not participate because they lack human capital is very low, as human capital is usually higher in such countries; thus, there is more support for public goods.

Based on this result, one would expect the citizens in Sweden (highly egalitarian) to favour redistributive policies; US (slightly unequal) citizens would favour less of this type of policy; and citizens in Latin America (highly unequal) to favour redistribution. In actual fact, of course, highly egalitarian places like Sweden favour redistribution, and little happens elsewhere. Thus, one has to wonder if Sweden is egalitarian in part because it has favoured redistribution in the past. If this is the case, a closer look at the dynamics of politics and redistribution over time seem appropriate.

The politics of inequality: parties – internal dynamics

If the interaction of socio-economic conditions and participation in Latin America favour redistribution, why do we see so little of it? Two more explanations for failure to appeal to the median voter will be dealt with here. The first explanation focuses on the internal dynamics of parties, in which conflicts between leaders, activists and voters produce policy positions that deviate from the preferences of the median voter. Indeed, under certain conditions, such conflicts can lead parties to deviate even from the preferences of their own voters. This literature will be discussed below. A second explanation focuses on the possibility for competition among parties along multiple dimensions, in which competition along a second dimension can pull parties off of the median voter position on the Left-Right dimension. This explanation will be modelled formally and applied to the Latin American, regressive privatisation case. A third explanation might highlight the dynamics generated by competition among more than two parties. This explanation will not be discussed extensively here, as the typical electoral system in Latin America (presidentialism with run-off) creates a tendency towards two-party competition for chief executive contests. Of course, presidential systems create their own dynamics, some of which will be dealt with below. It is mentioned simply to be sure that future work, referring to other political systems, takes such possibilities into account.[4]

Internal partisan dynamics: simple version

One set of literature focuses on the internal partisan dynamics. The basic story is that different echelons within party organisations have slightly different preferences. As a result of strategic behaviour among the echelons and between parties, the policy positions of the parties may not reflect the interests of the median voter. In fact, if the conflict among echelons within a party follows certain patterns, party positions may not even reflect the position of that party's voters.

Early discussions of internal party dynamics contrasted party leaders and followers. Resource constraints, socialisation, or simply the requirements of organisational preservation led to distinctions between the leaders and followers within parties.[5] Leaders were concerned with presenting policy positions and sustaining a partisan organisation with themselves at the helm. Followers were subsets of the electorate who identified with the leaders that were closest to their own ideological preferences.

There were two basic versions to the distinction between leaders and followers (see Figure 6.1). In one version, party leaders were more ideologically extreme than their followers.[6] Such extremist leaders exaggerated differences between themselves and their opponents to differentiate themselves from competitors, mobilise cleavages and polarise the electorate. Alternatively, others saw leaders as more Centrist than their followers. Centrist leaders were ambitious entrepreneurs who sought to appeal to the median voter, cooperate with other leaders to attain office, and subdue extremists among their support base.[7]

How well do these portrayals apply to the case of regressive privatisation in Latin America? Both portrayals could explain why parties fail to appeal to the median voter within their party. In the extremist version, leaders would drive their parties to distantly opposed policy positions. In most contexts, this strategy does not occur, or if it does occur, it is followed either by polarisation and breakdown or by attempts to fill the gap in the centre. If this were the explanation for regressive privatisation, one would expect regime breakdown or the appearance of centrist alternatives.[8] Over the last decade, neither has occurred. Rather, the general story in Latin America is that Centrist

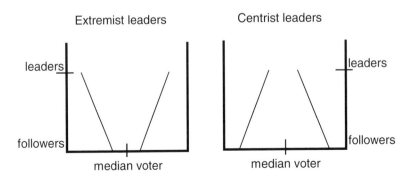

Figure 6.1 Distinction between leaders and followers

and Rightist leaders have offered regressive privatisation policies and voters have supported them.

We can also ask if the Centrist leader description explains regressive privatisation. According to this explanation, leaders drive their parties to the centre, and the appeals of different parties become virtually indistinguishable. This describes many Western European democracies, but it does not fit the regressive privatisation model very well. In Latin America, Left parties continue to favour redistribution, while Right and Centre parties offer regressive options. These Centrist and Rightist parties have continued to enjoy support despite the fact that they do not appeal to the median voter on distributive issues.

Internal partisan dynamics: more complicated versions

To understand regressive privatisation and continued voter support, greater nuance has to be added to the operation of internal party dynamics. Instead of simply distinguishing between leaders and followers, another set of party literature has distinguished between leaders, activists and voters and attributed different preferences to each. The earliest application was May 1983, who argued for a 'Special law of curvilinear disparity' (see Figure 6.2). According to this law, voters were largely clustered around the median voter in the centre of the issue space. Activists, by contrast, were socialised and selected for greater convictions and motivation to do the grunt work of political parties, and were far more extreme ideologically. The political leaders at the top of the party, however, were located somewhere between activists and centrist voters. They were pulled away from the centre by their links to extremist activists, but their desire for office drew them back towards the median voter. The result was political platforms that lay slightly to either side of the median voter.

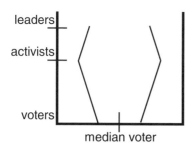

Figure 6.2 Special law of curvilinear disparity

Later variations on this theme formalised the logic that determined the interests of the echelons of parties. Aldrich (1983) explains the extremism in the activist echelon by noting that activism requires overcoming obstacles to participation (for example, indifference and alienation). Only individuals with convictions strong enough to overcome these obstacles will become activists, thus leading to strong distinctions between the activist's echelon of different parties (in fact, overcoming indifference leads to greater extremism than overcoming alienation) (p. 984).

The intuition that selection mechanisms contribute to the degree of extremism of different echelons of parties led Kitschelt to a further observation (1989). He observed that partisan actors are motivated by a combination of organisational, programmatic, and strategic interests and can be distinguished as 'pragmatists' or 'ideologues'. Pragmatists seek a more moderate combination of organisational resources, programmatic agenda and strategic positions. Ideologues are the opposite (p. 406). The key to this model is that echelons within parties seek different types of benefits and are motivated to participate for different reasons. Depending on the weight of different interests, the special law of curvilinear disparity need not apply equally in all parties. In short, the degree to which leaders are pulled away from the median voter position is determined by the relative strength of ideologues within a party. Thus, according to Kitschelt, it would be possible for some parties to be pulled farther from the median voter position than others. Laver and Hunt (1992) surveyed experts on parties and confirmed that parties showed different characteristics. They found that parties varied significantly in the degree to which they prioritised 'office' or 'policy'.

The conditions that determine the relative importance of different interests within parties remain an open question, however. When will ideologues dominate and when will pragmatists dominate? Tsebelis (1990: especially Chapter 5) argues that the outcome of diverging priorities between echelons of a party depends on the institutional rules for candidate selection and the strategic conditions in a given jurisdiction.[9] Thus, the dominant position of the National Executive Committee (NEC) of Britain's Labour party allowed them to pick candidates who were generally close to the median voter position in marginal districts. In 'safe' seats, the NEC would allow more radical extremists to pick candidates, knowing that Labour would win anyway. In 'safe' conservative seats, the NEC would also allow extremist activists to pick the candidate, knowing that they had no chance of victory. Thus, the overall position of the party would depend on the relative number of safe, marginal, and losing seats.

A more complete model of the determinants of party type is offered by Kaare Strom (1990). Strom connects the divergent internal echelons of parties to different types by focusing on vote-seeking, office-seeking, and policy-seeking incentives. Strom argues that all parties include some combination of these interests. The determinants of which interests will dominate include inter-party conditions (relative strength), intra-party institutions (leadership accountability, candidate selection mechanism, recruitment patterns), organisational resources (capital or labour intensive, sources of finance) and social conditions (number of dimensions, degree of fragmentation in the polity). Vote-seeking parties either maximise total votes or seek a plurality. Office-seeking parties maximise the organisational benefits of office perquisites. Policy-seeking parties maximise their impact on programmatic policies.

How well does the model of internal party dynamics fit the choice of regressive privatisation in Latin America? If vote-seeking interests dominated within Latin American parties, they would offer progressive policies, close to the preferences of the median voter. Rightist and Centrist parties, however, have offered regressive privatisation models, far from the preferences of the median voter. Surprisingly, they have been rewarded, and voters have elected Rightist and Centrist candidates, despite the campaign platforms of regressive privatisation.

One explanation follows Kitschelt, Tsebelis and Strom, and suggests that extremists within the Right and Centre parties are more influential than extremists in the Left. Such an explanation would suggest that Rightist extremists have pulled their party leaders away from the median voter position. This begs the question, however, of why voters have not supported Leftist parties? Shouldn't they have opted for the parties closer to the median voter preference, in this case, the Left? Also, why were extremists within the Right and Centrist parties more influential than their counterparts within the Left parties? Most common understandings of Left parties in Latin America suggest that it is extremists in these parties who are the most influential. A history of repression and evolution from revolutionary or anti-authoritarian movements has meant that most parties on the Left exhibit far higher party discipline and links to activist bases than Rightist or Centrist parties. If any party were to be influenced by its extremists, one would expect it to be parties on the Left.

Internal party dynamics alone cannot explain why Centre and Right leaders win even though they offer regressive privatisation policies far from the preferences of the median voter. Left parties, despite locating themselves closer to the median voter on distributional issues, often fail to win majoritarian elections. The Right has been electorally successful and has implemented regressive privatisation models. The Left has been successful in major urban centres (San Salvador, Managua, São Paulo); is often a significant force in national legislatures; and has achieved national successes once regressive privatisation has been installed (Chile, Brazil, Ecuador,

Venezuela). Still, we need to consider other explanations for the electoral success of political leaders who offer regressive privatisation models. What is surprising is that the Left does not win on an anti-privatisation platform.

Inequality through multi-dimensional agendas

Roemer (1998) extends the idea of the median voter to a context where the electorate has concerns over economic and as well as other dimensions. Such dimensions can include economic stability, racism or ethnic ostracism, and in Roemer's example, he focuses on religion. Voters and parties operating in a multidimensional issue space can produce surprising patterns of voter support.

Assume, for sake of clarity, that the Leftist party represents those below mean income and the Rightist party the opposite. If the poor majority support redistribution and redistribution is the decisive issue in people's vote, then the Left will win. If, however, the decisive issue is something else on which some people below mean income join with wealthy voters, Rightist parties will win. In Latin America, Rightist parties have generally been able to attract voters on two key issues: security and fiscal stability.

Roemer's model also allows for party factionalisation, in which some members of the party could be reformers, some opportunists and still others militants. The central idea here is that parties have to decide how forcefully they should prioritise different dimensions in their party platform. Roemer's model provides a link between party factions and party choices on different dimensions. He suggests that the intersection of views of internal partisan factions becomes the party preference on each dimension. The party system rests at equilibrium when no one in a party has an incentive to deviate from the party platform when they consider the positions of other parties. Roemer calls this equilibrium party unanimity equilibrium (PUNE). This may be an extreme notion of party unity, but it is functional to arrive at an equilibrium solution.

A non-trivial PUNE is where neither party stands to win an election with a probability of 1. In short, even taking into account party factions, there can be a non-trivial equilibrium where the holders of a median view on fiscal stability or security issues are the decisive voters. As a result, they are able to limit redistribution. In this case, one can imagine a non-trivial PUNE when the dynamics of internal factions lead to neither party offering a strong platform regarding redistribution.

This result can be used to understand why viable Leftist parties moderate, lose or have only recently begun to win elections. The Chilean example might be an example in which the Left has won elections by downplaying its redistribution stance and moving to the Centre on fiscal stability issues.

In Brazil, a similar, but slightly different, dynamic might be at play. The Workers' Party lost several elections when it tried to prioritise redistribution at times of great fiscal instability. Recently, however, they both moderated, and perhaps found voters less worried about fiscal stability. In addition, they found Centrist alliance partners to placate worries about fiscal stability. Also, eight years of relatively low inflation may have lowered the importance of fiscal stability for voters, and turned their attention to issues of redistribution. In Peru, Fujimori first promised populist policies, and on winning office, distracted voters with issues of security and fiscal stability.

A final scenario could be that voters care neither about fiscal stability nor redistribution, yet party factionalism does not allow any partisan response. In Colombia, a more left wing candidate, Serpa, had held an electoral lead until guerrilla attacks intensified. While voters and opposition parties began to focus on security, factionalism among the Serpa party prevented them from developing their own position on security and convincing the voters that redistribution was still important. As a result, they lost the election on security issues.

Presidentialism, delegative democracy, and executive– legislative relations

The prior discussion has focused attention on parties and party systems and the way dynamics in these institutions can prevent politicians from using redistributive policies to appeal to the poor majority. A final note on the nature of another key institution, presidentialism, deserves attention. The behaviour of presidential systems clearly interacts with party systems. Much ink has been spilled on the potential stalemates and policy immobilism can emerge from divided governments in which different parties control president and legislature. For some observers, though certainly not all, presidentialism lies at the heart of problems of unstable democracy and poor development performance. It would be too great a task to consider all of the literature but a few patterns are worth considering here, especially with respect to the likelihood of pro-poor policies.[10]

Here, the impact of presidentialism will be considered within the notion of governability, understood as forming a government and governing. In terms of forming a government, presidential systems have the advantage of choosing the chief executive through the electoral process. Presidents automatically have a mandate, even if only a slim one, because they must achieve a majority (or at least plurality) of votes. In addition, presidents have relative security of tenure, because, barring impeachment, they can only be replaced at the next elections. In parliamentary systems, by contrast, the executive only emerges from negotiations within parliament, and there is a possibility that government will be difficult to form or that it will be disbanded at any moment.

The problem, of course, is that presidential systems in Latin America have been prone to patterns of 'delegative democracy' (O'Donnell, 1994). Delegative democracies are democracies that have settled at an unsatisfactory, partially consolidated, degree of democracy, and there is every indication that they can remain in this condition for long periods. Such democracies are characterised by a president who, even if elected by the slimmest of margins, governs with absolute authority, as though there were an overwhelming mandate. They legislate through decree, seek extra-legal avenues to impose policy, and basically operate in an entirely unaccountable manner. In some cases, this allows the president to advance difficult policies that promote major changes. There is no guarantee, however, that such policies will be pro-poor. In fact, delegative democracy allows presidents to win elections on pro-poor platforms, as Menem did in Argentina, and then govern in a completely anti-poor manner, a complete separation of rhetoric and reality. The centralisation of power, the lack of accountability and the disdain for the rule of law weaken democracy in general and create incredible fragility for the regime. At the slightest downturn in performance, the president is open to abandonment and attack. Problems that were evident but not problematic at one moment, such as corruption, can lead to the fall of governments in the next, as seen in Collor (Brazil), Perez (Venezuela), and Fujimori (Peru).

A second issue of governability is actually governing, i.e. the drafting, passing and implementing legislation. Presidentialism has great difficulty in government operation, especially when the legislature is polarised, fragmented, or in opposition to the president, as is often the case in Latin America.[11] Electoral rules exacerbate these problems, as parliaments are necessarily elected from different districts and rules to the president. To pass legislation, the president must constantly remake a support coalition among legislators who do not necessarily share similar roots.

In parliamentary systems, by contrast, the relations between the executive and legislature are mostly resolved when MPs form a 'minimum winning coalition' to form a government.[12] The government can usually count on support from its coalition, and in the rare event of widespread opposition, a new coalition and government can be formed. Presidential systems may be particularly handicapped when it comes to redistributive policies. Such policies incite serious conflict, and are difficult to pass in any legislature. In the context of presidentialism, executives wishing to pass difficult policies have turned to trade-offs that weaken policy, corruption to buy votes, and delegative democracy to rule by decree. None of these promote or sustain progressive redistribution.

Propositions

The political economy of inequality suggests a number of political constraints on progressive policies. These constraints can emerge from several roots. We have covered several:

- economic segregation
- status quo bias
- unequal participation
- intra-party leader–follower dynamics
- intra-party leader–activist–voter dynamics
- multidimensional inter-party competition
- presidentialism, delegative democracy, and executive-legislative government.

The list is not meant to be exhaustive. Rather, it suggests the multiple institutional and dynamic reasons why poor majorities may not get their preferences represented. To what degree have poor majorities failed to receive distribution in Latin America? Before one can examine the causes of inequality, it is first necessary to examine its degree of intensity. In particular, we examine the extent to which inequality is continued and deepened as a result of privatisation of utilities in Latin America. The patterns are mixed. Initial results in some countries suggested an expansion of access, which can be seen as progressive but tariff increases (especially fixed rental charges) seem to tax more the poorest segments of the population. However, the overwhelming impression from the record of privatisation in the continent is that it proceeded in a regressive fashion. The poor majority was not privy to the process, and their preferences were not reflected in the way in which privatisation unfolded.

Regressive privatisation

Starting in the late 1980s, a wave of privatisation took place throughout Latin America affecting the main utilities – electricity, gas, telecommunications, water and sanitation, etc. Prior to privatisation, state-owned enterprises were in charge of production and delivery to final users of telecommunications, water and electricity services. Tariff for those services were heavily subsidised and did not allow enterprises to recover costs. In general, state intervention in the utilities sector was justified by the existence of market failures – sunk costs, externalities, and increasing returns to scale. Also, in countries like Brazil, state provision of utilities fit into the state-led growth model prevailing after the Second World War.

However, under public provision, the goal of universal access to services remained elusive. Lack of investment seriously undermined service expansion. As a consequence, the proportion of the population unable to access the networks grew over the years. Subsidised tariffs did not benefit the poor, who lived in areas not yet connected to the main utility networks. The final recipients of these subsidies were richer and middle classes. Poor households were paying in real terms even more than well off ones to access services of lesser quality through 'informal' providers.

Latin American countries in general enjoyed a level of access to services that did not correspond to the average level of income per-capita. Table 6.1 shows the level of access to water and sanitation sectors in the decades prior to reforms. Numbers show that in spite of some steady increase over the years, services did not reach a sizeable proportion of the population. Furthermore, numbers show big disparities of access between urban and rural areas. Services were also poorly run.

The main motivation behind the privatisation drive was allegedly the need to attract private financing in order to alleviate the burden of public services on the budget. This all happened at the time when increased liberalisation of services worldwide made it possible to attract substantive inflows of foreign direct investment to these sectors. Indeed, infrastructure services experienced a dramatic increase in international transactions. During the late 1990s, trade in the service sector was the fastest growing sector in the world economy. The inward stock of FDI to sectors like electricity, gas and water to countries in Latin America increased from 0 per cent in 1988 to 11.2 per cent of GDP in 1999 (UNCTAD, 2001). Latin America led in the growth of private infrastructure activity during the 1990s (see Figure 6.3). On average, Latin America accounted for almost half of the investment commitments in infrastructure projects with private participation during the last decade. After the USA, Spain has been the largest source of FDI in Latin America.

The extent of privatisation

Table 6.2 presents an overview of the privatisation processes in Latin America up to 1998. Chile pioneered the movement towards privatisation of the utilities, passing already in 1970 laws to transform the sectors. Other countries in the region followed the Chilean example. Argentina launched in 1989 a wide-ranging privatisation programme covering the main utilities. Water privatisation in Argentina took place in 1993. Peru also initiated a process of privatisation of telecommunication and electricity in 1994. However, privatisation of water sectors was halted. Brazil started the privatisation process relatively late, in 1997 with the privatisation of TELEBRAS.

Table 6.1 Access to water and sanitation facilities (percentage of the population)

Country	Access to water							Access to sanitation						
	Total			Urban		Rural		Total			Urban		Rural	
	1970	1980	1990	1980	1990	1980	1990	1970	1980	1990	1980	1990	1980	1990
Argentina	56	54	64	65	73	17	17	85	79	89	89	100	32	29
Bolivia	33	36	53	69	76	10	30	13	19	26	37	38	4	14
Brazil	55	72	87	80	95	51	61	55	21	72	32	84	...	32
Chile	56	84	87	100	100	17	21	29	...	85	99	100	...	6
Colombia	63	86	86	...	87	79	82	50	66	64	100	84	4	18
Guatemala	38	46	62	89	92	18	43	22	30	60	45	72	20	52
Honduras	34	59	64	50	85	40	48	24	60	62	40	89	26	22
Mexico	54	73	89	64	94	43	...	23	38	...	51	85	12	...
Peru	35	50	53	68	68	21	24	36	37	58	57	76	0	20
Venezuela	75	86	92	91	...	50	36	45	87	...	90	...	70	72

Source: World Development Report 1994.

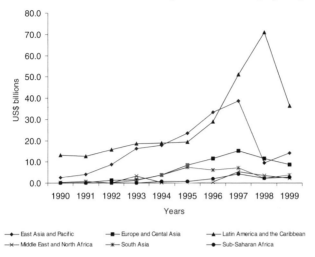

Figure 6.3 Private investment in infrastructure by region

Table 6.2 Privatisation across Latin America in 1998

Country	Telecom	Electricity[1]	Water
Argentina	X	X	X
Bolivia	X	X	X
Brazil	X	X	X
Chile	X	X	X
Colombia	X	X	
Costa Rica	P	P	
Dom. Rep.	X	P	
Ecuador	P	P	P
El Salvador	X	P	X
Guatemala	X	X	
Honduras	P	X	P
Mexico	X	X	X
Nicaragua	P	P	
Panama	X	X	X
Paraguay	P	P	
Peru	X	X	P
Uruguay	X		
Venezuela	X	P	P

Source: Torres and Hakkola (1999).

Notes
X: Privatisation executed or started in the sector.
P: Plans for partial private sector involvement.
1: Includes generation, transmission or distribution.

It is clear from Table 6.2 that privatisation was less advanced in countries of Central America in the mid-1990s. This was reflected in the flow of foreign direct investment directed to these countries. According to the Inter-American Development Bank, the share of FDI to Central America shrank in the total FDI to the whole Latin American region. The share went from 5 per cent in 1989–93 to 2.5 per cent in 1994–5 (*Financial Times*, 10 June 1998). Privatisation started up slowly due, on one side, to legal constraints in selling off state property. On the other hand, privatisation has also faced strong opposition by labour and political groups.

Acceleration of privatisation process in Central America took place towards the end of the 1990s, as countries in the region were subject to structural adjustment programmes.

The proceeds from privatisation have been sizeable. In Argentina, the total proceeds (including roads, ports, airlines, etc.) reached US$18 billion (7.6 per cent of the 1993 GDP). Proceeds from *telecom, electricity* and *gas* companies accounted for US$10.7 billion, or about 60 per cent of the total income generated by privatisation. Transfer of the telecom company alone produced US$3.5 billion, and privatisation of the electricity and gas utilities procured US$4.1 and 3 billion, respectively (Delfino and Casarin, 2001). In Peru, by the year 2000, total proceeds from privatisation reached US$8,100 million. In 1997, 82 per cent of total proceeds from privatisation were concentrated in the following sectors: telecommunication, generation and distribution of electricity and hydrocarbons (Macroconsult, 2000).

In Bolivia, privatisation took the form of capitalisation. The Bolivian government transferred shares equivalent to 50 per cent of a firm to the investor with the winning bid. Private pension funds received 45 per cent and the remaining 5 per cent went to the company's employees. A noticeable aspect of the process is that under the capitalisation scheme, the government did not earn disposable income. Fifty per cent of proceeds from the bid were re-invested entirely in the company. The incumbent private operator had to carry out this investment within a specified period (six to eight years), and agree to fulfil obligations of expansion and quality goals.

Capitalisation was possible in Bolivia because privatisation was not seen as a means to cover fiscal deficits, but rather as a way to attract foreign investment and to improve management in key areas of the economy (Barja and Urquiola, 2001). The process of capitalisation of utilities raised a significant amount of capital. For instance, in 1995, capitalisation of three electricity distribution companies and ENTEL raised about US$750 million.

In sum, SOE's poor economic performance, the need to bring in capital for new investment to the utilities sector, and the threat that the budget deficits represented for macroeconomic stability were the most important reasons advanced to justify state subsidiarity and privatisation throughout the region.

Privatisation also signalled a commitment to reforms by newly elected governments (as those in Argentina and in Peru). State retrenchment was necessary for the countries to obtain access to foreign capital markets and to multilateral organisations' lending.

The effects of privatisation on the fiscal stance were thus anticipated. The impact on the poor and the distributional effect that privatisation can bring about were not. In fact, the need to regulate was underestimated. Regulation appears crucial to ensure an equitable outcome because of the ensuing market structure in which private utilities will operate. Networks used to supply electricity and water to final users are natural monopolies. After the selling of state assets or the signing of concession contracts in the case of water, the incumbent private operators unavoidably became monopolist. Regulation in those cases is needed to curb monopoly power and to allow efficiency gains to spread to consumers under the form of lower tariffs.

Access to utilities and consumer surplus in selected countries[13]

One way to approximate welfare gains from privatisation and to observe the pattern of distribution of these gains is to measure the increase in the number of new connections to utilities services after privatisation and to calculate changes in the consumer surplus by income quintile. This exercise has some limitations as we will see below. Results from these calculations need to be interpreted with caution. However, it provides a rough approximation of the distributive impact of reforms of the utility sectors in South America. Information below concerns three countries: Argentina, Bolivia and Peru. The three countries show some similarities but also some contrasts. Privatisation in Argentina and Peru was undertaken as a means of fiscal adjustment in the early 1990s. Bolivia started the process under the auspices of a better macroeconomic situation, which clearly gave the Bolivian government more room to inject capital and restructure public entities. On the other hand, utility networks in both Bolivia and Peru had not yet reached most of the population. In Argentina, a richer country, most of the population was already connected to utility supply networks.

Calculations on the basis of household surveys for Bolivia and Peru show that access – the number of households connected to the network – increased after privatisation for the three utilities under study. In Bolivia, the most noticeable increase was in telephones as shown in Table 6.3. But most importantly, statistics show that the increase in access has not by-passed poor households. In the case of electricity, information disaggregated by income quintile shows convergence in the rate of household access across

Table 6.3 Bolivia departmental capitals and El Alto: percentage of households connected to basic services, 1994–9

Service	Percentage of households with access		
	1994 (a)	1999 (b)	% change
Electricity	95.8	98.4	2.7
Telephone (fixed and mobile)	20.0	44.6	123.0
Water	80.7	92.8	15.0
Sewerage	62.6	70.9	13.3

Source: Barja and Urquiola (2001). Calculation on the basis of information from the LSMS.

Table 6.4 Argentina Greater Buenos Aires area: new users connected to basic services

Service	Thousands		
	T1	1999	% change
Electricity	3516	3997	14
Telephone	1274	2920	29
Water	5758	7669	33
Sewerage	4663	5744	23

Source: Delfino and Casarin (2001). Calculation from Annual Statistics and published reports by the companies.

Note
T1: Electricity 1992; Telecomm 1989; Water and Sewerage 1993.

income quintiles. The same is observed for water. In the case of telephones, the rate of increase in connections for poor households is higher than for the richer ones. Changes in access for Argentina were also positive (see Table 6.4).

Concerning changes in tariffs, privatisation resulted in new pricing schemes for the utilities. It is recognised that, prior to privatisation, basic services were not free for poor people either in terms of money or in terms of time and effort. For children in particular, the opportunity cost in terms of forgone education is enormous. Free or subsidised, albeit rationed, water services were available for richer/middle-class households. Poor households had to pay higher fees than richer ones to access services of lesser quality. This has been taken as evidence of poor people's ability/willingness to pay for the services (see Whittington *et al.*, 1988 and 1990). In order to understand the effects of utilities' pricing on the poor's well-being we need to distinguish between poor households having access to the service through the main utility provider prior to privatisation and those who were not connected to the main network.

When households were supplied by the state-owned company, privatisation/reform of the sector could bring a price shock. Private operators inherited a distorted tariff structure and a complex scheme of subsidies that was abolished after privatisation. Prices increased dramatically after the new regime of provision took place. Tariff increases have been observed virtually in all sectors after privatisation. However, it is difficult to know how much of the price increases is actually due to the need to correct distortions or whether they reveal the existence of monopoly power.

In the case of Argentina, Figure 6.4 summarises the change in real tariffs for all the privatised utilities including telecommunication, electricity, gas and water and sanitation. The values shown are deflated with the CPI. In the case of telecommunication, the price of the unit charge decreased while there is a substantial increase in the value of the fixed charge. In the case of electricity, the increase in the fixed charge was accompanied by a significant increase in the unit charge, particularly hitting low-demand households. Water and sanitation shows the smallest tariff adjustment in real terms.

In Bolivia, with liberalisation of entry and competition in the mobile telephone market, prices started to fall. In addition, new entrants offered free connection and other special plans to attract consumers. Price reductions

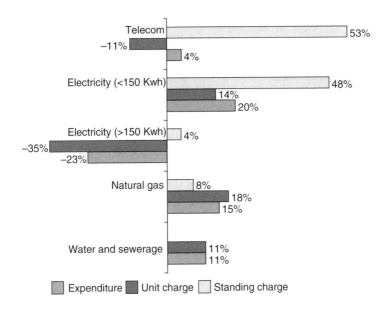

Figure 6.4 Argentina: changes in utilities' real tariffs

combined with the availability of low-cost cellular phones dramatically lowered access prices. This is particularly evident in comparison to the past pricing policies of local telephone co-operatives when a fixed connection cost about US$1,000. In the case of electricity, as Table 6.5 shows, residential tariffs have increased in real terms. Nevertheless, this trend seems to be reversing. With regard to the water and sanitation sector, the concession operating in La Paz did result in higher tariffs per m³.

In Peru, the telecommunication privatisation agreement allowed a re-balancing period in order to gradually reduce the existing tariff distortions. The pattern is similar to that observed in Argentina. The re-balancing considerably increased monthly fixed charges, while reducing the unit cost of local calls and national and international long-distance calls (see Table 6.6). Residential tariffs for electricity increased from US$ 0.07 per kWh at the beginning of 1994 to US$ 0.12 by the end of 1995. Tariffs remained stable until 1997 when they started to decrease slowly due to the decrease in tariffs charged for generation. At the beginning of 1998, residential tariffs were about US$ 0.10 per kWh. Altogether, the level of residential tariffs in Peru seems to be above those charged in Bolivia and Colombia, but below the level prevailing in Chile, Brazil and Argentina (Campodónico Sánchez, 1999).

Consumer surplus changes can be calculated on the basis of the information presented above, but only for households being provided by the main utility operator before and after privatisation. This means that the effect of price changes for households newly connected remains unseen. This approach clearly underestimates welfare changes, especially in the cases of Bolivia and Peru, where new connections are important to assess the effects of privatisation in facilitating access to services to the poor.

Table 6.5 Bolivia evolution of electric tariffs (residential) (index numbers (from average real values))

	Electropaz *La Paz/El Alto*	*ELFEC* *Cochabamba*	*CRE* *Santa Cruz*
1992	100.00	100.00	100.00
1993	108.59	98.22	100.45
1994	116.16	100.71	102.47
1995	123.48	107.47	109.21
1996	127.27	111.21	122.47
1997	134.85	112.28	128.31
1998	144.95	118.33	128.31
1999	153.54	114.77	124.04

Source: Barja and Urquiola (2001).

Table 6.6 Peru evolution of telecommunication rates (index numbers in 1995 prices)

	Rent	Local	Long distance Domestic	Long distance International
1993	100.00	100.00	100.00	100.00
1994	207.84	91.79	112.54	68.84
1995	232.27	89.37	106.61	65.30
1996	353.63	85.99	89.83	55.31
1997	484.31	83.09	82.37	47.25
1998	538.47	85.99	57.12	43.05

Source: Torero (2002). Author's calculations.

Note
1995 averages. Otherwise end of period.

In Peru, the sharp increase in fixed charges for telephones offset welfare gains obtained from unit tariffs reductions for local and long distance calls. The net effect was negative (welfare losses) for all households, in particular for the poorest quintile. In Argentina, the effect of rebalancing telephone tariffs was also regressive. Consumer surplus was negative for households in the first income quintile (the poorest one). The other segments of the population experience surplus gains.

In the case of electricity, the negative effect of tariff increases was mainly concentrated in the poorest households in Buenos Aires. In Peru and Bolivia (except for the city of Cochabamba), substantive surplus losses were observed across quintiles. This time, the impact on the poor did not appear to be as severe as for the richest households. Finally, in the case of water supply and sanitation, surplus losses were observed affecting rich and poor households in Buenos Aires and in the area of the concession of La Paz/El Alto. It is interesting to note that, in Bolivia, consumer's surplus losses were smaller in the area of La Paz/El Alto served by a private concessionaire than in other departmental capitals where the system of water and sanitation had not been subject to reforms (Ugaz and Waddams Price, 2003).

Assessing the reforms is not easy as there is mixed evidence depending on the country and on the sector studied. First, the initial conditions in each of the countries are different and processes of sector transformation across countries are not homogeneous. Second, each sector – telecommunication, electricity and water and sanitation – has its own characteristics, which may ultimately determine the success of the privatisation and regulation. Such is the case of the telecommunication sector that is at the forefront of radical transformation in all countries, and is commonly seen as a success story. The telecommunication sector is characterised by very fast technological progress and presence of a substitute (mobile telephone) that is unique to this sector. These aspects are absent from other basic infrastructure sectors, especially the water and sanitation sector. Generalisations based on the performance of the telecommunication sector are misleading.

Regulation

Because of the urgent macroeconomic situation, Latin American countries had to privilege the platform of fiscal stability, which had clout among voters. However, the speed at which public utilities were privatised allowed little time to assess the redistributive impacts of reforms. In particular, it underestimated the complexity of putting together an effective system of regulation that is essentially a redistributive tool.

The way regulation has been performed so far needs to be improved. The understanding of regulation as a public – as opposed to a government – institution, may take some time to gain momentum. Regulation is public because it operates in the public space and acts on public issues – tariff setting, service quality, service levels and standards of provision. However, lack of transparency still surrounds regulatory decisions. This is reflected in persistent (and regressive) tariff increases documented in this chapter. The findings of this chapter suggest that under the 'new model' of regulated private provision, affordability is an important barrier to service access especially by poor people.

Governance of regulation remains difficult to address. Governance refers to the way transparent and predictable regulatory systems can be put in place and sustained over time (Stern, 1997: 70). In this context one aspect of governance of regulation that requires further attention is participation (Stern and Holder, 1999). Participation in this framework means that all relevant parties in the process – governments, firms and consumers in particular – contribute effectively to improve the quality of regulatory decisions (see Ugaz, 2003). This remains a major challenge in the years to come, especially in countries where strong executives tend to circumvent channels of participation, preventing citizens from exercising their rights to reclaim access to basic utility services.

Conclusions and implications

State reforms in Latin America were triggered by fiscal and ideological considerations. Faced with inefficiency and debt, policy makers prioritised fiscal adjustment and adopted principles in which government performed only those tasks that the private sector was unable or uninterested in assuming. This approach was expressed most clearly in the rapid privatisation of publicly owned utilities. Regulation and other distributive mechanisms were largely an afterthought. The neglect of regulation is especially puzzling given the experiences of countries such as the UK where regulation was shown to be critically important to the success of the process. In Latin America, severe inequality demands a greater attention to equity, yet governments largely implemented regressive privatisation strategies. Even more surprising, voters tended to support these moves. This chapter uses models from the political economy literature to explain the persistence of redistributive policies in a context of highly unequal societies, as is the case of Latin American countries.

To understand the pattern of regressive privatisation in Latin America and to seek improvements, it is necessary to look into the political economy of policy decisions. Despite the overwhelming number of poor voters, Latin American policy makers have chosen privatisation policies that often exclude the poor. In the current study, we examined a number of the economic and social factors that contrive to exclude the poor from decision making. First, we explored the tendency for citizens to segregate by income, systematically concentrating public goods for the rich and excluding the poor. In addition, we examined limited access to information and uncertainty about future outcomes that create a status-quo bias that further disenfranchise the poor. Finally, we explore the idea that the link between inequality and political participation creates barriers that prevent the poor from advancing their demands in equal weight to the rich.

More explicitly, political factors further distort policies away from the preferences of poor voters. Internal partisan dynamics can drive party platforms away from the preferences of the poor as different echelons of parties compete to control the agenda. When these intra-party dynamics are joined with inter-party competition, the results are even more perverse. Competition along multiple issue dimensions can generate majorities for regressive policies, especially when policy makers prioritise non-redistributive dimensions, such as fiscal adjustment or security. These political economy analyses suggest that policy interventions will have to be well timed and sharply targeted if they are to be successful.

Even in the best case, however, presidential systems in the region create difficulties for advancing a progressive agenda. Presidents in the region tend to rule by decree, and when they operate through the legislature, progressive agendas are watered-down. Worse, the lack of accountability that generally characterises presidential regimes in the region makes it possible for presidents, even those that promise redistribution in their campaigns, to advance regressive policies.

The policy interventions associated with a more progressive privatisation are not complex. There are fairly standard solutions such as universal provision, progressive tariffs, improved regulation on service quality, and oversight involvement of pricing. External donors could assist by funding training, personnel exchanges, and stronger regulatory regimes. Such regimes might include multiple mechanisms of oversight, including executive agencies, legislative committees, and civil society organisations.

For these interventions to occur, however, political economy analysis suggests local political support may not easily emerge. In particular, multiple dimensions of partisan competition may distract poor voters from progressive alternatives. One aspect of the current historical juncture may provide a unique opportunity to mobilise support for redistribution. The fiscal adjustment dimensions of political competition are now less salient, as most countries have committed to relatively sound fiscal policies. In addition, outside Colombia, the region no longer faces serious internal conflict.

Policy makers can now engage in the important work of addressing inequality. This will only occur, however, if politicians interested in redistribution, especially actors in the legislature, can develop the capacity to hold chief executives accountable. This may be the moment to repair those policies that ignored equity when they were put in place. In the context of utilities, this means addressing shortcomings, especially in the area of regulation.

Our emphasis on the need for capable and powerful regulation draws out one more political economy wrinkle to the discussion. When ownership was public, states could set prices, control market structure, and determine access. A capable bureaucracy helped to accomplish these tasks, but it was not necessary. In fact, public ownership frequently emerged exactly because the state had limited capacity. Even a weak state with limited administrative capacity and few resources could influence the utility sector if utilities were publicly owned.

With privatisation, non-state actors control prices, market structure and access to the utility sector. These non-state actors tend to be large and powerful. To regulate to advance distributive goals, the state must be capable. Weak states cannot do it. Only capable states can effectively privatise and regulate. Without ownership, states require significant capacity to influence powerful utility sectors. Such powerful private actors easily overwhelm weak states. Privatisation, which shrinks the state, can only be progressive if the state is strong. This is the paradox of privatisation.

Notes

1 Schlesinger (1984) defines parties as an 'office seeking team'.
2 The median voter rule was originally demonstrated for conditions of two-party competition (Downs, 1957) and formalised in Davis *et al.* (1970).
3 For example, instead of the 50th, the 55th poorest voter in a population of 100 would be the median if the 10 poorest do not vote.

4 For a more extensive discussion of the impact of electoral rules on the number of parties see Lijphart (1984) and in Latin America, see Shugart and Carey (1992). For a discussion of polarising behaviour in multiparty systems, see Sartori (1976).

5 Michels described a socialisation process that distinguishes leaders from followers, an Iron Law of Oligarchy (1966: 205–11) and Duverger contrasted parliamentary parties to mass parties (1959: 190–2).

6 See R.J. Dalton (1985) for an argument that candidates are more radical than voters.

7 For an early statement of the leaders as extremists, see Schattschneider (1942). A portrayal of party leaders as moderate office seekers can be found in Laver (1981).

8 Some might consider Chavez's rise in Venezuela as an example of regime breakdown, but it did not follow any sustained attempts at policies such as regressive privatisation (Coppedge, 2002). Early views on Fujimori in Peru were that he had filled the ideological centre between polarised alternatives (Levitsky, 1999). His subsequent performance showed him to be far more to the Right than the Centre, however, and he continued to enjoy electoral support even after implementing regressive privatisation.

9 Kitschelt (1989: 407–10) suggested that social cleavages, political regime, competitive position, and past performance would determine the relative strength of ideologues within a party.

10 See, Linz (1990); Riggs (1992). For a balanced defence of presidentialism, see Shugart and Carey (1992: 28–54).

11 As they exist in many Latin American countries, proportional electoral rules for parliament and majoritarian rules for the presidency perhaps exacerbate the problem by creating different patterns of representation for the two branches.

12 For an example of the minimum winning coalition literature, see Baron and Ferejohn (1989).

13 The contents of this section are a summary of the findings presented in Ugaz and Waddams Price (2003).

Bibliography

Aldrich, J.H. (1983) 'A Downsian Spatial Model with Party Activism', *American Political Science Review*, 77, 974–90.

Barja, G. and Urquiola, M. (2001) 'Capitalization, Regulation, and the Poor: Access to Basic Services in Bolivia'. Paper presented at the UNU/WIDER meeting on The Social Impact of Privatization and Regulation of Utilities in Latin America, 6–7 October. Helsinki: UNU/WIDER.

Baron, D.P. and Ferejohn, J.A. (1989) 'Bargaining in Legislatures', *American Political Science Review*, 83(4), 1181–206.

Bénabou, R. (1993) 'Workings of a City: Location, Education and Production', *Quarterly Journal of Economics*, 108 (August), 619–52.

—— (2000) 'Unequal Societies: Income Distribution and the Social Contract', *American Economic Review*, 90(1), 96–129.

Borjas, G.J. (1992) 'Ethnic Capital and Inter-generational Mobility', *Quarterly Journal of Economics*, 107(1), 123–50.

—— (1995) 'Ethnicity, Neighborhoods and Human-Capital Externalities', *American Economic Review*, 85(3), 365–90.

Campodónico Sánchez, H. (1999) *La Inversion En El Sector Petrolero Peruano En El Periodo 1993–2000,* Santiago de Chile: CEPAL.

Collier, R. and Collier, D. (1991) *Shaping the Political Arena: Critical Junctures, the Labor Movement, and Regime Dynamics in Latin America*, Princeton, NJ: Princeton University Press.

Coppedge, M. (2002) 'Venezuela's Vulnerable Democracy', *Journal of Democracy*, 3(4), 32–44.

Dalton, R.J. (1985) 'Political Parties and Political Representation: Party Supporters and Party Elites in Nine Nations', *Comparative Political Studies*, 18, 267–99.

Davis, O.A., Hinich, M. and Ordeshook, P.C. (1970) 'An Expository Development of a Mathematical Model of the Electoral Process', *American Political Science Review*, 64, 426–48.

Delfino, J.A. and Casarin, A.A. (2001) 'The Reform of the Utilities Sector in Argentina'. Paper presented at the UNU/WIDER meeting on The Social Impact of Privatization and Regulation of Utilities in Latin America, 6–7 October. Helsinki: UNU/WIDER.

Downs, A. (1957) *An Economic Theory of Democracy*, New York: Harper and Row.

Duverger, M. (1959) *Political Parties: Their Organization and Activity in the Modern State*, translated by B. North and R. North. New York: John Wiley & Sons.

Fernandez, R. and Rodrik, D. (1991) 'Resistance to Reform: Status-quo Bias in the Presence of Individual-Specific Uncertainty', *American Economic Review*, 81(5), 1146–55.

Kitschelt, H. (1989) 'The Internal Politics of Parties: The Law of Curvilinear Disparity Revisited', *Political Studies*, 37, 400–21.

—— (1994) *The Transformation of European Social Democracy*, New York: Cambridge University Press.

Laver, M.J. (1981) *The Politics of Private Desires,* Harmondsworth: Penguin.

Laver, M. and Hunt, W.B. (1992) *Policy and Party Competition,* New York: Routledge.

Levitsky, S. (1999) 'Fujimori and Post-Party Politics in Peru', *Journal of Democracy*, 10(1), 78–92.

Lijphart, A. (1984) *Democracies: Patterns of Majoritarian and Consensus Government in Twenty-One Countries,* New Haven, CT: Yale University Press.

Linz, J. (1990) 'The Perils of Presidentialism', *Journal of Democracy*, 1(1), 51–69.

Loury, G. (1981) 'Inter-generational Transfers and the Distribution of Earnings' *Econometrica*, XXXIX(1), 843–67.

Macroconsult, S.A. (2000) 'Determinantes de los Arreglos Contractuales en la Participación Privada en Infraestructura: el Caso Peruano'. Research Network Working Paper # R-390. Washington, DC: Inter-American Development Bank.

May, J.D. (1983) 'Opinion Structure of Political Parties: The Special Law of Curvilinear Disparity', *Political Studies*, 21(2), 135–51.

Michels, R. (1966) *Political Parties,* New York: Free Press.

Meltzer, A. and Richard, S. (1981) 'A Rational Theory of the Size of the Government', *Journal of Political Economy*, 89(1), 914–27.

O'Donnell, G. (1994) 'Delegative Democracy', *Journal of Democracy*, 5(1), 55–69

Piketty, T. (1995) 'Social Mobility and Redistributive Politics', *Quarterly Journal of Economics*, 110(3), 551–84.

Pinheiro, A. and Giambiagi, F. (1999) 'The Macroeconomic Background and Institutional Framework of Brazilian Privatisation', in A. Pinheiro and K. Fukasaku (eds) *Privatisation in Brazil: The Case of Public Utilities*, OECD Development Centre. Mimeo.

Pinheiro, A. and Fukasaku, K. (eds) (1999) 'Privatisation in Brazil: The Case of Public Utilities', OECD Development Centre. Mimeo.

Putterman, L. (1997) 'Why Have Rabble Not Redistributed the Wealth? On the Stability of Democracy and Unequal Property' in Roemer, J. (ed.), *Property Relations, Incentives, and Welfare*, London: Macmillan.

Riggs, F.W. (1992) 'Presidentialism: A Problematic Regime Type', in A. Lijphart (ed.) *Parliamentary vs. Presidential Democracy*, Oxford: Oxford University Press.

Roemer, J. (1998) 'Why the Poor do not Expropriate the Rich: An Old Argument in New Garb', *Journal of Public Economics*, 70(3), 399–424.

Sartori, G. (1976) *Parties and Party Systems: A Framework for Analysis*, New York: Cambridge University Press.

Schattschneider, E.E. (1942) *Party Government*, New York: Holt, Rinehart, and Winston.

Schlesinger, J.A. (1984) 'On the Theory of Party Organization', *Journal of Politics* 46, 369–400.

Shugart, M.S. and Carey, J.M. (1992) *Presidents and Assemblies: Constitutional Design and Electoral Dynamics*, Cambridge: Cambridge University Press.

Stern, J. (1997) 'What makes an Independent Regulator Independent?', *Business Strategy Review*, 8(2), 67–74.

Stern, J. and Holder, S. (1999) 'Regulatory Governance: Criteria for Assessing the Performance of Regulatory Systems. An Application to Infrastructure Industries in the Developing Countries of Asia', *Utilities Policy*, 8, 33–50.

Strom, K. (1990) 'A Behavioral Theory of Competitive Political Parties', *American Journal of Political Science*, 34(2), 565–98.

Tandon, R. (2002) 'Linking Citizenship, Participation and Accountability: A Perspective from PRIA', in J. Gaventa, A. Shankland and J. Howard (eds) 'Making Rights Real: Exploring Citizenship, Participation and Accountability', *IDS Bulletin*, 33(2), April.

Torero, M. and Pascó-Font, A. (2000) 'The Social Impact of Privatization and Regulation of Utilities in Peru'. Paper presented at the UNU/WIDER meeting on The Social Impact of Privatization and Regulation of Utilities in Latin America, 6–7 October. Helsinki: UNU/WIDER.

Torres, H. and Hakkola, T. (1999) *Municipal Privatization*, Washington, DC: World Bank, Private Sector Development Department, January.

Tsebelis, G. (1990) 'Why Do British Labour Party Activists Commit Political Suicide?', in *Nested Games: Rational Choice in Comparative Politics*, Berkeley, CA: University of California Press.

Ugaz, C. (2003) 'Liberalisation of Utilities Markets and Children's Rights to Basic Services: Some Evidence from Latin America', Innocenti Research Centre – UNICEF. Mimeo.

Ugaz, C. and Waddams Price, C. (eds) (2003) *Utility Privatization and Regulation: A Fair Deal for Consumers?*, London: Edward Elgar (May 2005).

UNCTAD (2001) *The World Investment Report: Promoting Linkages*, Geneva.

Weyland, K. (1996) *Democracy Without Equity: Failures of Reform in Brazil.* Pittsburgh, PA: University of Pittsburgh Press.

Whittington, D., Briscoe, J., Mu, X. and Barron, W. (1990) 'Estimating the Willingness to Pay for Water Services in Developing Countries: A Case Study of the Use of Contingent Valuation Surveys in Southern Haiti', *Economic Development and Cultural Change*, 38(2), 293–311.

Whittington, D., Lauria, D., Okun, D. and Mu, X. (1988) 'Water Vending and Development: Lessons from Two Countries', WASH Technical Report no. 45. Washinton, DC: USAID.

7 Overcoming inequality in Latin America

Conclusion and policy recommendations

Patricia Justino and Ricardo Gottschalk

This book has discussed and reviewed the importance of inequality for social and economic development and argued for the need to reduce economic, social and political inequalities in Latin America (and in other developing regions) through better macroeconomic policies, paced liberalisation reforms, sound programmes of redistribution of incomes, assets and wealth, as well as social and political rights.

Latin America has one of the highest levels of economic, social and political inequalities in the world. These inequalities are predominantly dysfunctional, arising mostly from political connections, inherited wealth and power and discriminatory acts against specific population groups. Dysfunctional inequalities imply that particular regions, groups and individuals are excluded from accessing public goods and services and from participating in the political process of decision making. This situation has, in turn, impacted negatively on the prospects for increasing economic growth and reducing poverty in Latin American countries and will have serious negative implications for the achievement of the Millennium Development Goals, as the living standards of poorer segments of the population will not improve if these groups are prevented from accessing key economic, social and political institutions and rights.

The (persistently) high levels of inequalities have thus been a major characteristic of development patterns across Latin America, a region formed by countries that have incomes above the average in the developing world. However, those levels of income lag significantly behind those of North America and Europe. As implied above and more generally throughout the book, the level of inequalities in the Latin American region must have been an important factor as to why the region's economies did not perform better in recent decades. The experience of Latin America shows clearly that increases in inequality must be avoided, as high levels of persistent inequalities have negative consequences on important economic, social and political variables:

- High inequalities make more difficult the implementation of efficient macroeconomic management policies.
- High inequalities restrain the demand capacity of poor and middle-income countries.
- High inequalities magnify possible negative distributional impacts of international economic shocks.
- High inequalities decrease the stock of human capital available in each economy as it leads to the persistence of illiteracy and poor health amongst disadvantaged groups.
- High inequalities increase social discontent and, consequently, the propensity of individuals and population groups for engaging in criminal activities, violence and even civil wars.
- High inequalities hinder widespread political participation of deprived households and poor local communities.

The Latin American experience thus suggests that the rise of inequality that may result from the development process is not, under any circumstances, desirable if that inequality is largely dysfunctional. Although some level of inequality will result from the fact that market economies will reward successful risk-taking strategies and skill acquisition, most types of inequality that took place during the development process of Latin American countries were largely dysfunctional.

Successful development strategies can only occur when economic, social and political inequalities are reduced or avoided altogether. The reduction and avoidance of high inequalities require a combination of policies that simultaneously establish just distributional systems (of financial resources and social and political rights), guarantee equal access to social and economic opportunities across all segments of the population and eliminate all forms of discrimination and segregation. The implementation of such a policy framework will depend on the coordination of efforts, not only from national governments and the civil society, but also from the international community.

In Chapter 2, we identified three particularly important areas where the intervention of governments is of crucial importance for inequality reduction in Latin America:

- The establishment of progressive tax systems, whereby income gets transferred from the rich to the poor.
- The promotion of equal opportunities by, for instance, implementing universal primary and secondary education and universal access to

primary health care and basic social security benefits; and the improvement of the quality of the services provided, especially to the poor.

• The encouragement of change in social attitudes regarding the discrimination, segregation and exclusion of certain population groups from key economic, social and political institutions. This involves: (i) the guarantee of equal access to job opportunities by all groups in the population (men and women, individuals of different cultural backgrounds and so on); (ii) the protection of cultural differences; and (iii) the establishment of equal rights of access to socio-political and legal institutions by all population groups (including indigenous people and African descendants).

The implementation of this three-tier system of policies amounts, thus, to effectively increasing the redistribution of not only income, assets and wealth, but also of social and political rights.

Redistributive policies – of either financial resources or social and political rights – are notoriously difficult to implement, as those policies may be constrained by a lack of political will for redistribution or pure opposition to redistribution by political and social elites, as well as by weak economic conditions and instability. Also, some types of financial redistribution may introduce distortions that may be deemed counter-productive (for instance, capital taxes that discourage investment).

However, redistribution does not necessarily mean – at least not only – static transfers. Other forms of redistribution include what Chenery *et al.* (1974) referred to as 'redistribution with growth' and, more recently, Killick (2002) called 'dynamic redistribution'. These include the promotion of rural development, research and incentives to encourage labour-intensive investments, infrastructural investment to reduce the remoteness of many of the poorest, social policies to promote educational, health and social capital, measures to eliminate biases against women as producers and consumers, improved access to capital through financial sector reforms of micro-credit schemes, avoidance of macroeconomic crisis by sound macroeconomic management (Killick, 2002). Policies such as these would reduce the extent of economic, social and political inequalities due to both their material and non-material dimensions. Moreover, they would enhance the poor's physical, human and social capital thereby enabling them to respond better to shocks and in this way reduce the likelihood that they slip further on the distributional scale. The implementation of these policies thus can contribute towards social stability and lay the foundations for a more efficient and legitimate market economy.

As discussed in Chapters 3 and 4, more recently the Latin American experience has also shown that financial crises resulting from rapid capital account liberalisation have had, in some countries, the power to reverse very rapidly any positive equality gains that may have occurred in the first half of the 1990s. This highlights the fact that there is a need in the region for policies that can address deep rooted inequality as those suggested above, but also for policies that do not worsen inequality even further. Clearly, liberalisation policies concerning the capital account of the balance of payments contributed to an increase in inequality in those countries where they resulted in deep and prolonged financial crises, as was the case in Argentina during 2001/2.

In view of these outcomes, Chapter 3 draws attention to the need for domestic policies that can reduce the inequality effects of financial crises, or to avoid such crises happening in the first place. These policies include a cautious approach towards capital account liberalisation, with the maintenance of capital controls on those flows that are short term and easily reversible, the strengthening of financial regulation and supervision, so that domestic financial systems can withstand sharp currency devaluation, and counter-cyclical fiscal policy, which can be adopted in times of crises to attenuate their contractionary effects. Moreover, social safety nets should be in place to be activated when a crisis occurs, to protect the poor and the most vulnerable.

Chapter 3 more broadly highlights the need for flexibility in the macro-economic framework so that different mechanisms can be quickly activated when an economy is hit by a financial shock. The need for a flexible macro-economic framework is true not only for countries that suffer financial crises caused by sudden reversal of private capital flows, but also for countries that suffer from external shocks such as terms of trade shocks and natural disasters. Low-income countries in Latin America fall under the latter category of countries, but unfortunately their macroeconomic frameworks are too rigid, thus lacking the mechanisms required to deal with shocks.

There is therefore the need for flexibility in the macroeconomic framework of both middle-income and low-income Latin American countries, to enable them to deal with the negative effects of shocks on poverty and inequality, and to ensure a truly stable macroeconomic environment that includes reduced volatility in key macroeconomic variables such as output levels, employment and real wages. As argued in Chapter 6, a more stable macroeconomic environment – achievable only through appropriate macro policies that take due account of external shocks – would open space for poorer population groups to become more active in pursuing more extensive redistributive programmes. This could be done through the political process, whereby voters may start supporting more clearly those political parties that favour redistributive welfare spending. A more active participation of the poor in support of pro-poor policies through the electoral process (and directly as well), is an essential factor in the reduction of inequalities in Latin America.

Chapter 5 also argues that macroeconomic stability that includes a stable and competitive exchange rate is key to successful trade policy reforms, both in terms of growth and better income distribution. A competitive exchange rate in addition may ensure reduced economic and social costs in the short to the medium term, often associated with job losses among import-competing industries. Unfortunately, Chapter 5 shows that the 1990s in Latin America saw a perverse combination of rapid trade liberalisation and highly volatile real exchange rates, which in all probability may have contributed to inefficient resource allocation, and increased poverty and inequality, at least in the short and medium terms.

This book, especially in Chapter 4, argues strongly that policies in support of better income distribution should be pursued at the international level as well. International financial institutions such as the International Monetary Fund (IMF), the World Bank (WB) and the Inter-American Development Bank (IADB) have a particularly crucial role to play in the fight against economic, social and political inequalities in Latin America. Although it is recognised that the extent of economic, social and political inequalities constitutes a serious constraint to economic growth and poverty reduction in Latin America, very little has been done by the international financial institutions to address directly those inequalities.

The IMF has a central role in supporting international financial stability. Moreover, it has an institutional commitment to poverty reduction, and should have a similar commitment to inequality reduction as well. However, the IMF commitment to poverty reduction has not been matched with policies that are pro-poor. The reality is that of economic policy advice that is not sensitive to the needs of poor people. The IMF has made some efforts in the recent past to mainstream poverty and inequality concerns. This has been, however, limited to its programmes in low-income countries, through the creation of the PRGF and the PRSP processes. It would be important that the IMF do the same as regards middle-income countries. In the case of Latin American countries, inequality is a very real problem and should therefore be given prominence when the Fund is putting together loan agreements for such countries.

As regards the IMF's role in supporting international financial stability, the Fund should provide emergency liquidity to countries facing financial instability. By doing so, it can contribute to crisis prevention and containment and, consequently, to the reduction of poverty and inequality impacts of financial instability. In addition to liquidity provision, the Fund should change the conditionality that traditionally accompanies rescue packages in order to include higher concerns for strong social safety nets in periods of crisis.

Recent financial crises have in fact called for the need of a broader range of social policies to help countries deal appropriately with the economic and social crisis effects. Examples of such policies include unemployment insurance, income support, public works programmes, price subsidies, nutrition programmes, social service fee waivers and micro-finance programmes. Because it is difficult for governments to finance these policies, especially in times of financial crises, the international community should provide financial assistance to help countries to deal with the effects of such crises – and, of course, of other crises as well, caused by terms of trade shocks and natural disasters.

Another way in which international agencies can increase their role in the process of inequality reduction in Latin America is to increase awareness of national policy makers for the problem of inequality and the need to resolve it. They can also participate in building governments' technical capacity to deal with the various issues, by providing technical advice and support to individual governments in the design of the following policies:

- Progressive tax systems that can be feasibly implemented in countries that experience serious budget constraints.
- Policies that counteract the power of elites and their antagonism towards the redistribution of income, assets and wealth and social and political rights.
- Policies aimed at promoting larger efficiency in administrative tasks (more qualified staff, wider use of computers, etc.).
- Social polices that increase the availability of equal opportunities for all social groups. Particular importance should be paid to the establishment of universal secondary education, the increase of efficiency in the administration of public health systems and better targeting systems in the distribution of social benefits and other socially protective policies.
- Policies aimed at directly reducing discrimination and segregation in the labour markets and in the access to social and judicial services, such as more transparent procedures in job applications and the use of indigenous languages in the design of legal documents.
- Creative financial arrangements that provide credit, and thus higher financial auto-sufficiency, to poor people and small and medium enterprises. These enterprises have an important role in the provision of local employment and should thus be further encouraged through better access to credit and larger technical support.

Building governments' capacity for dealing with the persistence of inequalities in Latin America will not be sufficient without a more active participation of the civil society and a change in social attitudes of both elites and the rest of the population. The international community (e.g. international organisations, NGOs, other advocacy groups) and various national stakeholders should thus aim to work together on reducing persistent inequalities and their consequences for the welfare of both elites and more disadvantaged groups. This can be achieved through collaborative work with the following groups and institutions:

- Local small and medium enterprises. These are important sources of employment in Latin America. Without a change in attitudes in local labour markets towards discrimination, segregation and other bad job practices little will be achieved in terms of reducing social inequalities in Latin America.
- Local governments that may need explicit advice in the adaptation of national policies to specific community problems. These can range from a more efficient implementation of food programmes to the strengthening of local legal procedures.
- Labour unions. These can play an active role in the protection of political representation of member workers. Labour unions can have a powerful part in the reduction of inequalities, as well-organised unions will be able to influence both local job practices undertaken by public and private enterprises and lobby for the interests of otherwise disadvantaged groups in the design of national policies. In order to perform those tasks, labour unions need, however, to be well organised, benefit from efficient communication channels, have well-managed and transparent accounts and be able to voice actively the demands of the workers they represent.
- Local communities and citizens' associations. It is particularly important that local communities are mobilised to increase their demand for better and more extensive redistribution of incomes and social and political rights. Population groups in several Latin American countries have implicitly supported and tolerated, through the voting process, the implementation of regressive policies. The political participation of local communities and the strengthening of their demands for more redistributive policies are thus crucial for the reduction and avoidance of persistent inequalities in Latin America.

Bibliography

Chenery, H., Ahluwalia, M.S., Bell, C.L.G., Duloy, J.H. and Jolly, R. (1974) *Redistribution with Growth: Policies to Improve Income Distribution in Developing Countries in the Context of Economic Growth*, London: Oxford University Press.
Killick, T. (2002) *Responding to Inequality*, Inequality Briefing Paper no. 3. London: DFID and ODI.

Index

Overcoming inequality in
Latin America : issues
2006.